Opposing Democracy in the Digital Age

WEISER CENTER FOR EMERGING DEMOCRACIES

Series Editor

Dan Slater is Professor of Political Science,
Ronald and Eileen Weiser Professor of Emerging Democracies,
and Director of the Weiser Center for Emerging Democracies (WCED)
at the University of Michigan. dnsltr@umich.edu

———————————

The Weiser Center for Emerging Democracies (WCED) Series publishes cutting-edge research in the pivotal field of authoritarianism and democratization studies. We live in a historical moment when democracies seem increasingly fragile and authoritarian regimes seem
stubbornly resilient across the globe, and these topics continue to be a central part of research in the social sciences. The WCED Series strives to collect a balance of titles on emerging democracies and enduring dictatorships, as one cannot understand the conditions under
which democracies live and thrive without comprehending how they die and remain unborn.

The WCED Series is interested in the full range of research being conducted on authoritarianism and democratization, primarily in political science but at times from history, sociology, and
anthropology as well. The series encompasses a global geographic reach. We invite works that are
primarily qualitative as well as quantitative in approach and are interested in edited volumes as
well as solo-authored manuscripts.

The series highlights the leading role of the University of Michigan Press, Weiser Center for
Emerging Democracies, and International Institute as premier sites for the research and production of knowledge on the conditions that make democracies emerge and dictatorships endure.

———————————

OPPOSING DEMOCRACY IN THE DIGITAL AGE

The Yellow Shirts in Thailand

Aim Sinpeng

University of Michigan Press
Ann Arbor

Copyright © 2021 by Aim Sinpeng
All rights reserved

For questions or permissions, please contact um.press.perms@umich.edu

Published in the United States of America by the
University of Michigan Press
Printed and bound by CPI Group (UK) Ltd, Croydon, CR0 4YY

First published March 2021

A CIP catalog record for this book is available from the British Library.

Library of Congress Cataloging-in-Publication data has been applied for.

ISBN: 978-0-472-13235-5 (Hardcover : alk paper)
ISBN: 978-0-472-03848-0 (Paper : alk paper)
ISBN: 978-0-472-12856-3 (ebook)

To Marc

Contents

Digital materials related to this title can be found on the Fulcrum platform via the following citable URL: https://doi.org/10.3998/mpub.11666233

Figures

Tables

Preface

It was around 9 p.m. in the evening of September 19, 2006. Like many Thais, my Mom and I were watching an evening soap opera on TV. Suddenly the TV show was interrupted. A group of military generals appeared. They sat calmly with portraits of the king and queen behind them. For a moment I thought it was a déjà vu. I'd seen this "image" before . . . when I was young. The generals announced that they had taken over from the government and that everything was going to be alright. But I knew this would not be alright.

The story of Thailand is personal to me. Not simply because it is my birth country, but because my life has been directly affected by its democratic collapses. In 1991, at the age of nine, I experienced firsthand a collapse of democracy when a group of military generals dislodged a democratically elected government. I remember the vivid scenes I witnessed as a child, of army tanks rolling down the streets of Bangkok, and the hundreds of armed soldiers occupying key areas of the city. My father was a high-ranking army officer at the time, and the simple thought that "men in uniform" dressed just like him were responsible for such chaos and the killing that ensued was entirely confusing to me. My siblings and I grew up in a military household. We were thankful to the institution that had provided my father a good career that allowed us to have a good life. Were these men in uniform the very same that did those evil things? As I grew up and lived through several coups d'état, I became even more baffled and haunted by this question. It often perplexes me how a country that had become more prosperous over the decades could subsequently have been drawn into a descending spiral of sometimes weak, sometimes overbearing, civilian governments that alternated with periods of authoritarian rule.

Just a year prior to the coup of 2006, I was working at the Government House of Thailand during the prime ministership of Thaksin Shinawatra. The antigovernment protests were becoming frequent and serious. I remember the many occasions that I was unable to reach my workplace via the main entrance since it was blocked by the protesters. One day, as I squeezed myself through the back entrance along the canal, trying to make an exit, it occurred to me that I had no idea why they were protesting. Maybe I should listen in. And so I did. That was the day my interest was sparked in what would later become the "Yellow Shirts."

The People's Alliance for Democracy (PAD)—more locally known as the "Yellow Shirts"—is one of the most contentious and sustained political movements in contemporary Thai history. Its title notwithstanding, this antidemocratic movement centers around a powerful monarchy and army, a distinct conception of "democratic politics," and a weakly institutionalized party system. This study analyzes the relationships among these three components and situates them in the overall development of the modern Thai polity. It argues that blockage in formal and informal democratic institutions drove the PAD movement to appeal to nondemocratic institutions, which contributed to the collapse of Thailand's democracy in 2006. By exploring the forces and conditions that promoted this antidemocratic movement, and by showing how its emergence and decline has shaped Thailand's experience with democracy, the study seeks more generally to elucidate factors that undermine democratic political regimes.

The PAD eventually evolved into another political movement—the People's Democratic Reform Committee (PDRC). The PDRC was even more antidemocratic than the PAD and it was a truly digitally networked movement. Some of the PDRC leaders became social media influencers with millions of followers online. The fact that this popular movement opposing democracy could thrive online challenged our conventional wisdom that social media is a democratizing tool.

Three convictions underpin this book. The first is that there is no such thing as overthrowing democracy for the sake of democracy. A coup d'état is irreversible. Democracy cannot be "taken away" from the people and "returned" to the people in its same shape and form. Rolling back democratic rights, no matter how small and seemingly insignificant, can take a nation down a dangerous path. Democracy is difficult and messy, and publics can have many reasons to be disillusioned. But one must not give in to the urge for "order" in the face of temporary chaos and inconvenience by allowing democratic rights to be curbed. Second, procedural democracy—fair elections, real power for elected officials, and basic human and civil rights—is worth pursuing. By deterring the abuse of power, by allowing the exercise of popular sovereignty, and by making it easier for the disadvantaged to influence and benefit from public policy, democracy promotes the free development of human capabilities. The third conviction is that social structures, historical legacies, and political arrangements can be changed by acts of human will. Political choices matter, and they will matter even more if those who make them understand the opportunities and constraints their predecessors have faced. A grasp of these opportunities and constraints can help such actors identify, and thus more easily overcome, obstacles that otherwise overwhelm them.

While this book examines the emergence and development of the PAD and the PDRC movements between 2005 to 2014, its implications remain relevant to understanding the future of democratic politics in this Southeast Asian country. The contribution of this empirical work will not only help us to understand why democracy collapses, but it also lends insights into the flaws of democratic regimes more generally.

The failure of democracy in Thailand, despite decades of trial and error, provides some key lessons to newly democratizing states and warns us that institutionalizing procedural forms of democracy provides no guarantee for democratic survival. Extraconstitutional institutions ought not to be strong enough that they compete for political legitimacy with democratic institutions. In the Thai case, both the military and the monarchy have been institutionalized as powerful sources of authority and legitimacy both in politics and society to remain crucial power brokers in Thai politics. It is not that democracy cannot thrive as long as the monarchy and the military remain on stage. More problematic is that their authority is able to contend with that of democratic institutions. In the digital age of politics, we also cannot expect tools like social media to democratize us if we do not believe in democracy ourselves.

PART I

ONE

Introduction

How and why do people in democracies oppose democracy? Does social media facilitate democratic collapse? Since the mid-2000s, democratic breakdowns and recessions have occurred around the world alongside an explosion of social media adoption. While the phenomena of antidemocratic movements that induce democratic collapse are perennial questions for scholars of democratization, these are further complicated by the arrival of new media. Earlier optimism that social media would be a boon for democracy has been seriously questioned by recent revelations of its central role in facilitating foreign electoral interference; electing radical, right-wing candidates; and fueling ethnic and religious conflicts around the world. Yet much of the current scholarship on regime transition has left an important gap in our understanding of how social media may contribute to democracy's downfall.

This book is about understanding in the first place why and how people in middle-income democracies mobilize against democracy. The main argument of this book is that people *strategically* mobilize against democracy when they feel permanently excluded from democratic institutions. Disenchanted with their inability to gain access to power through democratic bodies such as parliament, ordinary people in young democracies where democratic values and experiences remain immature are inclined to embrace an authoritarian turn. Emerging democracies tend to be plagued by the perennial problems of weak institutions, political instability, polarization, frequent executive changes, and low levels of civil and political liberties. After years of intense struggles and difficult reforms, these new

democracies suddenly reach the promised land: democracy is finally working! Its people enjoy greater freedoms and political participation more
than ever, while its executives also have improved power and capacity to
govern. This, unfortunately, in turn leads to a clash of two incompatible
visions of democracy: power-sharing versus majoritarianism. On the one
hand, there is greater inclusion: citizens are not only afforded regular and
routinized elections where they can exercise their voice and vote; they also
feel empowered by greater rights and freedoms. Yet, on the other hand,
their executives are becoming too powerful and prone to abusing their
power with little constraint from below.

Despite the ideological contentions that may prompt the masses to turn
against their elected governments, the decision to oppose democracy is
often strategic. This means that the movement *decides* to oppose democracy. Becoming an antidemocratic movement is a choice, not an inevita-
bility. New democracies are trapped in this dilemma: wanting both more
inclusion and more constraint on the executive (Schedler, Andreas, and
Plattner 1999). Elites are also confronted by the fact that they may have
to finally redistribute resources and power in order to maintain power and
prevent widespread unrest (Acemoglu and Robinson 2006). While elites
squabble over who will redistribute, and over how and how much, ordinary
people, in contrast, fight over what kind of democracy they want to live
in. Invariably, this means the majoritarian version of democracy in which
the wishes of the majority matter most, or the power-sharing democracy
where its people are included in political decision-making and its executives restrained. Disputes arise not just between elites and the masses, but
also within each group itself. As the costs of staying with the current democratic regime rise above the anticipated benefits of a new regime, democratic breakdown becomes likely.

But the story of how today's democracy dies is incomplete without taking seriously the role of social media. Social media is a tool for antidemocratic mobilization and the expansion of antidemocratic voices. Social
media can make coups cheaper. Popular mobilization increases and polarization magnifies through social media; combined, these radically reduce
the costs of mounting a coup. Ironically, by providing a new avenue for
people to express their opinions and participate in politics, social media
entrenches and sometimes worsens polarization—keeping societies divided
rather than bringing them together. It gives the masses the very weapon
most likely to deepen the conflict. Unlike other forms of mass communication tools like television or print, social media creates a "participatory culture" in which users are transformed into active participants and producers

of content (Jenkins 2006). Social media users can generate, share, edit, and produce whatever information and content they want—and they can do this at will. Social media is therefore an instrument in itself for empowering antidemocratic voices and allowing them to galvanize popular support for dictatorship. If we agree that today democracy is under attack in more ways than one, then social media must be added to the list of factors that heighten its vulnerability.

Since the Third Wave of democratization in the mid-1970s, little scholarly attention has been paid to popular mobilization against democratic governments, or against democracy more generally. Images of ordinary people rising up to challenge oppressive regimes and eventually toppling their dictators give us hope and optimism (Huntington 1993; Diamond 2003; Schock 1999; Collier and Mahoney 1997; Kim 2003; Bernhard 1993; Bellin 2012). The fall of the Berlin Wall set in motion by protests across the Eastern bloc, prodemocracy movements against President Joseph Estrada in the Philippines, protests against dictatorial Indonesia and Burmese rulers, and the 2011 Arab Spring all remind us of the "people's power" in the collapse of authoritarian regimes.

Yet, on closer inspection, empirical evidence presents a rather mixed picture regarding the democratic orientations of mass political movements in contemporary times. Popular movements have been regarded as contributing factors to the *loss* of democracy in the past decade in countries such as Bangladesh, Fiji, the Philippines, Thailand, Honduras, and Egypt. As such, not all political movements are prodemocracy. We have made empirical observations of cases of opposition movements that advocate against some aspects of the democratic system. But not all antidemocratic movements contribute to a democratic collapse. Some democracies are able to survive despite popular movements that push for regime change.

Opposition movements in Egypt successfully called for a military intervention that resulted in the removal of a democratically elected president, Mohamed Morsi, in 2013. Tamarod, one of the key anti-Morsi movements, rallied members to shore up support for the military-backed government of Adly Mansour, despite the autocratic nature of the regime. In Honduras, what started as an antigovernment movement led to the 2009 coup d'état when a group of soldiers broke into the presidential palace and forced President Manuel Zelaya to resign. The subsequent military-backed government reportedly enjoyed strong support from sections of Honduran society.[1] Some 70,000 people marched in the streets of Tegucigalpa in support of this new authoritarian government.[2]

The phenomenon of antidemocratic mobilization is real and has been witnessed more frequently in large, middle-income countries, such as Brazil, Egypt, Bangladesh, Turkey, and Thailand. Despite this increasing occurrence, existing literature cannot help us to make sense of how antidemocratic movements develop in emerging democratic countries. This book thus outlines a *concrete process* in which a once prodemocratic movement turns antidemocratic. I use Thailand as a showcase of the antidemocratization process. Thailand is a focus of this book not only because it suffers from the highest number of democratic collapses in recent years, but most significantly because of the critical role played by social media in the antidemocratic mobilization. At a nearly 100 percent penetration rate of online population, and alongside other developing democracies like the Philippines and Indonesia, Thailand ranks among the world's most social media active countries. More importantly, the origin and evolution of the "Yellow Shirts"—an antidemocratic mass movement that is the focus of this book—begins in the pre-social-media era and continues as social media becomes an integral part of the people behind the movement. Thailand thus provides an excellent case to examine how a mass movement comes to oppose democracy in a middle-income country and probes the role of social media in the process.

There is also a real gap in current studies on political transitions to dictatorship that take social media seriously. Much of the existing literature on political regimes and media and communication either focus on the contribution that digital media makes in political transitions to democracy or on the entrenchment of authoritarian regimes (Tufekci and Wilson 2012; Lim 2012; Pearce and Kendzior 2012). This book seeks to fill this empirical gap through the case of Thailand by providing rich and compelling research at the micro level on how democracy fails, and the contribution that social media plays in its downfall. Implications from this study are relevant to many developing countries around the world whose citizens are increasingly distressed and disenchanted by democracy and who take up their frustrations on social media. Some are dreaming of an alternative future in which life seems more orderly and secure, even if they must concede some of their hard-earned freedoms. Those having grown up in authoritarian times still have fond memories of the "good old days." Such authoritarian nostalgia has already been on the rise in Asia, as preferences for strong unelected leaders and military intervention in politics grow.[3]

There are three important research questions that guide this study and the subject matter of this book. First, under what conditions do people have antidemocratic attitudes? Second, when does antidemocratic mobilization occur? And third, when do antidemocratic movements succeed? In the next sections of this chapter, I consider answers to these three research questions. Following this, I discuss the current literature on social media and democracy and outline how social media amplifies antidemocratic attitudes, speeds up antidemocratic mobilization, and simultaneously brings down the costs of a military intervention—making coup possibilities greater and success more likely.

Opposing Democracy

Antidemocratic movements are but one type of opposition mobilization. I argue here that there are three *ideal* types of opposition movements in democracies: (1) proreform; (2) anti-incumbent; and (3) antidemocratic (table 1.1). What distinguishes these three types of movements is their goal. In general, an opposition movement forms to contest either a specific policy or the general direction of an incumbent government. Once formed, an opposition movement takes one of these three forms. This typology is an ideal type, thus in reality a movement can be a mixture of proreform and anti-incumbent. These ideal types, however, help to differentiate analytically and empirically the *nature* of opposition by distinguishing their goals. Proreform opposition movements look to propose policy alternatives, while anti-incumbent movements seek executive or government replacement. Neither is intent on subverting the democratic system.

Antidemocratic mobilization, which is the main focus of this study, is a distinct type of movement whose characteristics differ from other forms of opposition mobilization. To be clear: for an antidemocratic movement, government change is not a desired outcome. Instead, its goal is to overhaul the entire political system. Unlike other types of opposition mobilization, antidemocratic mobilization carries the highest costs and is sometimes considered a "last resort" strategy for a movement. It is important to note that not all electoral democracies are conducive to the emergence of antidemocratic movements. The theory set forth in this book outlines the conditions under which an antidemocratic movement can arise to successfully overthrow an elected government.

TABLE 1.1. Typology of opposition movement in democracies

	Goals
1. Proreform	Propose policy alternatives; voice grievances
2. Anti-incumbent	Oppose incumbent government; voice grievances
3. Antidemocratic	Subvert democratic system

Does antidemocratic mobilization account for the recent collapse of Third Wave democracies? Indeed, while some 60 percent of states today are electoral democracies, the world has become less free.[4] Serious signs of democratic rollback and incidences of breakdown have been on the rise within the Third Wave countries.[5] The rise of antidemocratic mobilization is, by definition, part of the explanation for why we see an increasing incidence of democratic reversal in some of these states. Understanding antidemocratic mobilization in these postdemocratizing states is, therefore, not only empirically relevant but also has implications for our understanding of the overall state of democracy in the world. In particular, middle-income democracies are supposed to be well placed to sustain democracy, yet we continue to see their democratic collapses. Why such relatively well-off democracies face mass antidemocratic mobilization and breakdown is the very puzzle this book examines.

Having antidemocratic attitudes is not enough to get a movement going without the ability to organize it. Mobilizational capacity—the ability to organize and mobilize supporters—is thus an additional and necessary factor for forming an antidemocratic movement. An antidemocratic movement with the potential to pose a credible threat to democracy is one that can galvanize sufficient popular support. As most mass movements are broad-based and eclectic, which is to say they are composed of a number of diametrically opposing groups and ideological bedfellows, the question is then one of which group will end up leading the overall movement. This is when mobilization capacity matters: success in the overall movement falls to those groups most skilled at rallying a majority of people behind their leaders and directing the movement agenda toward opposing democracy. Crafty and charismatic figures able to better leverage a variety of media channels to advance their agenda hold a distinct advantage over others. It is not who has the best idea but whose idea is heard by the greatest number of people. Media will play a critical part in understanding how antidemocratic attitudes spread and who is able to advance such ideas in a movement.

When opposition forces feel shut out from access to power, they rebel against such closures by appealing to nondemocratic actors to reverse or reopen democratic channels. Antidemocratic mobilization then serves as a vehicle for various opposition forces whose leverage has been reduced, or completely cut out, by an overpowering executive. If such mobilization succeeds in garnering support from nondemocratic authorities, then we see a complete breakdown of democracy. The existence of viable nondemocratic institutions, such as a monarchy, military, or religious bodies, is necessary for the mobilization of an antidemocratic movement. These

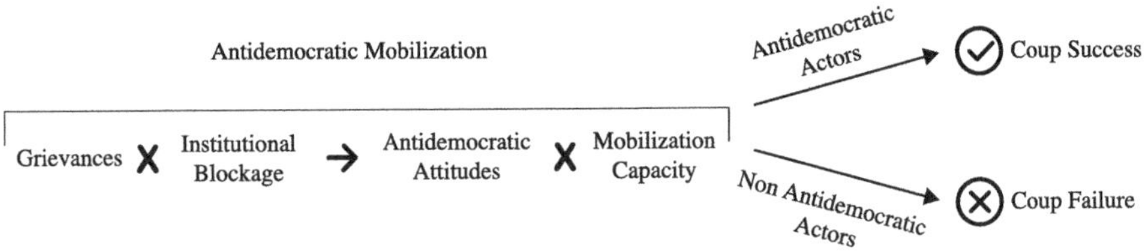

Figure 1.1. Antidemocratic mobilization and coup success

institutions often historically played a critical role in the politics of their respective countries during authoritarian times. Following democratization, such institutions continue to wield significant power despite their more limited role. These nondemocratic bodies will reassert themselves when (a) their interests are threatened and (b) they see a chance of success.

Antidemocratic mobilization is therefore more likely to succeed if it can appeal to nondemocratic actors, such as the military. A sudden democratic collapse usually happens via a military putsch; but coups état happen far less frequently than they once did. In the age of mass politics, mass support is crucial for the military to even consider staging a coup as the cost of coups is so high, especially if they fail (Svolik 2012). If antidemocratic movements can demonstrate their popularity and convince the military to take their side, this then contributes to the much stronger possibility of a successful coup. To demonstrate their popular appeal, antidemocratic groups tend to form extensive alliances with other opposition groups and persuade them or the opposition movement's leaders to accept the antidemocratic agenda. How well antidemocratic movements can both demonstrate their popularity and signal to the military their readiness to welcome its intervention is of great import to the overall likelihood and success of a coup d'état.

Not every new democracy witnesses a rise of antidemocratic mobilization. Likewise, only some democratizing countries will experience regime breakdown. While the vast research in the study of democratic transition points to the fragility and sometimes fleeting nature of newly established democracies (O'Donnell et al. 1986; Loveman 1994; Jones 1998; Bratton 1998; Bunce 2000), there is great variation in existing scholarship as to why some new democracies survive but others do not. I will canvas five key theoretical arguments that are advanced on democratic transition and stability. The most widely cited argument within the body of comparative literature on what explains the rise of an antidemocratic/antisystem mobilization is an economic one. When new democracies face severe economic crisis, the public reacts negatively toward the regime by supporting antidemocratic/

antisystem movements or political parties (Kitschelt and McGann 1997; Brustein 1991; Olukoshi 1998; Allen 1973). It is not the economic crisis per se that drives people to overthrow their democratic governments. Rather, it is how the people react to severe economic downturns that are purported to have implications for democratic stability. Times of war or major economic downturn in a democracy provide grounds for groups to organize in opposition to the political system in which they live. Much of this literature addresses more broadly the rise of "antisystem" movements, which include extreme right-wing, extreme left-wing, and fascist mobilization.

Second, the intraelite competition approach argues that the stability of democracy depends on elite unity. Democratic breakdown and democratic transition can occur as long as elites remain fragmented (Higley and Burton 1989; Lopez-Pintor 1987). An antidemocratic movement is thus largely reflective of the power struggle among rival elites (McCargo 2008; Ockey 2008; Nelson 2007). Traditional elites, such as the military, can be threatened by the rise of career politicians, for instance. The "men in uniform" then mobilize people to help them legitimize their seizure of power from a democratically elected government. Third, the class-conflict approach contends that what gives rise to an antidemocratic mobilization is the longstanding divide between the rural poor and the urban elites. Fearful of the rising political influence of the poor, the rich mobilize against them by seeking to subvert the democratic system that gives the former power in the first place. The antidemocratic movement is thus an upper- and middle-class reaction to the threat from below (Acemoglu and Robinson: 2005; Phongpaichit and Baker 2008; Pongsudhirak 2008; Funston 2009; Hewison 2012). An implicit assumption in this class-based framework is that economic positions shape groups in society along class lines and motivate their behavior. Unequal distribution of power across diverse groups in society also plays a key role in a class struggle.

Fourth, the extent to which a democratic regime survives depends on elite choices (Linz and Stepan 1978; O'Donnell, Schmitter, and Whitehead 1986; Muller and Seligson 1994; Ake 1991). This elite-centric approach argues that decisions made by elites are crucial to regime change. While recognizing the importance of structural factors, elites decide when a regime change occurs. When elites are not committed to democratic ideas, democracy is always unstable. One interpretation of the importance of political leadership to regime change concerns explanations for the rise of antisystem parties and ethnic conflicts. Ake (1991, 34) argues that "bad leadership" explains ethnic conflicts in Africa as elites mobilize people against adversarial groups. Bermeo (2003) contends that extremist parties in interwar Europe and Latin America are driven by elites, not the masses. Fifth, the political institutionalization approach argues that antidemocratic movements are most likely to thrive in places with weak political institutionalization (Huntington 1968; Berman 1997; Fiorina 1997; Armony 2004). When social mobilization outpaces political institutionalization, chaos and crisis will ensue.[6] When weak political institutions cannot respond to the public demand for meaningful political participation in public life, the people look for other alternatives to voice their grievances. As such, where institutions fail to meet the demands of a mobilized society, we see the rise of an antisystem movement (Berman 1997).

These existing theories provide important explanations as to why Thailand witnessed two popular antidemocratic movements and subsequent successful military coups in 2006 and 2014. Weak political institutions, the heightening of intraelite conflicts, and deep-seated and growing polarization within the middle class about what democracy is and should look like are all contributing factors to the country's recent political chaos. What this book offers in addition to existing analyses is the often-overlooked micro-level process of *how* antidemocratic mobilization emerged and evolved over time. It emphasizes the importance of understanding the *strategic* nature of the antidemocratic mobilization process that goes beyond considerations of structural factors. This book also takes seriously the role of media and communication, particularly social media, in understanding the emergence of digitally mediated antidemocratic movements.

Thailand

Thailand is among the oldest democracies in Southeast Asia, yet it has also witnessed the greatest number of coups. With the introduction of democratic politics in the 1970s, Thailand became the second democracy in the region, following the Philippines.[7] But Thailand has suffered multiple regime oscillations since military coups were frequent: a total of nineteen attempts from the time of its transition to a constitutional monarchy in 1932. Important reforms beginning in the late 1980s set in motion a series of initiatives to liberalize Thailand's polity. These reduced the political power of the military and instead expanded civil society and empowered ordinary people. Liberalizing reforms culminated in the first-ever "People's Constitution" of 1997—a new, people-oriented constitution that would strengthen democratic institutions and further help Thailand's democratic consolidation by focusing on the rights and freedoms of its people. Consequently, many held high hopes that Thailand of the 1990s would be the beacon of democracy in Southeast Asia following its longest spell without any threat of a coup, and its first constitution to be drafted by a power other than the military (Neher 1996; Bertrand 1998; Bunbongkarn 1999). If democracy were to survive in this previously coup-ridden nation, there was hope for neighboring states such as Cambodia, Malaysia, and Myanmar that a similar transition to democracy could be achieved.

Yet, paradoxically, by 2005, the very prodemocracy activists who fought tooth and nail for the 1997 People's Constitution found themselves at the helm of the country's largest antidemocratic movement. These activists, the so-called Yellow Shirts, spurred hundreds of thousands of supporters and demanded extraconstitutional interventions to dislodge a popularly elected prime minister, Thaksin Shinawatra, a billionaire cum politician who rose to power in 2001. He became the first Thai prime minister ever to win an absolute majority in parliament and to serve out a full four-year term. Thaksin was possibly Thailand's most popular prime minister of all time. Supporters renamed their villages after him and planted flags with his face all across populous northeastern Thailand. His remarkable leadership was marked by sweeping reforms, welfare policies, and corruption scandals. These drew both affection and revulsion from the public. By 2004, dissolution and opposition to his rule among some sections of the public was growing and various protest groups were spilling into the streets. When Thaksin went on to win the 2005 election in yet another landslide victory, opposition forces rapidly escalated. The breaking point was reached when Thaksin sold his family's Shin Corporation to Singapore-based Temasek Holdings for 73.3 billion baht ($2.4 billion) without paying any taxes—causing massive outcry among the opposition forces.

In 2005, sustained broad-based popular mobilization against the democratically elected government of Thaksin Shinawatra nearly brought the nation's capital Bangkok to a complete standstill. In fact, some of the demonstrators had been protesting since 2004, while more opposition groups steadily poured onto the streets to demand the resignation of Thaksin. By early 2006, oppositional forces to the Thaksin government had united under a loosely organized movement called the People's Alliance for Democracy (PAD), which is to say the more popularly known "Yellow Shirts," and began calling for the ouster of his government. As the situation intensified, leaders of the PAD movement appealed to the military and the much-revered monarchy to "step in" to resolve this political deadlock and draw Thailand out of this "tyrannical regime." The first intervention came from the judiciary when the courts annulled the results of the April

2006 election, which all major political parties had boycotted. Despite this, the Thaksin government refused to back down. Eventually, the military staged a coup d'état in September 2006 and successfully ousted the Thaksin administration. The PAD hailed this as a crucial success for the movement and moved to push for systematic reforms in the country's polity that would do away with some key aspects of the democratic system.

The 2006 coup government promised an anxious nation a swift election and a return to democratic politics soon after it took power. But the ousting of Thaksin in 2006 unwittingly, and unfortunately, gave birth to a countermovement to the Yellow Shirts: the "Red Shirts," a largely prodemocracy movement loyal to Thaksin's electoral base. The Red–Yellow conflict continued unabated in the intercoup period (between 2007 and 2014), with violence breaking out on both sides. After passing a new constitution to guarantee the military's immunity and strengthen the military's position in politics, Thailand returned to parliamentary rule with a general election in 2007. The result was devastating to PAD supporters: the Thaksin-aligned party, the People's Power Party, again won, which prompted a sustained period of antidemocratic mobilization. By 2009, the judiciary staged its own coup by backing the PAD's appeal to Thailand's monarchy for an intervention and banned the People's Power Party. The move prompted the takeover of the new government by the opposition party, the Democrat Party. The Red Shirts were outraged and again took to the streets in a bloody showdown between their movement, on the one hand, and the Yellow Shirt–backed government and the military, on the other. Eventually, an election was held again in 2011 and Thaksin's sister, Yingluck Shinawatra, and her newly formed party, Pheu Thai, won another landslide election. Thaksin and his successor parties had won four consecutive general elections in Thailand. Former groups within the defunct PAD movement reorganized themselves and officially partnered with the Democrat Party defections to form the People's Democratic Reform Committee (PDRC). The PDRC launched a full-scale antidemocratic mobilization from the start; they demanded no less than a cessation of elections and military and monarchy interventions into politics. After the massive protests that ensued between 2013 and 2014, the military again staged a coup in May 2014. Thailand remained under military rule until mid-2019.

Thailand became the richest nation to have staged a successful coup d'état in recent decades.[8] With its GNI per capita (purchasing power parity) close to $14,850, this "upper middle income" country, according to the World Bank's classification, should not have seen a day of army tanks rolling into its streets. Indeed, Przeworski et al. (1996,) predicted in their influential article "What Makes Democracies Endure," that "above $6,000, democracies are impregnable and can be expected to live forever: no democratic system has ever fallen in a country where per capita income exceeds $6,055." [9] The collapse of democracy in Thailand sent reverberations across the Pacific region: the Fijian coup leader, Commodore Voreque Bainimarama, cited Thailand as an "inspiration" for his successful coup in December 2006. As this research will show, the causes for the recent collapse of the Thai democracy were political, not economic. Understanding what happened in this relatively affluent and seemingly stable, important Southeast Asian nation helps reveal much about the state of democracy in the developing world.

Current theoretical approaches that explain the emergence of antidemocratic movements offer important but partial answers for the rise of the People's Alliance for Democracy and the People's Democratic Reform Committee. Known collectively as the Yellow Shirts, their emergence and evolution are clear symptoms of weak democratic institutions, deep-rooted intraelite conflicts, and class conflict. That Thailand has dealt with nineteen military coup attempts, frequent governmental and constitutional change, and the continued political power of nondemocratic actors like the monarchy and the military is indicative of a weakly institutionalized democratic system. To look at the party system alone, the majority of Thai political parties lack organizational depth, ideological goals, and strong societal ties, and rarely rise above the personal leadership of a particular individual (Hicken and Kuhonta 2014). Ironically, the two most institutionalized parties—the Democrat Party and Thaksin's Thai Rak Thai (TRT)—are at the center of the country's political crisis since the former faced a challenge by the latter.

The heightened intraelite conflict was exemplified by the leadership of Thaksin and his parties and the main opposition party, the Democrats. But it likewise concerned new versus old elites. Thaksin was part of a new group of business elites who had turned to politics after the country narrowly avoided bankruptcy in the aftermath of the 1997 global financial crisis. The group's meteoric rise disrupted the status quo of traditional nonelected elites—the monarchy, the military, and the bureaucracy—on the one hand, and the established career politicians who had become accustomed to working with this powerful trio, on the other. Not willing to play by the same rules, Thaksin both challenged and undermined the power and authority of powerful actors in the polity, riding on the back of his electoral popularity and growing nationwide fan base. The goal of both the 2006 and 2014 coups was crystal clear to its plotters: to rid Thaksin and his nominees from Thai politics for good.

Class-based analysis in part explains the conflict between the Yellow Shirts and their antagonists, the Red Shirts, the pro-Thaksin movement that emerged following his ousting after the coup. Unlike the widely accepted wisdom that Thailand's political crisis is marked by the division between the rich and poor, it is more aptly described as a conflict between the older, more established middle class and the upwardly mobile newer sections of the middle class. Some key grievances of the Yellow Shirts are best understood through the class lens: their privileged position in society—a secure and stable source(s) of income and voice in the democratic system—is being challenged by the rising lower middle class, which has been vying for the same economic and political benefits afforded to their upper middle-class counterparts. Thaksin empowered the lower section of the middle class through his redistribution programs and greater access to state coffers. Seeing the gains made by Thaksin's supporters as their loss, the Yellow Shirts saw no other means to reset the clock back to the "good old days" but to appeal for extraconstitutional interventions. While this class-based explanation is useful to outline the underlying grievances driving the mobilization of the Yellow Shirts, more nuances are required. The Yellow Shirts are made up of highly dynamic and eclectic sections of society that cannot uniformly or solely be understood along class lines. This book therefore attempts to provide a more nuanced appreciation as to who constituted the Yellow Shirts movement, and how their antidemocratic mobilization transpired.

The theoretical frameworks outlined above capture well why, but not *how* or *when*, a large-scale antidemocratic movement emerges in a democracy. Structural explanations like class, economic, and institutional perspectives can be deterministic and unable to fully capture the dynamism of antidemocratic mobilization emergence. The concept of institutional blockage and the process of antidemocratic mobilization detailed in this book brings us closer to understanding how and when people turn against democracy. The PAD was composed of and driven by actors and groups in society that were not only made worse off because of Thaksin's policies. Opposition channels that might have allowed these actors and groups to convey their grievances were closed off. This happened in both the formal and informal arenas. In the formal democratic institutions, opposition parties in the legislature and certain sections of the Senate joined forces with the PAD movement due to their inability to oppose or advance alternatives to the Thaksin-led absolute majority in parliament. The same went for the courts and key figures of the bureaucracy, whose powers were severed by Thaksin's rule. In the informal institutional channels, the nongovernmental organization (NGO) sector, labor unions, and media all experienced not only the loss of their political space; possibilities for them to present alternatives to government positions were marginalized. This resentment did not culminate in the PAD movement until Thaksin and his Thai Rak Thai party won their consecutive landslide election victory in 2005. Following this, the opposition became convinced they were permanently excluded from power due to Thai Rak Thai's electoral dominance and Thaksin's growing abuse of executive power. At this point, the PAD came together as a movement not merely to oppose Thaksin collectively but also to appeal to the monarchy and the military to intervene.

The People's Democratic Reform Committee—a successor movement to the PAD—was mobilized around similar grievances: feeling shunned from the formal democratic institutions as Thaksin's successor parties continued their electoral dominance. The PDRC, however, was fundamentally different from the PAD in two key respects: it was far more antidemocratic, and it was largely mobilized on social media. The PDRC took a more hard-line approach when it came to its core priorities: cessation of elections, a greater role for the monarchy and military in politics, and a return to a fully unelected house of review (the Senate) in the Thai National Assembly.

Why Social Media Matters

Social media is a game changer in understanding antidemocratic politics in democracies. I argue here that social media is a tool for antidemocratic mobilization. Social media also makes coups cheaper. Social media amplifies antidemocratic voices to reach more people in a much shorter time than any other form of media today. The costs required to mobilize hundreds of thousands of people in the pre-social-media era are sharply reduced by leveraging social media affordances. By making antidemocratic mobilization faster and much cheaper, social media directly contributes to bringing down the overall cost of launching a military coup.

Up until recently, social media was heralded as the "liberation technology": it empowers activists and ordinary people the world over to fight against oppressive regimes, it keeps governments accountable to their actions, and helps to increase civic and political participation (Diamond and Plattner 2012). Successful uprisings from the Arab Spring to Hong Kong have fostered early optimism that platforms like Facebook and Fire-Chat can expand the numbers of the politically engaged, particularly those previously disengaged from formal politics. Scholars who subscribe to this view that social media can mobilize new sections of society into politics have been encouraged by the rise of political engagement among youths in North America and Europe, whose participation in formal politics had long been in a decline (Vromen et al. 2016).

Social media should also help improve the quality of democracy by providing new ways to engage with elected officials, wherein citizens can offer feedback or hold officials accountable to their actions and thus foster greater transparency. For many countries in Asia where media freedom is low, social media should also offer avenues for ordinary citizens to challenge the dominant state-led discourses of information and make it harder for governments to suppress information online. Moreover, by talking online to people of diverse viewpoints, social media should help neutralize radical voices by subjecting them to public exposure and greater engagement with the mainstream.

Despite a long list of contributions that social media can make toward strengthening democracy, it also has a dark side. This book demonstrates empirically, through the rise of the People's Democratic Reform Committee and its subsequent contribution to the 2014 coup d'état in Thailand, that social media did not counter antidemocratic attitudes online. Instead, it amplified these and, moreover, helped antidemocratic factions to gain control of the broader movement and dictate its antidemocratic agenda. Analysis of political engagement by both the PDRC and the Red Shirts also shows that social media perpetuates political polarization and societal divisions by further sowing the seed of discord. Facebook groups under study demonstrate strong echo chamber effects whereby like-minded individuals only talk to one another and rarely engage with those with opposing views—dampening any opportunities for neutralizing antidemocratic attitudes. The mobilization of nearly a quarter of a million protesters on the streets during the 2013–14 Bangkok Shutdown was also largely facilitated online. All in all, social media did far more to strengthen the antidemocratic attitudes and facilitate antidemocratic mobilization than it did to contain them.

The major contribution of this book is the explanation to the puzzle: why we observe a successful antidemocratic movement in a middle-income country where social media hastened democratic decline. The incorporation of social media in this book serves primarily to demonstrate the positive impact that it has had on both the antidemocratic mobilization and coup prospects for Thailand. While not advancing any causal claim here, this work provides an empirically rich analysis of the role that social media plays in advancing nondemocratic discourse and mobilizing mass movements that seek to overthrow an elected government. This serves to fill an empirical gap in the study of social media and political regimes insofar as it directly and comprehensively discusses the ways in which social media can contribute to democratic breakdown.

Methodology

This research is based on fieldwork conducted in Thailand from 2009 to 2014, and it employs both qualitative and quantitative methodologies. Key qualitative research methodologies utilized in this work include participant observation, semistructured interviews, archival data research, statistical analysis, discursive analysis, and a public opinion survey. The majority of the interviews conducted for this book were drawn from fieldwork trips in 2010, 2011, 2012, 2013, and 2014. Interviews were targeted at the following groups: the PAD's and PDRC's top national and local leaders, activists, media, security forces, politicians, military officers, protesters, police, academics, and government officials. To obtain a balanced view on the political crisis in Thailand, interviews were also conducted with the Red Shirts, a pro-Thaksin movement that emerged following the 2006 coup. My interviews helped me gain a context-specific understanding of the relationships among the different forces that have contributed to the collapse of democracy in Thailand. Specifically, I have gained a nuanced understanding of the motivations and aspirations of ordinary people in joining this antidemocratic movement.

To test the argument on institutional blockage, I created a new database on protest activities across Thailand between 1991 and 2011. The statistical analysis based on this data allowed me to map the cycle of contention both before and after the democratic breakdown of 2006, categorized in types and modes of opposition. I was also able to identify "critical moments" in each period of the protest cycle as the movement ebbed and flowed over time. I also used a number of digital tools to map the PAD's and PDRC's membership and support base and predict their movement strategies. Frequently, the research was conducted at the Yellow Shirts' headquarters—Baan Pra Athit—and that of the New Politics Party, both in Bangkok. Over the span of a decade, I attended numerous PAD and PDRC rallies, which proved crucial to my analysis of their discourse. Given the dynamic and fluid nature of this political movement, it was imperative to be present at various activities of the movement to gain a nuanced understanding of the movement's goals, strategies, and discourse. The PAD was arguably the world's first *live* movement: its entire activities during much of its existence were broadcast through its satellite channels. There were many elements of the "production" of mass media involved. As such, understanding the message that the PAD and PDRC sent out to their respective members both at the rallies and in the online, digital space helped to cement a more complete understanding of the movement.

Social media data on Facebook and Twitter was collected and analyzed using both quantitative and qualitative methods. For social media, the key time frame of interest is from 2013 to 2017, given that the PDRC emerged in 2013 and its major activities ranged from mid-2013 until the coup in May 2014. Following the coup, Facebook data of procoup support groups until May 2017 were also analyzed to provide insights on the procoup groups in the postcoup politics. Prior to 2013, social media was available but not popularly used by the masses nor any of the key movements under study here. By examining the PAD, which was in the pre-social-media era, and the social media fueled PDRC, I can investigate what impact, if any, social media has had on antidemocratic mobilization. To collect Facebook and Twitter data, I used multiple data extraction methods to gather millions of data points as a basis for analysis. I then employed social network analysis, profile analysis, topic modeling, natural language processing, and content analysis to discern the role that social media, particularly Facebook, played in both the antidemocratic discourse of the movement and its online mobilization. I also analyzed the discourse and networks of the military dictatorship from May 2014 onward—namely, those who were mobilized for democratic breakdown—to see if and how such procoup sentiment might translate to military government support over time.

Plan of the Book

This book examines three critical periods: the emergence of the PAD movement from 2005 to 2011, the emergence of the PDRC movement from 2013 to 2014, and military dictatorship from May 2014 to May 2019. This time frame was chosen to reflect the four major periods of these yellow-shirted movements' development: the first, the PAD's emergence (2005–06); the second, the PAD's resurgence (2008–09); the third, the PAD's decline (2010–11); and the fourth, the PDRC's emergence (2013–14). The last chapter and its conclusion examine the post-2014 coup authoritarian environment and discuss future prospects of antidemocratic remobilization following a resurrection of electoral politics.

Opposing Democracy in the Digital Age: The Yellow Shirts in Thailand is divided into eight chapters. Chapter 2, "Opposing Democracy," provides a more detailed discussion of the concept of institutional blockage and how it operates within the antidemocratic mobilization framework. Given that my work is informed by the literature on civil society, political movements, and democratic breakdown, in this chapter the frameworks, arguments, and underlying theoretical assumptions will be spelled out in greater detail to allow for close examination. I will then show how these existing theories are important but incomplete to explain the emergence of antidemocratic movements in Thailand. I then briefly analyze recent examples of democratic breakdown in Venezuela to illustrate both its similarities and differences with the Thai case.

Chapter 3, "Crises and Coups," introduces Thailand as the main case in this study. It argues that Thailand's political and economic structures make its democracy conducive to a breakdown. Specifically, I discuss the importance of the military and the monarchy—key nondemocratic bodies in Thailand—to understand the trajectory of Thai politics. I then analyze other key factors that provide grounds for democratic collapse in Thailand: (1) frequent coups d'état; (2) support for nondemocratic figures and institutions among the public; and (3) previous episodes of antidemocratic mobilization. This chapter also charts the origin of the PAD movement as rooted in the contestation of democratic accountability visions. I argue that the ideological foundations that underpin the PAD originate in the 1990s following the 1992 Black May Uprising and its subsequent political and economic reforms. The tension among the reformists with regard to what type of accountability Thailand needed—horizontal, vertical, and moral—strained the reform process and gave grounds to the resurgent moral ideologists inside the PAD. Last, I outline how the conflicting notions of democracy and accountability so crucial to the foundational years of the PAD directly affected the development of its successor movement, the PDRC.

Chapter 4, "The Origins of the Yellow Shirts," chronicles the foundational years of the birth of the People's Alliance for Democracy. Specifically, it focuses on the reformist years when, following the 1991 coup, future PAD leaders took up the fight for democracy in Thailand. This chapter argues that while the prodemocracy reforms were largely successful, they nonetheless reflect tension between majoritarianism, on the one hand, and accountability, on the other. Such tension would sow the seeds for the eventual emergence of the PAD and its transformation from a pro- to an antidemocratic movement. Chapter 5, "Democratic Breakdown," discusses the process of antidemocratization of the PAD movement. The main argument is that the PAD movement resorted to nondemocratic sources of power and authority due to the failure of other strategies. I also advance the claim that the coup d'état in 2006 was a *choice*—that is, it was a product of numerous strategic interactions between opposition forces and the Thaksin government. It also addresses the postcoup PAD and its decline in 2010. This section employs the postcoup PAD mobilization as a within-case variation: an antidemocratic movement still remained, but democracy survived. The chapter's main argument is that the conditions of institutional blockage were not present during this period. As such, the PAD's opposition declined in both popularity and effectiveness. Opposition elites did not see the need to engage in extraconstitutional means.

Chapter 6 introduces social media in chronicling the emergence of the PAD's successor movement—the People's Democratic Reform Committee. In "Social Media and the New Antidemocrats," I argue that social media helped to remobilize the antidemocrats by making coordination cheaper, faster, and easier. Facebook, in particular, represents an important platform for antidemocratic ideas to spread. Social media helped to entrench and prolong political divisions in Thailand, making compromise impossible. Through a series of mass mobilizations both online and off, the PDRC successfully created conditions for the subsequent military coup in 2014. Chapter 7, "Crowdsourcing Dictatorship," maps support for the military government since the 2014 coup. I focus particularly on groups that were part of the broader PDRC movement and which demanded military intervention. By examining three years of data pertaining to their postcoup conversations on Facebook and comparing it to the precoup period, I uncover the extent to which these coup supporters remained supportive of the very government they helped put in place. I find that the hardliners were few in number but very committed, whereas the majority of the PDRC supporters began to lose their support for the movement and its leader, Suthep Taugsuban, following a series of unfulfilled promises. Ironically, even the antidemocrats expected accountability from the authoritarian government, suggesting that their support for overthrowing democracy was temporary and conditional. In the concluding chapter, I outline the implications of the PDRC's dwindling support for the junta government toward the prospect of a return to both democratic and antidemocratic politics in Thailand. The conclusion in Chapter 8 outlines the implications of Thailand's antidemocratic movements on understanding similar phenomena in other developing democracies.

TWO

Opposing Democracy

Since the publication of the seminal *Transitions from Authoritarian Rule* (O'Donnell et al. 1986), where scholars debated the possibility of and the way in which democratization occurs in authoritarian settings, the world has become much more democratic. Democracy has truly emerged as the dominant regime type, and sophisticated public opinion tools have shown greater popular support for democracy. In 1989, there were sixty-nine electoral democracies, accounting for 40 percent of the regime types worldwide. This figure jumped to 117 electoral democracies in 2012, accounting for 60 percent of the world.[1] This period, broadly speaking, is considered as "democratic ascendency" (Gilley 2010, 160) whereby the number of democratic regimes far outstripped that of their authoritarian counterparts. This should be cause for optimism for scholars of democratization.[2] Samuel Huntington's *Third Wave of Democracy* (1991) devoted significant space in its later chapters to warning scholars of the "reverse wave" that resulted from powerful militaries, authoritarian nostalgia, weak democratic values, and the breakdown of law and order. Francis Fukuyama's *The End of History and the Last Man* (1992) also cautions that the world will continue to be vulnerable to antidemocratic movements as long as human beings have a desire to dominate. It remains inconclusive that democracy is a final form of government.

Recent democratic breakdowns have raised the question not only of their causes but what such collapses tell us about the state of democracy prior to the regime breakdown. Indeed, understanding authoritarian resurgence should tell us as much about the authoritarian tendencies as the nature of the democratic regime prior to its collapse. This research seeks to contribute to a more nuanced understanding of conditions prior to democratic collapse. As O'Donnell, Cullell and Iazzetta (2004, xiii) argue, "The happy fact of the recent emergence of numerous democratic regimes cannot, and, should not, conceal the fact that the workings and impacts of the respective governments and states evince wide variations. Variations that run from acceptable to rather dismal performance have important consequences." Among the democracies that collapsed in the last decade, their pattern of breakdown has been one of tremendous variation. Some states were extremely poor, while others were as well off as any developing democracy. About half of these states had a presidential system, while the others were parliamentary democracies prior to the breakdown. Given that the collapsed democracies are situated across different continents, contagion does not seem to be driving these breakdowns. All in all, the variation that exists among the collapsed democracies is as great as among the ones still in existence (table 2.1).

Popular mobilization for democratic reversal has been crucial to the success of regime change in several countries in the last decade. After the Egyptian uprising that toppled the thirty-year-old regime of Hosni Mubarak, many of the Egyptian "revolutionaries" found themselves calling for extraconstitutional powers to remove their newly elected leader, Mohamed Morsi. In the summer of 2013, the army ousted Morsi from power, much to the delight of many Egyptians. In Bangladesh, the military intervention in January 2007 was "widely welcomed" by civil society and the international community.[3] "The aspiring new middle class is quite happy to use the military and unfair political means . . . to pave the way for their own entry into leadership position," explains Baladas Ghoshal of the middle class's support of the coup.[4]

How do we explain these recent examples of popular support for nondemocratic rule? Under what conditions do people in a democracy call for military intervention to oust their elected leaders? To answer these puzzling questions, my book advances the following claims. I argue that antidemocratic mobilization occurs when mobilized societal groups feel "cornered" and are unable to channel their grievances through democratic institutions. They form opposition groups to regain their access to power in a democratic polity. If the opposition forces perceive their exclusion from power to be permanent in the foreseeable future, they rebel against the system by appealing to nondemocratic institutions. And they do so by undermining the democratic polity. If these nondemocratic bodies respond to the opposition groups, a democratic breakdown occurs.

The choice made by nondemocratic institutions to ally with antidemocratic movements and do away with the democratic systems depends largely on their "perceived" level of public support for the opposition movement. In other words, if nondemocratic bodies see that the antidemocratic movement garners sufficient support to legitimize extraconstitutional acts, then democracy will likely collapse. As such, a mobilized, popular antidemocratic movement creates the conditions for a democratic breakdown. I show in detail in the empirical chapters how nondemocratic institutions in Thailand were *reactive* to the growing opposition mobilization against the democratic government. It was not the case that nondemocratic institutions were going to stage a coup regardless of whether or not people were calling for it. It was the antidemocratic movement that made a coup possible. Although Thailand had a long history of military-initiated coups devoid of the need to elicit popular support, the disastrous aftermath of the 1991 coup vastly increased the cost of future coups for the military. This is

TABLE 2.1. Incidents of democratic collapse by coup d'état, 2000–2015

Country	Year	Outcome	Type of government	GNP, PPP year of collapse	Support for democratic breakdown
Nepal	2002	Successful	Parliamentary	$1,280	Upper caste, palace circle
	2005	Successful		$1,500	
Venezuela	2002	Successful (short lived)	Presidential	$10,460	Business class, middle class, state enterprise
Thailand	2006	Successful	Parliamentary	$10,630	Civil society, middle class, labor, royalist-conservative groups
	2014			$14,850	
Fiji	2006	Successful	Parliamentary	$6,630	Rival ethnic groups
Bangladesh	2007	Successful	Parliamentary	$2,150	Civil society, international community, middle class
Honduras	2009	Successful	Presidential	$3,610	Political elites, United States, evangelicals, Catholic Church
Mali	2012	Successful	Presidential	$1,760	Farmers, civil society workers
Egypt	2013	Successful	Parliamentary	$9,900	Secular groups, Christian groups, students

* World Bank, GNI PPP per capita (current International)
Note: "Successful coups" refers to ones that result in a regime change and transfer of power.

due to the mass demonstrations and bloody confrontations that followed the 1991 coup, which eventually led to the military government stepping down. Since then, the military focused its efforts on staying well within their barracks (Bamrungsuk 2001).

This chapter proceeds as follows. The first section defines the main dependent variable—antidemocratic mobilization—and demonstrates a considerable variation in the makeup and orientation of antidemocratic movements in recent instances of democratic breakdown. I then provide a typology of opposition movements, categorizing these on the basis of mobilization goals. This typology will help to distinguish empirically and analytically the difference between anti-incumbent and antidemocratic movements.

In the second section I review the current literature on the determinants of antidemocratic movements, explaining how the rise of the People's Alliance for Democracy and the People's Democratic Reform Committee both builds on and fills empirical gaps in our understanding of antisystem movements. I emphasize here that my theoretical claims are both in line with an institutional approach and benefit from the prominent structural-based frameworks, such as class and intraelite causes. While I recognize the utility of these approaches to pinpoint the structural foundations of the grievances that underlie the PAD's and PDRC's emergence, they cannot account for why antidemocratic movements in Thailand arose when they did. More importantly, these approaches tend to be "structural" in nature and do not fully account for the "agency" of the movement. The emergence of this antidemocratic movement in Thailand is not a "natural progression" of the existing inequality or elite fragmentation in Thailand. Rather, it is contingent upon a number of strategic choices made by various societal groups.

The paradox of the Thai case, for the study of comparative politics, is not merely that the PAD and PDRC emerged and succeeded in overthrowing a democratic regime in a middle-income country. It is also that both movements were largely supported by the middle class and civil society agents. While neither of the movements denotes an explicitly class-based mobilization, the major role played by the Thai middle class in the makeup of each movement has important implications for our understanding of the relationship between the middle class and democratic stability. Moreover, the emergence of the PAD was initiated and widely supported by civil society actors. Again, why civil society agents would support antidemocratic mobilization presents an additional puzzling fact of the Thai case.

The third section discusses the evolution of the PDRC and how similar conditions facing the PAD at the onset in early 2006 were experienced by PDRC supporters. It also notes the PDRC's far greater antidemocratic orientation in comparison to the PAD. While there was some initial ambivalence in propagating the antidemocratic agenda within the PAD, especially within the leadership, the PDRC was early and upfront about its antidemocratic proposals: not just to throw out the elected government through extraconstitutional intervention, but a cessation of electoral politics altogether. The last section briefly discusses the novel ways in which this research breaks new ground in the study of Thai politics, most notably as it relates to the current and ongoing political conflict and to the broader contributions it makes to the study of regime transition globally.

Typology of Opposition Movements

I adopt the minimalist definition of democracy advanced by Przeworski et al. (2000). This is a procedural definition that focuses on the issue of "contestation." According to Przeworski (2000, 19–20), democracy is defined as followed:

1. Ex-ante, a possibility that an incumbent may lose an election;
2. Ex-post irreversibility, an assurance that an election winner will take office;
3. Elections must be repeated.

Democracy is thus "a regime that fills executive and legislative bodies through free and contested elections; has more than one party and the opposition has some chance of winning" (Przeworski et al. 2000, 19). Given that this is a minimalist definition of democracy that largely focuses on the mechanism of free and fair elections, it becomes an "easy" test to determine what would constitute an antidemocratic movement. If a movement forms that opposes the principle of holding elections and supports extraconstitutional interventions, then it is "antidemocratic." I choose to use this procedural definition because it presents a clear-cut yardstick to measure against. For analytical purposes, it is more advantageous to use this basic definition than other more substantive, and ultimately complex, definitions of democracy that can encompass a multitude of factors to the extent that these become a slippery slope.

Antidemocratic mobilization refers to a movement of individuals and groups mobilized to subvert the political system's holding competitive, free, and fair elec-

tions. Movements that support extraconstitutional measures to undermine a democratic regime are also regarded as antidemocratic. These factors represent a *minimum* requirement for a movement to be considered as opposing the democratic system. There are other indicators that would qualify a movement as being antidemocratic as well. These indicators include (a) support for extraconstitutional intervention; (b) support for unelected political leadership; (c) support for strong involvement in politics from nondemocratic institutions/actors; and (d) support for an appointed legislature. These indicators help to analytically and theoretically distinguish antidemocratic mobilization from anti-incumbent movements. Sometimes it is unclear to what extent a particular movement actually opposes the principles of democracy or merely opposes a particular elected government. There are many reasons why ordinary people would protest against their elected government, but one needs to be able to discern whether they are against the democratic system per se or simply want to remove the incumbent.

The case of antidemocratic mobilization is far more dangerous to the stability of the democratic system than other types of antiestablishment or antigovernment movements because the former seeks to subvert the democratic regime. The anti-Morsi movements in Egypt were calling for the military to step in: they were unhappy with President Morsi, but at the same time also actively supported extraconstitutional intervention. As such, these movements are considered antidemocratic.

Opposition movements are neither monolithic nor unidirectional. In much of the literature and empirical work on opposition politics, opposition movements are often perceived positively as a collective action against something "bad": be it a regime, a government, or a leader.[5] I argue here that there are three key types of opposition movement—each with its own characteristics and raison d'être for mobilization. In general, an opposition movement forms to contest either a specific policy or the general direction of the government. Once formed, an opposition movement takes on one of these three forms: (1) proreform; (2) anti-incumbent, and (3) antidemo-

TABLE 2.2. Indicators for antidemocratic mobilization

Minimum	Oppose competitive free and fair elections
	Support for extraconstitutional intervention
Additional Indicators	1. Support for unelected political leadership
	2. Support for strong involvement by nondemocratic institutions in politics
	3. Support for an appointed legislature

cratic. These typologies help to differentiate analytically and empirically the *nature* of opposition by distinguishing the goals, channels, and methodologies of opposition mobilization. Proreform opposition movement seeks to propose policy alternatives, while anti-incumbent movements seek executive or government replacement. Neither is committed to subverting the democratic system.

Antidemocratic mobilization, which is the main focus of this book, is a distinct type of opposition movement whose characteristics differ largely from other forms of opposition mobilization. For an antidemocratic movement, government change is not the desired outcome. Unlike other types of opposition mobilization, an antidemocratic movement carries the highest costs and is considered a "last resort" strategy. The theory set forth in this study outlines the conditions under which an antidemocratic movement can form with the goal of overthrowing an elected government.

Opposition movements that are proreform seek to address their grievances through proposing policy alternatives to those of the incumbent government. They channel their demands through formal institutional means in a democratic system, such as petitioning their members of parliament (MPs), holding demonstrations, lobbying relevant stakeholders, and campaigning. It is imperative that proreform opposition movements offer policy alternatives. The option of proreform as a strategy for mobilization for opposition movement is most likely to occur in a democratic setting where public channels for voicing grievances are available. A more decentralized system provides greater numbers of access points for citizens than does its centralized counterpart.

An anti-incumbent movement is a more contentious form of opposition politics, whereby groups are mobilized to demand a change in leadership. The incumbent, for the opposition, has failed to deliver desired political outcomes and should no longer be in power. Contrary to the proreform opposition movement, its anti-incumbent counterpart does not necessarily propose policy alternatives. In many cases, anti-incumbent movements demand leadership resignation or a new election. The movement would cite reasons for its opposition both in broad and specific terms, such as incumbent corruption, vote rigging, a poor economy, and bad policies.

There is no reason why proreform, anti-incumbent, or antidemocratic types of mobilization should logically follow each other. One can empirically observe opposition movements that have the characteristics of being both proreform and anti-incumbent. Alternatively, a particular opposition movement can first be one of proreform and then evolve into an anti-incumbent movement, or vice versa. Typically, however, an antidemocratic movement should be the last option used as a result of the failures of the other two options precisely because it is the costliest option for an opposition movement. Subverting an entire political system requires a complete regime change, which means a politicized military must be willing and available to make it happen. Those with power, especially if elected, will not give up such coveted positions so easily. Moreover, appealing to powerful, nondemocratic sources of power is not always an available option for opposition movements and may entail serious risks.

Explaining Opposition to Democracy

Examining how democratic institutions give rise to a popular antidemocratic movement is the key task that this research accomplishes. How do democratic institutions shape the behavior and strategic calculation of political actors in such ways that they may seek to overthrow the regime altogether? Why do ordinary people and civic groups join forces to subvert the democratic system? This research paints a complex, yet often overlooked, picture of how the public plays an important part in its country's democratic demise. Tracing the antidemocratic movement's emergence and development lies at the heart of this work.

Existing scholarship highlights that there are three key factors that explain the rise of antidemocratic and antisystem movement in new democracies. The most widely cited argument is an economic one. When new democracies face a severe economic crisis, the public reacts negatively toward the regime by supporting antidemocratic/antisystem movements or political parties (Berg-Schlosser 1998; Kitschelt and McGann 1997; Brustein 1991; Olukoshi 1998; Allen 1973). It is not the economic crisis per se that drives people to overthrow their democratic governments. Rather, it is how the people react to severe economic downturns that could have implications for democratic stability. Sartori (1976) argues that severe economic adversity prompts people to vacate the center and move toward the extreme left or right wings of the political spectrum. Sartori's argument found traction in a number of later works, particularly those that seek to explain the rise of fascism, communism, and Nazism in Europe (Saich 1990; Lewis 1997; Daalder 1984).

In *The Nazi Seizure of Power* (1973), William Allen concluded that the dire economic situation was a driving force behind the success of the Nazi movement: "There is no doubt that the progressive despair of the jobless, as reflected in the longer and longer periods of unemployment, weakened the forces of democracy. . . . In the face of the mounting economic crisis, Thalburgers were willing to tolerate approaches that would have left them indignant or indifferent under other circumstances."[6] Similarly, Lyttleton (1973, 41) argues that the professional classes in Italy joined the fascist movement as they were "faced with a serious decline in living standards and with their social function denied by proletarian socialism."[7]

A second approach, political leadership, argues that leadership failure accounts for the demise of democracy. Nancy Bermeo's seminal work, *Ordinary People in Extraordinary Times* (2003), investigates seventeen cases of democratic collapse in Europe and Latin America to show that although people may throw democracy off course, they rarely do so through their vote. Political elites either misunderstand or manipulate public polarization (i.e., protests, strikes, opinion polls) for their own gain and act on their own convictions to the demise of democracy. Bermeo refers to this condition as "elite ignorance" (2003, 228). People in states like Weimar Germany, interwar Italy, or crisis-prone Argentina mobilized against democratic governments in the first place due to a multitude of factors that are located above and beyond economic crises. No matter how people become polarized, she argues, elites are the ones that bring down democratic regimes. The fascist movement in Italy, for example, despite Benito Mussolini's efforts to appeal to the masses, did not come close to achieving a popular mandate. The real breakdown of democracy in Italy came as a result of miscalculations by the monarchy—and it is these that essentially empowered Mussolini.[8]

Bermeo's approach fits well with broader arguments made by many scholars: democratic transitions and breakdowns are ultimately the product of elite choices (O'Donnell et al. 1986; Lopez-Pintor 1987; Linz and Stepan 1978). Linz and Stepan's (1978) oft-cited work, *The Breakdown of Democratic Regimes*, argues that structuralist approaches like the macrosocial and economic conditions used to explain democratic breakdowns are too deterministic. These authors purport, rather, that poor leadership quality—particularly incumbent democratic leaders—contributes to the collapse of democratic regimes.[9] Democratic rulers must believe in the persistence of democratic institutions for the regime to survive.[10]

A third alternative theory, from which this book extends, argues that antidemocratic movements are most likely to thrive in places with weak political institutionalization (Huntington 1968; Berman 1997; Fiorina 1997; Armony 2004). When social mobilization outpaces political institutionalization, chaos and crisis will ensue (Fukuyama 2006).[11] When weak political institutions do not respond to the public demand for meaningful political participation in public life, citizens are driven to look for other alternatives to voice their grievances. Haunted by the shadow of their authoritarian past, some countries begin their journey down the democratic road in having to bring with them powerful, entrenched nondemocratic institutions that continue to undermine their democratization prospects (Hicken and Kuhonta 2014).

One interpretation of this Huntingtonian argument on "political decay" is made by Sheri Berman (1997). She argues that democracy can break down when the regime cannot meet growing public needs in a highly mobilized society. Berman believes the poorly designed and weak political institutions in the Weimar Republic exacerbated social cleavages, which in turn prompted mobilized and organized Germans to devote their energies to associational life. Weimar collapsed because of the party system's failure to channel the conflicting demands of a very vibrant civil society. The Nazi movement, in contrast, was able to appeal to German associational life and take over where political institutions had failed. The rapid mobilization of social forces and slow development of political institutions can create instability and disorder in several ways (Huntington 1968). First, traditional sources of power may intervene to restore "order" when faced with social instability. The military and the civilian bureaucracy, if more developed than political institutions, will be encouraged to "intervene" because of the incompetence of politicians and political institutions (Riggs 1964; Huntington 1968).

Many scholars agree that institutionalized party systems are a cornerstone of strong democracies (Mainwaring 1999; Randall and Svasand 2002). Low party institutionalization means that parties do not have deep anchors in society; electoral volatility is high; party organization is shallow; and voters do not have strong party identification or feel that parties are legitimate (Croissant and Volkel 2010). More institutionalized party systems produce better outcomes for their citizens in terms of public goods delivery and in providing meaningful ways to hold those in office accountable. But the Third Wave democracies are particularly noted for their weak party roots in society as politicians prefer to deliver private goods (Mainwaring and Torcal 2006). The problem becomes even more acute when accountability problems are caused by both an abusive executive, on the one hand, and the lack of credible restraints on the executive, on the other (Diamond, Plattner, and Schedler 1999).

Two major case-specific explanations to the rise of this antidemocratic mobilization are worth noting. The most well-known arguments among observers of Thai politics are class-based ones. This approach is centered on socioeconomic structural arguments that contend that the long-standing divide between the rural poor and the urban elites is what has given rise to the mass mobilization and the ongoing crisis in present-day Thailand (Phongpaichit and Baker 2008, 2012; Pongsudhirak 2008; Funston 2009; Hewison and Kittirianglarp 2009; Aeosriwong 2010; Montesano et al. 2012; Hewison 2012). Phongpaichit and Baker (2012, 221–25) convincingly argue that the middle class and the powerful oligarchic elites were threatened by Thaksin and the poor that he had empowered. While Hewison (2012, 145) does not claim a direct link between class and political movements, he stresses the importance of class as a key structural factor to explain political activism in Thailand. The class-based explanation of the current Thai conflict is buttressed by the powerful concept of the "tale of two democracies" advanced by Anek Laothamtas (1996). He flags the existence of a division between how the Bangkok middle class and the rest of the country each understand democracy.

Alternatively, other scholars view the PAD and the PDRC as largely reflective of the power struggle between traditional versus new elites. Elite disunity can breed political instability and create a condition under which government executive power can be subject to seizure by force (Sanders and Handelman 1981; Higley and Burton 1989; Londregan and Poole 1990). Coups d'état occur because military elites' interests are under threat or neglected by political elites in the democratic system. Thus, the former overthrows the latter to regain its prominence (Nordlinger 1976; Li and Thompson 1975; Kennedy and Louscher 1991). The traditional power holders in Thailand, the monarchy-military-bureaucracy trio, came under threat following the emergence of business elites. This threat prompted them to mobilize an antidemocratic mass movement. The Thai business class pursued active political involvement in the wake of the Asian Financial Crisis of 1997, which further threatened the interests of the traditional power brokers. The latter conservative establishment perceived the new business elites as a threat to their own power, and so mounted a series of opposition actions to Thaksin's regime, including mobilizing the PAD movement.

Additionally, democracies are more likely to break down in an environment of severe polarization (Baldassarri and Gelman 2008; Hare and Poole 2014). Political polarization in this case extends beyond its narrow but widely adopted definition: the ideological differences between political parties. Political polarization, in a widened conception, is "the process . . . whereby polarization is activated when major groups in society mobilize politically to achieve fundamental changes in structures, institutions and power relations" (McCoy, Rahman, and Somer 2018, 16). While some level of political polarization can be good for democracy for its tendancy to increase political participation and strengthen political parties (LeBas 2011; Campbell 2016), severe polarization is threatening to democracies because it divides society into two camps with ideologically irreconcilable differences, undermining social cohesion and increasing political instability (Baldassarri and Gelman 2008). Such vicious polarization unites otherwise disparate groups of people under a single identity in order to construct and mobilize against "the other" (McCoy, Rahman, and Somer 2018). In severely polarized societies, politics is seen as a zero-sum game where mutual benefits and compromise between the two camps become impossible. In a case where one side of the political divide becomes increasingly authoritarian and hegemonic, democratic breakdown may emerge as a reaction to such severe polarization (Kongkirati 2018).

For the economic crisis approach to be correct, the PAD and the PDRC movements would have had to emerge following a major financial crisis. And their supporters would have cited economic hardship as a key driving force for movement participation and mobilization. Movement leaders would have engaged in economy-centered discourses to mobilize their mass support. The leadership failure approach would be suitable for the Thai case were we to ascertain a divergence on ideological orientations and voting preferences of both the masses and the elites of the PAD and the PDRC. Elites also would have shown little commitment to democracy, demonstrable through analysis of their behavior or discourse. Moreover, for the weak institutionalization approach to hold for the Thai case, the PAD and the PDRC would have mobilized at a time when its democratic institutions remained weak vis-à-vis their nondemocratic counterparts, its party system institutionalization low, and its government increasingly unable to meet the demands of the public.

For these case-specific explanations to hold true for the PAD and the PDRC movements, we would expect to observe the following conditions. For the class-based approach to explain these antidemocratic movements, we would anticipate the PAD and the PDRC to be mobilized based on class interests. If the movements are composed of upper- and middle-class members, then their interests would be shaped by fear of losing economic interests and power to the rural poor and would prompt the urban rich to subvert the democratic system. As for the intraelite conflict approach, we would expect elites' interests to play an important part in the mobilization of both the PAD and the PDRC. The monarchy, military, and bureaucracy would play a major role in driving the opposition forces.

There are a number of reasons why both existing theoretical and empirical approaches discussed above cannot fully account for the emergence of the PAD and PDRC movements in Thailand. However, I acknowledge the importance of the structural, institutional, and class conflict explanations in providing the theoretical basis to understand why Thailand's democracy is conducive to a breakdown. To be clear: the contribution that I make to the existing literature on the institutional blockage concept and the process of antidemocratic mobilization is an additional lens through which to understand *how* a democratic collapse happens, particularly following a series of reforms that are designed to strengthen the prospects of democratic survival.

The PAD movement arose during periods of sustained economic *growth* in Thailand. For the economic crisis argument to hold, economic downturns need to be the driving force behind antidemocratic mobilization. Yet, between 2002 and 2006, when opposition against the Thaksin government began, GDP growth in that country was 6 percent (see figure 2.1). Following the 1997 Asian Financial Crisis, which left Thailand nearly bankrupt, not only did Thaksin's administration restore the economy, it succeeded in paying back the IMF loans that had forced previous governments to cut critical social spending. While economic growth was not on par with that of the precrisis period, overall economic conditions when the PAD emerged were good. Consequently, a major flaw with the economic crisis approach is precisely that it cannot explain antidemocratic mobilization during an economic boom. More broadly, the approach can similarly fall in the opposite direction: many countries that face severe economic downturns do not see mobilization against democracy (Roberts and Wibbels 1999; MacIntyre 2001; Levitsky and Murillo 2003).

The elite-centric approaches correctly flag the crucial role played by opposition elites in both facilitating and mobilizing antidemocratic movements. This was more evident the second time around, that is, when the PDRC came together, given that it was primarily led by key figures from the main opposition party, the Democrats. The conflict between the new business elites under Thaksin's leadership and the old powerhouses under monarchical and military tutelage, as a contributing factor in the coups of both 2006 and 2014, is well documented in the literature (McCargo 2005; Pongsudhirak 2008, Chachavalpongpun 2011; Chambers and Waitoolkiat 2016). However, elite-centered explanations tend to downplay the agency of the masses in impacting the elite's strategic calculations and overlook the masses–elite tensions in antidemocratic mobilization. I show here, through the cases of the PAD and the PDRC, that these movements' interests and those of their elite allies were interactive but often in contradic-

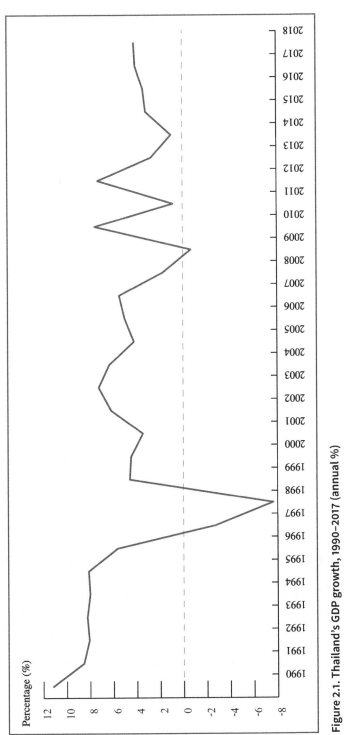

Figure 2.1. Thailand's GDP growth, 1990–2017 (annual %)

tion. Antidemocratic appeals were often "bottom-up" not top-down: it was the masses inside the movement that first demanded and pushed for an antidemocratic agenda, often resulting in ambivalence from the movement leaders themselves and those of allying elites.

The Huntingtonian arguments on weak institutions do provide background context for why Thailand is so susceptible to regime breakdown. The powerful monarchy and military—both nondemocratic institutions—have long served to stifle and intervene in politics and compete with the burgeoning democratic institutions, denying the latter a fair chance to strengthen. The frequent coups d'état interrupted and stunted any democratic progress that had been achieved previously. The Thai party system fares no better as it ranks the highest in terms of electoral volatility, according to Hicken and Kuhonta (2014), signifying its low level of institutionalization. Thai parties have always been mere shells of their leaders: they lack organizational depth, party roots, and are largely void of programmatic policies (Ockey 2005). The party system appeared incapable of accommodating social and political tensions. Opportunities for political participation for ordinary people were neither sufficiently open nor meaningful (Croissant and Volkel 2012). In this sense, the historical legacies of authoritarian institutions, frequent democratic breakdowns, and inchoate democratic institutions that sat alongside well-established nondemocratic institutions seemed all to combine in denying democracy a chance in Thailand.

But things seemed to be improving when the PAD rose up and demanded to dislodge the elected government of Thaksin Shinawatra. There had not been a coup in almost fifteen years—the longest stretch of democratic rule since Thailand became a constitutional monarchy in 1932. Thaksin was widely popular and was the first prime minister in the country's history to serve out his full four-year term and be subsequently reelected in a landslide victory. Unlike previous governments, Thaksin's policies were responsive to many of the Thais who voted for him. He delivered on his campaign promises and successfully enfranchised many Thais for whom prior engagement in politics was limited to mere voting, encouraging them to be an active part of the Thai political arena. He gave voice to millions of Thais who had always felt "neglected" and did not understand the value of their political membership. The electoral success of the Thai Rak Thai party had also meant a significant decrease in electoral volatility—an important indicator of a stronger party system institutionalization. What, then, went wrong?

Thailand's democratic development under Thaksin was at a crossroads: some aspects of democratic quality were vastly improving, while others were simultaneously, and quickly, deteriorating. This democratic improvement, from institutional perspectives, included stronger parties, a more empowered and engaged citizenry, more stable and more responsive governments, greater political participation, fewer elections and changes in government, and new independent institutions to provide further checks and balances. The negative aspects, the focus of this book, included the marginalization of opposition voices, growing executive abuse of power, and a sharp reduction in interparty competition. The primary accounts of the rise of both the PAD and the PDRC provide additional crucial details of how things went awry: why the good democratic progress achieved eventually lost out—twice—to the nondemocratic forces that Thaksin and his political successors had unleashed.

That class plays a key role in accounting for various episodes of political mobilization in Thailand is unquestionable. Chapters 3 and 4 provide a rich account of the nondemocratic tendencies among the Thai middle class that culminated in the formation of the Yellow Shirts. My own empirical accounts of the PAD and the PDRC movements also reveal a strong class component in the makeup of the movements' supporters, together with its discourse. However, the main contribution of this research is not to dispute class as a key structural factor for mobilization, but to question the utility of "class" as a framework to explain the *timing* and the *sequence* of antidemocratic mobilization. Class cleavages, driven largely by economic inequality and hierarchical societal structures, are "constant" features of the Thai polity. Since the mid-1980s, inequality has been on the rise.[12] But we did not witness *antidemocratic* mobilization for the entirety of this period. In the same vein, the existence of powerful nondemocratic institutions in Thailand should make the country susceptible to constant democratic breakdowns. But, again, democracies do not fall apart all the time.

Structural factors such as class and a powerful military tend to be "overly deterministic": they assume that as long as there are large economic gaps or a formidable military, then there will always be political mobilization and coups. I argue that these structural factors matter insofar as they further our understanding of the foundations of grievances and the frequency of coups. They do not, however, avail themselves to explaining the "when" and the "how" of movement emergence. Structural factors lack the dynamism and agency that are crucial to understanding an ad-hoc and fluid movement such as the PAD. The emergence of the PAD was contingent on both structural and specific circumstances. More importantly, the development of the PAD over time suggests that its mobilization pattern was based largely on "strategic interactions" with its opponents. Decisions on mobilization (and when to mobilize), on adopting certain campaigns, and on using specific language are calculated to respond to a movement's *immediate* set of circumstances. I show in detail in chapters 4, 5, and 6 that the outcomes that emerged through the PAD and the PDRC mobilization did not happen in a vacuum but were also based on the interactions with the opposing sides. Structural analysis is useful for providing the broad picture of the political struggles, yet on its own cannot provide the nuanced explanation of such political mobilization.

Similarly, the rich-versus-poor argument oversimplifies the composition of both PAD and PDRC supporters. While the PAD and the PDRC were supported largely by the urban middle class, their economic positions alone did not drive their mobilization. What defines this conflict instead, and what accounts for why the PAD and the PDRC were, broadly speaking, a "conservative-royalist movement," was their vision of the nature of the state and its relationship to society. This is clearly a political/ideological conflict. Both movements regarded the monarchy as having a veto power and sought to preserve the status of the monarchical institution as the pinnacle of modern Thai polity. Their supporters also viewed the traditional power brokers, the military and the bureaucracy, as the protectors of the constitutional monarch. Such an illiberal and conservative view of the Thai political system is what defines the movement, not the economic class of its supporters.

There is no question that Thai politics have been marked by serious political polarization since the mid-2000s, epitomized by the openly violent conflicts between the Yellow Shirts and the Red Shirts. But one does not observe democratic breakdowns all the time, even when political polarization heightens such as the case of the Bloody May in 2010, where more than a hundred Red Shirt supporters were killed in one of the country's most bloody protests in recent decades. Where polarization plays a role is in intensifying conditions for democratic breakdown—but polarization in itself does not make democracies die. Online, polarization has a demonstrable effect of creating echo chambers, which further worsens existing political divisions. In the cases of the PAD and the PDRC movements, polarization contributes directly to its formation and mobilization as *antigovernment* protests, while the choices to become *antidemocratic* were strategic.

Institutional Blockage and Mobilization Capacity

What is an institutional blockage? I define institutional blockage as *the attempt by the incumbent government to marginalize opposition voices in ways that make them feel shut out of democratic institutions.* In a multiparty system, political opposition, both in formal and informal institutions, is afforded a number of channels and platforms to air their grievances. A democratic system also provides guarantees for such fundamental civil liberties as freedom of speech, freedom of the press, and freedom of association. Institutional blockage occurs when the incumbent weakens the ability of the opposition forces to act as an effective check on the abuse of government power. Further, the opposition feels that when their basic freedoms have been encroached upon and cut short by the incumbent, its right to oppose is undermined by a democratic government.

Various opposition forces that normally have access to power in some form or other will seek to influence policy through formal democratic channels. Mechanisms for opposition through formal democratic channels include lobbying, bargaining, participating in the policy-making process, engaging the media, and using personal connections to influence government policy. If the government blocks the opposition's access to power within established democratic channels, this is considered formal institutional blockage. Note that opposition forces can come from *both* outside and inside formal democratic channels. Opposition within the formal democratic institutions might include opposition MPs, opposition senators, or independent bodies that would normally serve the purpose of placing checks on the executive. Opposition external to the formal institutions inside the democratic polity includes interest groups, pressure groups, and labor unions, to name but a few.

Is the opposition marginalized because of the incumbent's majoritarianism or institutional exclusion? The key difference between a weakened opposition because of a majority incumbent and institutional exclusion is whether some basic democratic freedoms have been eroded. An incumbent that seeks to intentionally shun opposition voices and violate civil liberties is critical to the institutional exclusion approach. If a government is both majoritarian and violates certain democratic freedoms, then it closes channels for the opposition to effectively voice their grievances. This type of opposition marginalization is dangerous to the democratic system because it erodes civil liberties.

How does institutional blockage produce antidemocratic mobilization? I further argue that when oppositions are blocked from democratic institutions, they tend to develop antidemocratic attitudes. These antidemocratic attitudes need to combine with the capacity to become organized in order to produce an outcome of antidemocratic mobilization. As defined in chapter 1, mobilization capacity refers to the ability of groups to get organized and mobilized. Such capacity stems from organizational learning, leadership skills, and past experiences. In the process of becoming an antidemocratic movement, we see the formation of opposition alliances of various groups that have been adversely affected by the incumbent. When opposition actors and groups feel they are shut out from accessing power now and in the foreseeable future, they may appeal to nondemocratic alternative sources of power to reverse, or at minimum halt, the process of institutional blockage. If these nondemocratic institutions respond to the opposition forces, then we may see a complete democratic collapse.

The assumptions here are twofold. First, that there exist functioning democratic institutions in the polity. Examples include a national assembly, the judiciary, and independent bodies. This theory does *not* apply to countries that are in transition from an authoritarian regime to a democracy; it only applies to electoral democracies—states with routinized elections and established and functioning democratic institutions. Second, "opposition" at the initial stage of mobilization is a loose term: it refers to actors or groups that seek to offer alternatives or oppose government policies. These opposition forces have *prior* access to power in the sense of being able to wield some degree of influence over policy in the past. Some of the actors have direct bargaining leverage with the government, while others, less powerful, can indirectly shape or put pressure on a government's policy outcome. Lastly, there must be nondemocratic sources of power and authority in the polity that coexist with democratic institutions.

The institutional exclusion concept makes an analytical distinction between *formal* and *informal* institutional blockages. Such a distinction recognizes the political reality of so many electoral democracies today—that is, there are more routes than formal democratic ones for opposition voices to be heard. Formal democratic channels include institutions such as the National Assembly—which includes the lower house, the House of Representatives, and the upper house, the Senate—and independent bodies (e.g., election authority, anticorruption agency). Conversely, informal ones comprise civil society organizations, labor unions, nongovernmental organizations, community groups, and the like. The formal institutional channels exemplify the *representative* dimension of the democratic polity, while the informal one represents a *participatory* one. When actors in the political arena feel that their interests are no longer represented, nor can they participate in the bargaining process with the government, they feel "choked" and thus have "no choice" but to resort to nondemocratic sources of power.

The key factors that drive the process of institutional blockage are two-fold. The first is the *relative change in access to power or distribution of power, or both*, within formal democratic institutions and between formal and informal ones. In a parliamentary system, relative change in the distribution of power among the executive, legislative, and the judiciary, for example, can induce formal institutional blockage. In the informal institutional setting, this can occur between the government and civil society organizations. The key thing to remember is that these actors or groups must have some power or, at a minimum, access to power prior to this change. It is their *loss* of access to power due to the institutional blockages that will set them off to look for alternative routes. The second and more important mechanism is the *perceived permanent exclusion from power*. Antidemocratic mobilization will occur in a democratic system when actors in both formal and informal institutional arenas perceive their relative loss of power vis-à-vis other institutions as permanent or likely to persist indefinitely. This perceived exclusion from power, due to institutional blockages both formally and informally, will drive these actors to nondemocratic sources of power to reduce and completely halt this process of institutional blockage.

In order to determine whether my concept of institutional blockage adequately explains the rise of the PAD and the PDRC movements, the following implications should be observed. Opposition actors must lose access to power relative to what they used to have. Channels for demands by organized groups and key political actors are closed off in the formal democratic institution. Means for opposition, such as a no confidence vote or Question Period in parliament, for instance, are closed to or rendered ineffective for the opposition. Organized groups are unable to lobby for support from the formal institutions, nor can they bargain with the government to provide them with a platform to voice their grievances. This clogging of opposition channels should drive the various groups to form an anti-incumbent mobilization. We should observe an upsurge of antigovernment protest activities over time, increasing in frequency and intensity as the opposition forces become more desperate. The opposition should be calling for the resignation of the current government or leadership.

The viability and availability of powerful nondemocratic institutions are crucial to the success of democratic collapse. First, nondemocratic institutions ought to be present in a polity to which antidemocratic movements can appeal. These appeals are more credible if such nondemocratic institutions are powerful and politicized. This means that countries with historical legacies of strong nondemocratic institutions are far more likely to see a successful creation of antidemocratic mobilization. By orchestrating support for antidemocratic solutions, through the mobilization of a large-scale movement, the costs of extraconstitutional interventions are effectively reduced. This makes it even more likely for nondemocratic elites to intervene successfully. Of course, nondemocratic elites would intervene if they also felt adversely affected by the elected government. In this sense, their interventions are seen as an important means to protect their interests. The dynamic interactions between the antidemocratic movement, on the one hand, and the antidemocratic actors, on the other, is what this book seeks to capture.

Institutional Blockage in Thailand

The Thai political structure remains rather centralized, with few access points to political power and influence. Open channels for public engagement prior to the Thaksin era were essentially obtained through the MPs of both national and local governments, senators (elected and appointed), and the state bureaucracies. The availability of access points to power and influence was increased as a result of the 1997 constitution. This development provided additional public participation in politics through the legislature and the newly created independent bodies (a list of them is provided in chapter 4). Despite this, there are no feedback mechanisms between the public and powerful nondemocratic institutions such as the courts, the military, or the monarchy. While this seems intuitive, the fact that nondemocratic institutions are highly powerful (and popular) but in no way accountable to the people that legitimize them remains an unusual feature of the Thai political system.

Despite the rather centralized state, opposition groups find ways to voice their grievances. Thailand in the 1990s was marked by a period of sociopolitical liberalization. Opposition movements, which had been instrumental in the Black May Uprising in 1992, sought to instigate several reform initiatives aimed at liberalizing the Thai political arena and increasing public participation in politics. The opposition found some measure of success in its reformist agenda, most arguably in pushing for the adoption of Thailand's most democratic constitution to date—the so-called People's Constitution of 1997. Following the Asian Financial Crisis that same year, more economic-oriented reforms were also implemented to restructure the economy. Throughout this period, waves of both proreform and anti-incumbent protests occurred, resulting in short-lived governments and frequent dissolutions of the House of Representatives. This more inclusive and open, albeit rather unstable, political arrangement increased public participation in politics and increased the capacity of more groups to champion their causes.

The coming to power of Thaksin Shinawatra, the first prime minister to be elected under the new 1997 constitution, dramatically altered opposition politics (chapter 4). During his first term, opposition movements by and large were engaged in anti-incumbent mobilization. This strategy had been primarily used because proreform politics already preceded the period, and many opposition figures and groups believed a reformist agenda would find no outlet in this powerful, absolute majority government. Opposition groups employed confrontational, sometimes violent, tactics aimed to depose Thaksin and his government. Opposition leaders called for the resignation of Thaksin and his cabinet. It was not until Thaksin's second electoral victory that the opposition movement recognized that neither proreform nor anti-incumbent mobilization had what it took to depose Thaksin.

The People's Alliance for Democracy (PAD) was a clear case of an antidemocratic movement, albeit not initially. When the movement began loosely mobilizing in 2005, it saw itself, by all accounts, as a "prodemocracy" movement. Soon after its emergence, the movement began to adopt a number of antidemocratic measures. First, the PAD called for installing a royally appointed prime minister to replace the popularly elected government of Thaksin Shinawatra. Second, the movement endorsed implicitly (and later more forcefully) both military intervention in politics and the coup d'état of 2006. Third, the PAD's ideology was explicit about the kinds of political reforms it envisioned. These included unelected legislators, senators, and a prime minister, and veto power by the monarchical institution in Thailand's political system. Fourth, the PAD sought a temporary cessation of elections to rid the system of corrupt politicians and "rotten politics." Finally, the PAD prioritized the notion of a "good leader" over an "elected leader."

The Thai case greatly problematizes the notion that civil society will or should inevitably promote and strengthen democracy. The PAD initially emerged largely as networks of NGOs, labor unions, opposition media, and religious networks, which formed an alliance to oppose the Thaksin administration. Several of the major networks of NGOs were those that had been key players in the political liberalization and democratization reforms in the 1990s. Their involvement and prominence in the PAD leadership provided strong empirical evidence against existing scholarship that links civil society to democratic stability (Diamond 1996; Putnam 1993, 2000;

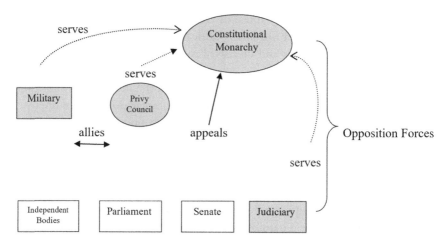

Figure 2.2. Opposition alliance formation

Arato 2000). The NGO-led antidemocratic movement of the PAD shows that there is no necessary connection between civil society and democracy, and, most saliently, that civil society can have antidemocratic effects.

The PAD movement is not alone in its antidemocratic orientation when compared to other opposition movements in posttransition states. In Venezuela, the anti-Chávez movement was supported by sections of civil society organizations (the middle class and labor unions) that pushed for an extraconstitutional intervention that eventually led to a bizarre forty-seven-hour coup in 2002. The opposition forces in Venezuela too felt "blocked" and "excluded" from access to power (Encarnacion 2002). With President Hugo Chávez looking to stay in power "forever," the opposition movements began to appeal to nondemocratic institutions such as the military and the courts to intervene. Although the coup government took power only very briefly, the success of the anti-Chávez movements in mobilizing key support from groups that should otherwise be supportive of democratic politics has had negative consequences for the country's democratic development.

Why was antidemocratic mobilization a plausible strategy for the Thai opposition movement? Chapter 3 outlines in detail the structural conditions in the Thai political system that make it conducive to democratic breakdowns. Of note are factors such as a history of frequent coups d'état and undemocratic tendencies among the public, since these have significantly reduced the cost of a follow-on coup and made military intervention a favorable option for conflict resolution. As such, military intervention is a real possibility in Thai politics—one whereby successful coups outnumber failed ones. However, the backlash against the coup government in 1992 has increased the cost of coups, making it imperative for the military to guarantee prior popular support for its intervention. The opposition movement—having failed to change the situation through anti-incumbent and proreform strategies—redirected its efforts to the last possible alternative: the call for military and royal intervention. The opposition had thus embarked on an antidemocratic path that would later shatter the country's democratic development.

The PAD movement was composed of and driven by actors and groups in society that had not only been made worse off as a result of Thaksin's policies, but whose opposition channels to convey their grievances were closed off. This happened in a highly arbitrary manner in both the formal and institutional arenas. In the formal democratic institution, opposition parties in the legislature, that is, certain sections of the Senate and independent bodies, joined forces with the PAD movement for the following reasons: (a) inability to provide effective opposition to the government; (b) failure to provide effective checks on the executive; and (c) inability to propose alternative policies. There is, in essence, a breakdown of opposition mechanisms inside formal democratic institutions that "cripple" opposition voices. The judiciary, in fact, was best positioned to mount an opposition against the Thaksin government and intervene it did, with palace support, to weaken the executive and the Thai Rak Thai–dominated legislature.

Informal institutional channels, too, the NGO sector, labor unions, the media, and various other social groups, all experienced not just the loss of their political space. The possibility of presenting alternatives to government positions was marginalized. During the pre-Thaksin period, many of these groups were able to lobby and put pressure on governments, senators, and independent bodies to represent their interests, albeit with varying degrees of success. During the Thaksin administration, however, a number of access points to formal institutions were blocked for the opposition: parliament, the Senate, and independent bodies. All of the resultant resentment did not, however, materialize into a movement until Thaksin and his Thai Rak Thai party won their second consecutive landslide election victory in 2005, which gave the opposition the perception of permanent exclusion from power. It was at this moment that the PAD came together as a movement to collectively oppose Thaksin, and likewise petition the monarchy and military to intervene.

But why did the opposition resort to nondemocratic institutions?

What were the options available to the opposition during that critical moment? There were essentially two options available to the opposition when faced with institutional blockage: (1) fight or (2) give up. The first stage of opposition mobilization was intended to increase their own bargaining power vis-à-vis the government by forming an alliance with other opposition groups. Such an alliance was considered a means to not only aggregate their interests and grievances but also to exert more pressure on the government. When such a strategy no longer yielded desirable results, they increased pressure by engaging in more coercive activities, such as mass protests. "Street politics" then becomes a confrontational strategy of choice for these opposition groups that seek to recruit supporters from the public at large.

In the third stage, the decision for the opposition to continue fighting as opposed to relinquishing depends on two factors. The first is what I call the "zero-sum game" motivation. Groups that remained in the PAD movement by this time were those that perceived their future to be dim should they not fight. Simply put, the stakes were too high to give up. The second factor is more strategic (and less desperate): the "no turning back" motivation. Essentially, opposition groups that have engaged in high-risk protest activities for quite some time, and gained popular support along the way, find themselves having gone too far to turn back—they simply cannot abandon the movement and lose momentum. Giving up would not only hurt their overall support but it also would delegitimize their cause for any future protests. Staying on course was perceived by some groups to be their only option, even though it meant putting their own ideals and demands aside. The PAD movement began to appeal to nondemocratic institutions when they perceived their loss of access to power to be permanent. There was no other choice but to press forward.

Opposition elites also have their own strategic considerations when faced with the problem of institutional blockage. Their main concern is similar to other opposition actors: if they feel threatened by the relative loss of access to power vis-à-vis other actors, they will intervene to change the situation. Opposition elites from both within democratic and nondemocratic institutions are those that rebel against their loss of access to power. Their major interests are shaped by their ability to (a) influence the decision-making process; (b) influence the policy discourse and policy-making process; and (c) provide an alternative agenda. For nondemocratic institutions, their interests are gravely threatened if there are systematic attempts to weaken their political power, shrink their political space, or undermine their institutional independence.

In the Thai case, opposition actors from the parliament, Senate, and independent bodies first began to show support for opposition forces in the informal institutional arena. They then began to appeal to nondemocratic institutions: the military, the Privy Council, and the monarchy. The judiciary, on the other hand, normally highly independent and insulated from political pressure, aligned its interests with those of the constitutional monarchy and sought to intervene to stop the process of institutional blockage. This entailed removing key actors and severely delegitimizing them. The military did the same and formed an alliance with the Privy Council—the monarchy's de facto representatives. The constitutional monarchy became the place where opposition elites coordinated their interests. Should measures by opposition elites not work, then the latter would look to form an alliance with other opposition forces in society to increase their own popular support base and hence the legitimacy needed for the intervention in the democratic regime.

The People's Democratic Reform Committee (PDRC), the PAD successor movement, was both more popular and more antidemocratic in orientation than its predecessors. Having failed to achieve the ultimate goal of uprooting Thaksin's political legacies from the Thai polity even after the 2006 coup, the fear of being shut out of democratic channels returned when Thaksin's sister, Yingluck Shinawatra, won a landslide 2011 election victory and formed yet another majority government. Attempting to alleviate fears of a Thaksin repeat, Yingluck initially kept democratic channels open to opposition voices. During the initial period of 2011–13, while more radical antidemocratic voices attempted to regroup and reform, there was a lack of mass support behind them because too few people felt shut out of the system. But by mid-2013, when Yingluck began to reempower her base, the Red Shirts, and showed signs of following the same route as her brother, the opposition was reignited, and the antidemocratic mobilization grew quickly, thanks largely to the power of social media. Within the span of weeks, the whole of Bangkok came to a near complete halt. Both online and off, millions were demanding an end to democratic politics. The military finally stepped in, via a martial law declaration, and democracy once more collapsed in 2014.

Conclusion

This chapter has provided an overview of the typology of opposition mobilization and has situated Thailand within the broader pattern of opposition movements in a Third Wave democracy. There are three types of opposition mobilization: (1) proreform; (2) anti-incumbent; and (3) antidemocratic. I argue that the conditions under which a movement adopts a proreform or anti-incumbent approach are neither exclusive nor chronological. In fact, a movement can both promote reforms and oppose incumbent government at the same time. However, the conditions under which a movement becomes antidemocratic are contingent on the unavailability or ineffectiveness of other approaches. Moreover, becoming an antidemocratic movement is not always an option available in all democracies.

This research advances a theoretical concept that I call "institution blockage." This is a process whereby both formal and informal channels of opposition in a democratic regime are perceived to be, and are in fact, closed. The result is a perceived loss of bargaining leverage by actors in the polity. When the opposition is or "feels" blocked from access to power, it rebels against such real and perceived closures in the democratic system by appealing to nondemocratic alternative sources of power to reverse, or at a minimum halt, this institutional blockage. Antidemocratic mobilization then serves as a vehicle for various opposition forces whose leverage has been reduced, or completely eradicated, by the process of institutional blockage that unfolds. If such mobilization succeeds in attaining extraconstitutional intervention from nondemocratic authorities, then we see a complete breakdown of democracy.

THREE

Crises and Coups

Why is Thailand known for its frequent military coups? Why does democracy in Thailand experience a disproportionate rate of breakdown? This chapter provides a background to Thai politics after its transition to constitutional monarchy in 1932. It focuses on outlining reasons for Thailand's frequent coups d'état, the political and symbolic power of the monarchy, and major episodes of popular discontent prior to the emergence of the People's Alliance for Democracy. The main argument of this chapter is that there are several structural and institutional conditions that make Thailand's democracy susceptible to breakdown: (1) a politicized military; (2) a powerful monarchy; and (3) the middle class's contingent support for democracy. Thailand has had many coups d'état in its political history. Coups were seen by political elites as a mechanism for crisis resolution and a "legitimate" form of government transition. Given that much of contemporary Thai history is marked by authoritarianism, a coup d'état accomplishes its purpose in the sense that, by force, it transfers power from one group of elites to another.

There have been two major popular uprisings during Thailand's constitutional monarchy, both of which have affected civil–military relations. However, here I argue that only the Black May Uprising in 1992 had *direct* impacts on the later emergence of the antidemocratic mobilization during the Thaksin period. Black May significantly weakened the military's position in the political arena. This is particularly true when considering the power of the military vis-a-vis the public, the monarchy, and career politicians. The second and related point is that the cost of coups d'état as a mechanism for regime change has dramatically increased for the military. Third, the Uprising set in motion a process of political liberalization, driven by reformist elites who had risen to political prominence following Black May.

In her seminal article "Contingent Democrats: Industrialists, Labor, and Democratization in Late-Developing Countries," Eva Bellin rightly points out that support for democracy among late-developing nations is ambivalent at best.[1] Indeed, Thailand has a history of mobilized middle-class movements that were simultaneously both pro- *and* antidemocratic: they supported some aspects of democratic reform all the while defending other aspects of the authoritarian status quo. Black May is a case in point: the uprising was *not* in opposition to the coup d'état per se. It was, rather, an opposition to the military staying on in power. Moreover, the public's support for a royally appointed prime minister underscores as much the immense power of the monarchical institution as it illustrates public acceptance of political leadership that does not originate in democratic processes. These tendencies among the public are not new in Thai political history, and thus demonstrate continuity rather than change, in this respect.

Lastly, the monarchy has become the ultimate source of power and legitimacy vis-a-vis other democratic and nondemocratic institutions in the Thai polity. The king, namely, served as the arbiter of political conflict and brought major violence to an end during popular uprisings in both the '70s and '90s. The immense power wielded by King Bhumibol created a dependency on the monarchical institution as an institution of "last resort." While the monarchy has become the symbol of national unity, its extraordinary power has also been used, at times illegitimately, as a tool for mobilization and empowerment. This latter point is crucial to understand how the PAD movement emerged at once as a promonarchy *and* an antidemocratic mobilization.

In the wider debate on the quality of democracy, Diamond and Morlino (2004, 21) note that two types of accountability matter to the "procedural" quality of democracy: vertical and horizontal accountability. Vertical accountability refers to the ways in which political leaders answer to their citizens, irrespective of whether they represent the very constituents that elect them. Horizontal accountability, on the other hand, requires political leaders to answer to other institutions designed to provide checks and balances in the political system. Dan Slater correctly notes that vertical and horizontal accountability are not always mutually reinforcing: in some cases, they are in tension with one another.[2] A tension between vertical and horizontal accountability emerged following the major political reform efforts of the Black May aftermath. The reform process reflected serious disagreement over what kind of democratic accountability was needed in Thailand: inclusiveness or constraints.

Brief History of Thai Politics

Democracy in Thailand has taken a tumultuous, oscillating, path. Despite the end of absolute monarchy in 1932, Thailand's democratic political system did not prosper until the 1970s, and even then only briefly. When King Prajadiphok abdicated the throne following a coup in 1932, he asked that the power not be given to a single individual or group(s), but to all the people of Siam. The reality could not have been further from the king's wish. From 1938 until 1973, military generals took turns ruling the kingdom. "Elections" were neither free nor fair. In fact, political parties were not legal entities until the 1950s. Politics was oligarchic in nature, with the majority of the populace remaining disenfranchised despite the introduction of universal suffrage. The armed forces were highly factionalized, and most coups during this period were launched by one military faction against another. Fred Riggs (1966) famously refers to this period as the "bureaucratic polity," whereby bureaucratic leaders, military and civilian, were responsible for running the Thai state.

Yet Thai politics in the 1970s were far from calm. And the people were far from docile. Indeed, Thailand witnessed its first popular mobilization against the military regime in 1973, known as the October 14 Incident. Frustrated with the repressive and highly oligarchic rule of Field Marshal Thanom Kittikajorn, what began as a modest demand for improvement for university students rapidly evolved into a large-scale antigovernment demonstration. The government refused to give in to the movement's demands, opting instead to exercise brutal repression against the many thousands on the streets. This resulted in numerous injuries and deaths (Musikawong 2006). The incident has come to be revered as a landmark event against dictatorship and the heroic protesters were dubbed the "October 14th Generation." Their power and influence continue to the present day.

The brief democratic period that followed the October 14 Incident provided space for a rapidly expanding civic activism. Between late 1973 and 1976, students, peasants, and workers all organized and mobilized to demand change. Protest became the order of the day: "Literally hundreds of other student groups and associations blossomed after the October 1973 incident" (Morell and Samudavanija 1981).[3] Meanwhile, numerous students adopted left-wing ideological positions that advocated sweeping social reform. The growth in left-leaning protesters terrified the military elites, particularly since it occurred during the Cold War period and Communist Party victory in Vietnam. The state responded with right-wing countermovements such as the Red Gaur, Nawaphon, and the Village Scouts. These attracted nearly two million supporters to counteract the leftists (Jamrik 1997).

Meanwhile, the elected governments during this three-year period—four in total—proved highly unstable and ineffective in their governance. On October 6, 1976 the right-wing forces, with the implicit consent of the cabinet, massacred students on the campus of Thammasat University in broad daylight, leaving scores dead and thousands humiliated as they were stripped and had their hands tied. General Sangad Chaloryoo staged a coup in the name of the Administrative Reform Council Resolution (ARCR). The ARCR appointed a privy councilor, Thanin Kraivichian, as prime minister. Following another coup by the ARCR a year later, the right-wing general Kriangsak Chamanan took over the leadership, a move that ended Thailand's experiment with democratic politics.

In the 1980s, Thailand reembarked on a road toward democratization through gradual political liberalization.[4] Under the leadership of an *unelected* prime minister, General Prem Tinsulanond, Thailand was ruled for nearly a decade by an appointed leader who carefully balanced the interests of the military, career politicians, and the monarchical institution. Prem—highly respected by the military top brass, the king, bureaucrats, and career politicians—engineered a power-sharing agreement with the political elites. This "pact" allowed Prem, himself committed to remaining "neutral" and "nonpolitical," to satisfy key elites and keep the country moving forward without another coup d'état. The generals were handed authority over defense and national security matters; the politicians were authorized to run domestic affairs; while the bureaucrats enjoyed bigger budgets and better pay. The technocrats were able to implement major economic development plans and Thailand gradually democratized its politics.[5] Power-sharing in Thailand worked for nearly a decade because the military began to recognize that in an increasingly globalized world, they could no longer afford to govern through the barrel of a gun. As Neher (1995, 197) argues, there was a "rising view among the military that the country's new economic complexity and international standing required a sharing of power between technocrats, business persons, trained bureaucrats and politicians."

Thailand did not return to full democracy in the post-Prem period, despite claims by some scholars (Bunbongkarn 1992; Jamrik 1997; Boonmee 2007). Although Prem refused to stay on as the country's leader following the 1988 election, paving the way for the first democratically elected government under Chatchai Choonhavan, the "elected" prime minister's legitimacy and power remained squarely with both previously unelected prime minister Prem and the military. The sole reason for Prem's decision to allow the country's transition into a "full" democracy was because he knew that the Chatchai government was supported by the army. Chatchai himself had announced that he would not intervene in any military appointments or transfers, and would approve whatever the military proposed; but he also admitted to turning to the generals for their approval.[6] General Chavalit, the army chief, confirmed: "I set up this government with my own hands."[7] The Chatchai government represented a failure of political liberalization in the late 1980s and paved the way for a full return of the military to politics.

The loss of military backing spelled the end of Chatchai's government and the demise of Thailand's democracy. The power-sharing agreement that Prem had built and worked hard to keep was collapsing. The government was plagued by internal infighting, a sour relationship with the military, and many corruption scandals. The military top brass eventually felt threatened by the possibility of removal from power by the Chatchai government and staged a coup in February 1991.

The 1991 coup d'état and subsequent uprising, known locally as "Black May," was a key turning point in the history of civil–military relations. Taking the Black May Uprising of 1992 as the watershed event in Thai political history, one that had both direct and indirect consequences in the emergence of antidemocratic mobilization and the 2006 coup, this chapter seeks to situate Black May in the historical development of Thailand. A decade later, Black May had direct ramifications for the emergence of the PAD movement.

On February 23, 1991, the upper echelon of the armed forces seized power from the Charchait government. Chatchai and General Athit Kamlang-ek were held at gunpoint while on a plane to Chiang Mai for an audience with the king. The Constitution was scrapped, martial laws were imposed, and the National Assembly was dissolved. The coup was led by General Sunthorn Kongsompong and most of Class 5 from the elite (U.S. West Point–style) Chulachomklao Military Academy, the members of which occupied most major positions in the armed forces. The putsch likewise had the support of the Academy's Class 11 and 12 (Maisrikrod 1992, 328; 1993). The coup plotters named themselves the National Peace Keeping Council (NPKC) and promised an election soon. The NPKC cited large-scale corruption within the Chatchai government and the protection of the monarchy as justification for their action.[8] The military generals cobbled together seasoned politicians, retired generals, and those close to the NPKC to form the Samakhi Tham Party (STP). The STP competed in the March 1992 election, and it won. In what was dubbed Thailand's "dirtiest election," a reported US$100 million was spent on vote-buying.[9] The STP-led five-party coalition[10] came to power and one of the coup leaders, General Suchinda Kraprayoon, eventually became prime minister.

On the surface, the coup d'état of 1991, which subsequently led to the Black May Uprising, was not unlike the many coups that had come before it (table 3.1): a handful of military generals roll in on their tanks to Bangkok, the country's capital, and take it under siege. The men in uniform claim that the elected government is too corrupt, and that failing their restoration of order and stability, the country would descend into chaos. The elected government is overthrown and the military government takes over—promising a return to democracy "soon." A new constitution is written up that gives impunity to the coup plotters, a bogus corruption investigation into the previous government is launched, and the military receives a massive boost to their budget. Meanwhile, civic and political rights are curbed with periodic curfews.

There were two major causes for the 1991 coup d'état: (1) serious conflict between the Chatchai government and military top brass; and (2) a high degree of unity among the armed forces. Coup rumors began to surge in 1990 and government–military relations turned for the worse. Military chief General Sunthorn Kongsompong warned that politicians had no right to shuffle military rankings. "I will never meddle with military appointments," Prime Minister Chatchai claimed. "Why would I? I ask approval from both General Suchinda and General Sunthorn every time if it's ok."[11] However, even General Chavalit had a fallout with another minister, which led to his eventual resignation. Sukhumbhand Paribatra, advisor to the prime minister, resigned because he did not get on well with the army chief. Chatchai sought to resolve the crisis by himself resigning, but the parliamentarians continued to back him as prime minister as he clung to power.

What began as a hunger strike to protest the military-installed government of General Suchinda Kraprayoon soon expanded into a full-blown uprising. Opposition leaders, the media, and nongovernmental organizations wanted a new election and a more democratic constitution. At the height of the crisis, more than 200,000 protesters occupied the main arteries of Bangkok (Callahan 1998). The government mobilized pro-Suchinda rallies in the provinces, particularly in the Northeast. They refused to concede to the people's demands and began to retaliate against the demonstrators. The violence quickly escalated in the days leading up to the massacre of May 17–20, 1992. Some 600 people were reportedly killed at the hands of the military, although actual figures are believed to be much higher. The Black May Uprising only ended when the king summoned General Suchinda and opposition movement leader Major General Chamlong Srimuang and "advised" them to end the political conflict.

The failure of the 1991 coup and the subsequent Suchinda government had three major consequences for Thailand's political development. First, coups became costlier and would now require popular support. The Black May debacle created internal division within the military itself; this significantly raised the cost for future coups. Coups d'état are more likely when the military is unified, particularly in the Thai case (Tamada 1995). After Black May, several young officers began to challenge the military hierarchies. They called on the top brass to take responsibility for the May crackdown (BBC Black May, 385). Moreover, military-initiated coups devoid of any regard for public backlash were simply no longer viable. Black May was the first massive outcry since the mid-1970s against military dominance in politics, and it tarnished the public image of the military as an honorable institution in Thai society. This would prove a crucial game changer in military strategic calculations as one of the most powerful entities in Thailand: not only regarding whether to stage a coup, but *when* to stage it. It would no longer be the case—as it was in the lead-up to the '70s—that a coup is justified because one faction of the military is in conflict with the other.

Second, the king's intervention in ending a conflict between the military and the people's movement demonstrates the power of Thailand's monarchical institution. That the monarchy remains today the most powerful institution in Thailand is not merely on account of a centuries-old tradition. It is also, and crucially so, the personal cultivation of the late monarch, King Bhumibol Adulyadej. Suwannathat-Pian (2003) argues that King Bhumibol almost single-handedly brought the monarchy from a position of decline to one that represents a pinnacle of the nation. He did so by way of "personal dedication and devotion to the commonwealth, public relations tours of the country and foreign nations, royal-sponsored socio-economic welfare projects, and royal financial independence. Most of these means and methods are as much image-enhancing as they are altruistic."[12] Moreover, the long reign of King Bhumibol allowed him to cultivate a key virtue of political leadership: *barami*.[13] The late king was considered to have much barami (charisma) according to many Thais; this explained why his blessing was so critical to the success of many unelected prime ministers such as Prem Tinasulanond and Anand Panyarachoon. This informal "soft" power of the monarchical institution can shape and change political outcomes in times of crisis.

Third, Black May reinforced the ambivalence of the Thai middle class toward democracy. The coup did not garner much resistance from the public who felt that the coup was justified (Uthakorn 1993). Like previous coups, the 1991 coup did not elicit public outrage or negative response.[14] The Black May protests did not emerge until the coup leader and army chief, Suchinda Krapayoon, became prime minister himself. David Murray (1996) argues that what, significantly, had upset people was that the unelected leader came from the military—not that he was unelected. Had a more "acceptable outsider" like Prem or Anand assumed power, such a move would have been acceptable.[15] While there had been past cases of popular yet unelected prime ministers, such figures were usually appointed by the king as an interim measure following the fall of a coup government. Prem and Anand left such important legacies in Thai political history that their own personal clout and charisma had a significant impact on the emergence of both the PAD and PDRC movements.

Some sections of the middle class had previously shown support for nondemocratic actors during times of political upheaval. The successful student uprising of October 14, 1973, "motivated conservative elements and the elites to counter-mobilize" (Kongkirati 2006, 12). The right-wing groups, responsible for the massacre of students in 1976, formed organizations to counter the peasants, labor unions, and students in 1975 (Kasertsiri 1998). Ji Ungpakorn also argues that the military and anti-Communist groups actively organized and supported the nationalist Red Guar and Nawaphon.[16] The Village Scouts, officially endorsed by the state, was "the largest counter-movement with its membership of more than 20,000 drawn almost exclusively from the middle class in Bangkok" (Kongkirati 2006, 25). "In upcountry towns," posits Kongkirati, "the movement attracted local officials, merchants, and other well-to-do figures. In Bangkok, the wives of generals, business leaders, bankers, and members of the royal family took part."[17] While it is not uncommon for the middle class in Asia to be "contingent democrats"[18]—given that the middle class's expansion has tended to rise during authoritarian times—their support for antidemocratic actors still defied a large literature within the modernization school (Jones 1998; Sinpeng and Arugay 2015).

Black May also holds its contradictions: it confirms long-standing nondemocratic tendencies within the Thai polity. The uprising was *not* in opposition to the coup d'état per se, but in opposition to the military staying in power. Public support for the royally appointed prime minister underscored the monumental power of the monarchical institution. It also illustrated public acceptance of political leadership that did not derive from the democratic process. These tendencies among the public were not new in Thai political history—they instead demonstrate continuity, rather than change, in this respect.

Thailand's Susceptibility to Coups: Structural and Institutional Factors

Thailand is a classic case of a crisis-prone democracy susceptible to regime breakdown. The structural and institutional conditions of the Thai polity—frequent coups d'état and powerful extraconstitutional institutions—make democratic collapse likely. They provide the background conditions for the emergence of an antidemocratic mobilization. Key factors that make Thailand conducive to the rise of antidemocratic mobilization include (1) patterns of previous mobilization; (2) legacies of successful coups d'état; (3) past "popular" support for undemocratic tendencies; and (4) powerful extraconstitutional institutions. As I will later argue, these structural and institutional conditions make antidemocratic mobilization more likely; they do *not*, however, activate mobilization. In other words, Thailand's democracy does not always break down, even under conditions of severe economic crisis like the Asian Financial Crisis in 1997.

The Politicized Military

A politically active military and frequent coups have become a hallmark of contemporary Thai politics. Between 1932 and 2019, Thailand witnessed nineteen coup attempts—the highest number of coups d'état in the world. Thailand continues to be trapped in this cycle of coups and crises due to conflicts among political elites over access to spoils. Parliamentary politics are wrought with corruption, factionalism, and in-party fighting. The military, still the only institution capable of launching a coup, intervenes to protect its own interest and put an end to democratic politics with the promise of returning to it shortly afterward. Before elections can be reintroduced, a new constitution is written to promote the interests of the coup plotters and to provide them with impunity. An election is held and parliamentary politics resumes. Politicians pursue pork barrel politics, crisis ensues, and the vicious cycle continues.

The price tag for a military intervention, however, has risen significantly since the popular backlash of Black May. Although the frequency of successful coups d'etat in a polity increases, in theory, the chance of another coup (McGowan 2003),[19] coups are ultimately a means of power transfer that is *contingent* on certain favorable conditions. Prior to Black May, there were two major ways to successfully launch a coup d'état in Thailand, depending on the nature of the coup itself (table 3.1). In the pre-1970s period, where coups were launched by one military faction against another and the public remained largely disenfranchised, military factionalism was key to whether a coup will be launched or not. However, following the October 14 Incident in 1973, there was a rising expectation that military dictatorship was less desirable among the populace. As such, political consensus that a change of government is necessary, particularly among the military elites themselves, was critical to whether a coup is launched. This explains why coup attempts failed during the Prem years: some sec-

TABLE 3.1. Causes and consequences of successful coups in Thailand

Period	Coup Plotters	Against	Outcomes	Considerations before coup	Consequences
Pre-1970s	Military faction A	Military Faction B	Another military dictatorship	1. Manpower of faction A versus B	Dictatorship until another coup
1970s–1990s	Military	Civilian government	Promise of civilian government and election	1. Manpower 2. Some popular support; public opposition to current government 3. Support from some sections of elites	Mixed; military and civilian governments, no elected prime minister
2000s	Military	Elected civilian government	Promise of civilian govt. and election	1. Manpower 2. Significant popular opposition to current government 3. Support from some sections of elites and other nondemocratic bodies	Interim military-installed civilian government, then election

tions of the military top brass continued to pledge their support to Prem, leaving other factions that desired change hung out to dry.

Popular support for coups has become necessary following the backlash against the Suchinda coup government.[20] While a coup is still deemed at times "necessary" in the case of a crisis, some indication of popular support has proven critical to its success. It is no longer enough that there must be sufficient unity among the military top brass to launch a coup; the success of a coup hinges also on the perception of popular support for a coup. The Black May Uprising ultimately altered the calculus of a coup for the military. Because there have been so many successful coups in the past, coups will be a factor in Thai politics for the foreseeable future. However, from the 1980s onwards, there has been public expectation that the military must pledge its support to democratically elected governments (Samudavanija 1997 57). The military intervention is thus regarded as an "emergency only" measure—one that, moreover, must receive some degree of public support. Also, military governments are considered temporary only in nature, and their main task is to clean up the "mess" of the dislodged democratic government and to lead the country back onto its democratic path.

The Middle Class and Democracy

Although scholars have yet to reach a consensus on a direct measure for the "middle class," most agree that this class grew over time in Thailand—mirroring a growing trend across Asia (ADB 2010). Depending on the definition used, the Thai middle class in 2013 was between 20 percent to 40 percent of the population (ILO 2013). In addition, according to estimates published by the National Statistical Office, Thailand's middle class grew continuously between 2000 and 2013. A more detailed analysis of the middle class is beyond the scope of this book; suffice it to say, however, that the burgeoning middle class in Asia is often seen as a "hope" for more open and perhaps democratic politics.

Yet the middle class in Thailand has been both illiberal and ambivalent toward democracy. This is not uncommon in Asia, as much of the middle class in the region grew and expanded under authoritarian rule (Jones 1998). The role of the middle class during the Black May and earlier popular mobilizations suggests their ambivalence toward, and sometimes opposition to, democratic politics. Clearly the middle class in Thailand is not a unified group with a defined set of ideology or political preferences. However, examining its role in political upheavals sheds light on its preferences in ways that voting behavior cannot always do, particularly during nondemocratic times. An investigation into middle-class behavior and attitudes shows that the middle class, particularly those originating from Bangkok, has demonstrated support for antidemocratic regimes since its first manifest participation in popular politics in the 1970s.[21] The ways in which the middle class has shown its undemocratic stripes can be categorized in three key ways: (1) support for antidemocratic forces; (2) support for an appointed prime minister; and (3) support for coups.

On balance, the undemocratic nature of the Suchinda regime may not have been the key issue in the Black May Uprising. Thais had not been against the 1991 government that had risen to power via military coup one year earlier because it was deemed undemocratic. The reason, instead, is that it was generally acknowledged that the government was corrupt. In fact, the 1991 military coup was "widely accepted—almost popular."[22] In the words of a Thai academic, "it was like watching a piece of rotten fruit—everyone was expecting it to fall and no one is sad now that it has."[23] Puey Ungpakorn, a highly respected bureaucrat, argued that public apathy toward the coup was widespread and similar to previous coups, and credited the coup makers for brainwashing the public that the coup was the right thing to do (Boonbongkarn 1992). Suchit Boonbongkarn likewise laments, "As with other coups in Thailand, there were no large-scale protests. Only some academics and politicians who had lost their jobs quietly expressed resentment. For the general public, the coup seemed acceptable" (Asian Survey 1992, 131).

The mass protest movement that eventually led to the crackdown of May 1992 did not emerge until the coup leader and army chief himself, Suchinda Kraprayoon, became prime minister. This was some time after martial law was imposed, the constitution abolished, and civic rights extensively curbed. To therefore state that the antigovernment popular uprising was "prodemocracy" certainly requires important qualifications. The muted public response after the 1991 coup, much like previous public reactions to earlier coups d'état, indicates, in the main, public acceptance of coups as a legitimate means for political power transferal. It is no surprise then, that the coup in 2006 received close to 90 percent popular support, according to polls. Samudavanija (1997, 53), along similar lines, argues that the 1991 uprising was not so much prodemocracy as it was "a movement opposed to the possibility of a new alliance of the military and business leading to a dictatorship." Likewise, David Murray (1996, 181) contends:

> Although superficially the rallying cry [Black May Uprising] had been for an elected MP as prime minister, the real issue was that the

unelected MP came from the military—a military which, with considerable doubts, the people had entrusted with the task of cleaning up Thai politics and returning the country to a more democratic form of government. That it had failed to do this was the real issue. Had an "acceptable" outsider been nominated for the premiership— someone like Anand or even Prem—the populace would probably have accepted it, particularly given the poor quality of the leaders of the government coalition parties.

Indeed, some sections of the middle class were also actively involved in the right-wing countermovements against students in the 1970s. The successful student uprising of October 14 "motivated conservative elements and the elites to counter-mobilize" (Kongkirati 2009, 12). The right-wing groups, which were responsible for the student massacres of 1976, formed organizations to counter the peasants, labor rights groups, and students around 1975 (Kasertsiri 1998). Ungpakorn (1998, 61–64) also argues that the military and anti-Communist groups actively organized and supported the nationalist Red Guar and Nawaphon. The Village Scouts, officially endorsed by the state, was "the largest counter-movement with its membership of more than 20,000 drawn almost exclusively from the middle class in Bangkok" (Prajak 2009, 25). "In upcountry towns, the movement attracted local officials, merchants, and other well-to do persons. In Bangkok, wives of generals, business leaders, bankers, and members of the royal family took part" (Kongkirati 2009, 25).

Popular Unelected Leaders

Unelected prime ministers have been viewed favorably in Thailand. Given the highly unstable electoral democratic periods in the 1970s and the 1990s, in contrast with the stability brought on by the Prem leadership in the 1980s, there is a sense among the public that an impartial leader who can stay "above politics" is a marker of good leadership. Royally appointed prime ministers, in particular, are viewed in a positive light because they are perceived to possess three qualities: (1) royal blessing, (2) neutrality, and (3) incorruptibility. The idea of having an unelected prime minister is to provide an incorruptible "buffer" between different political groups that struggle to gain control of the government. A lofty ideal, perhaps, but an appointed premier must show that he does not seek political office for his own personal gain and that he maintains enough distance from the influence of both the military and political parties. Support for an unelected prime minister stems from the idea that both the military and politicians have been extremely corrupt when they govern and thus do not represent the needs of the people.

Royal blessing gives a political actor an immense leverage vis-à-vis his counterparts. The palace will support someone who can steer the country out of a crisis and can rise above politics—the constant competition over access to pork and patronage. When the king appoints someone to lead the country, he emboldens both that particular person's political power and status. This is called the process of "royal legitimization."

> Although the king does not have any political or administrative power under the system of constitutional monarchy, his role in times of political crises has been crucial. The Thais view the King as sacred and as a spiritual leader who serves as a symbol of unity. . . . Because of this the monarch remains an indispensable source of political legitimacy. A political leader or regime, even a popularly elected government, would not be truly legitimized without the King's blessing. (Maisrikrod 1992, 334)

Historically, highly respected individuals are appointed prime ministers in times of crisis—often after the fall of a particular coup government. They are meant to serve in a "transition" period of an authoritarian government and an electoral democracy in the near future. Two particular appointed prime ministers, Prem Tinasulanond and Anand Panyarachoon, have left such important legacies in Thai political history that their own personal clout and charisma have had a significant impact on the emergence of the anti-Thaksin movements, the 2006 coup, and the current ongoing political crisis—years after their administrations ended. Prem was known to be an acceptable choice by the palace, the military, the parliamentarians, and the public. Prem endured through eight years of rule, four administrations, two coup attempts, and an assassination attempt, while maintaining parliamentary politics the best he could. Because he never ran for election, he was able to position himself as being "above politics" or "nonpoliticized." He maintained equal distance from both the armed forces and the political parties, and he was able to choose persons whom he deemed most suitable to form coalition governments. Yet Prem was no democrat as, during his long rule, he did not allow a no confidence motion against him, for instance. A staunch supporter of Prem and a veteran politician, Prasong Soonsiri (2000, 267), shares a popularly held view of his premiership:

> Prem understands Thai society better than any career politician. Elected officials have a lot to learn from him. . . . Prem has a con-

science of a true democrat—more than those elected. He never abused his power even though he could have, with the military's backing and all. He solved problems not to benefit any political party, but the nation. . . . He never had businessmen or people with vested interests lobbying him. . . . He's the only prime minister who ended his term in grace.[24]

Indeed, part of the reason why Prem refused to stay in power after the 1988 election was because some doubts regarding his supposed neutrality emerged. This decision came after some public wariness about his administration. A petition signed by ninety-nine people, mostly academics, was submitted to the king. It stated: "We request Your Majesty's assistance with this matter to ensure that the political leader in the position of prime minister will strictly maintain his neutrality to any institution for the sake of protecting his political position."[25]

Anand Panyarachoon,[26] a soft-spoken, highly respected diplomat, served as a premier twice without once being elected. He was handpicked by the junta following the military coup in 1991 to restore Thailand's image abroad after much criticism from the foreign press with regard to the military takeover. Anand always portrayed himself as "neutral" and "apolitical"— which gained him widespread support. "I had no intention to be a prime minister and never had any aspiration to enter politics. In the past many people asked me to take up various ministerial positions but I always said no."[27] Anand was regarded as the nation's "savior" after the military coup in February 1991 (Surin 2005, 405). General Suchinda asked him to be prime minister because he needed someone acceptable to both the public and internationally—particularly because the foreign press was condemning the coup.[28]

Following Suchinda's resignation after the Black May Uprising, internal bickering inside the parliament eventually led to the nomination of Anand to take the leadership position until a new leader was elected. The House Speaker at the time, Athit Urairat, was expected to nominate General Somboon Rahong as premier but then shocked everyone at the National Assembly when Anand's name was announced. "It's one of the most commendable decisions Dr. Athit had ever made," writes academic Rangsan Pattanarangsan.[29] Prinya Tewanaruemitrakul, one of the leaders of the Black May Uprising, admits that choosing Anand as premier averted the crisis. "When Anand came he reshuffled a number of military positions that were directly involved with the crackdown and . . . the situation that could have exploded again in fact calmed down."[30]

This is particularly ironic given that part of the motive for the protest movements was against the coming to power of the "unelected" Suchinda, but the public was willing to accept Anand, whom they believed could resolve the crisis. Indeed, a group called "Friends of Anand" was formed among a small circle of elites at the time to support a "good" and "honest" person like him to stay as premier.[31] The group believed a "good person like Anand must be protected and cherished."[32] Some influential academics also joined in, including Jermsak Pinthong, Methi Krongkaew, Kasien Tejapira, and Rangsan Thanapornpan. The membership shot up in less than a week after its inception and the group held rallies such as "Run for Anand" or "Flowers for Anand."[33] Such activities to protect someone because he was a "good person" was a unique phenomenon to Thailand.

Some section of the Thai elites and the middle class favor unelected prime ministers precisely because there seem to be no "obvious" vested interests with the military. Theerayut Boonmee, a Thai academic, explains (Meksophon, 72):

> The middle class was motivated by a special situation in which the dark sides of both moral and democratic values centralized in one figure [General] Suchinda. They did not have anything against unelected prime minister before the outbreak of the [Black May] turmoil, or against any other unelected prime minister before that because they found this type of leader more accessible.

The Monarchy

That the monarchy is the most powerful institution in today's Thailand is not only the result of centuries-old tradition but also the personal cultivation of King Bhumibol Adulyadej, who until his death in 2017 was the longest reigning monarch in the world. Kana Ratsadorn, a group of military and civil officers, sought to undermine the power and legitimacy of the monarchical institution when it overthrew the absolute monarchy in 1932. Yet the monarchy was not completely deprived of its influence and dominance in the Thai polity as the new political order retained the role of the patriarchal king, who stands as the symbol of national unity and moral rectitude to his subjects.[34]

Nonetheless, the power of the monarchical institution remained weak in the first two decades of constitutional monarchy. This is evidenced by King Bhumibol's failed attempt to prevent Field Marshal Phibul from reinstating the 1932 constitution in 1951 (Chaloemtiarana 2007, 204). It was not until after 1957, during the long rule of Field Marshal Sarit Thanarat, that the position of the monarchy was elevated (Hewison 1997, 63). Suwannathat-Pian (2003) argues that King Bhumibol almost single-handedly brought the monarchy from a position of decline to one that represents a pinnacle of the nation. Likewise, the Thai government explained why King Bhumibol was deeply revered: "The love and reverence the Thai people have for their King [Bhumibol] stem in large part from the moral authority His Majesty King Bhumibol Adulyadej has earned during his reign, one that involves a remarkable degree of personal contact with the people."[35]

While formally the king enjoys a ceremonial position as the head of state, a careful reading of the Thai constitution reveals a much more powerful position. In the second chapter of the 2007 constitution, Section 8 says: "The King shall be enthroned in a position of revered worship and shall not be violated. No person shall expose the King to any sort of accusation or action."[36] Such an article in the constitution may seem at odds with the conventional understanding of a constitutional monarchy. Yet in the Thai case, such reference to the power of the king reflects both traditional and modern understandings of the Thai monarch—one whose actual power cannot be captured in words. Thai people refer to the king as "Phra Chao Yu Hua," which literally translates to "God upon our head." In this instance, the king continues to be perceived as the "Lord of the land" whose main duty is to preserve and protect the land and the people who live on it.

In normal times, the king serves as a symbol of unity and stability of Thailand and guides by moral suasion and example through words and writing. A prime example of this is the king's oath of coronation on May 5, 1950: "We shall reign with righteousness for the benefit and happiness of the Siamese people." This particular phrase has been frequently replayed in the past six decades and it became a yardstick for "good governance"—one that those with the constitutional powers to govern in the democratic system should follow. In times of crisis, however, the monarch is expected to play a role in resolving the situation. The Thai government describes the king's role in crisis management:

> His Majesty's moral authority was reinforced by his judicious interventions to put an end to widening political bloodshed. Two of the most crucial of those times occurred in 1973 and 1991. . . . Through these interventions, the King did not involve himself in the political problems, which should be and were resolved through political mechanisms. Rather, he stopped bloodshed among Thais when state machinery had failed to do so.[37]

The king's ability to resolve the conflicts, both in 1973 and 1991, speaks volumes to his power and authority above and beyond constitutional standing. But the king's power is a two-way street: on the one hand, it is how the king perceives it to be, while on the other, it is what the populace expects from their monarch. Clearly there are sections of the population that called out for the king's intervention in both incidents, thus, his actions are reactionary. However, each intervention leaves a legacy and builds future expectations. This will become particularly important when discussing the emergence of the promonarchy movement of the PAD.

Moreover, the long reign of King Bhumibol allowed him to build a key virtue of political leadership, barami. Barami, an important concept in Thai studies, means "virtue" and "innate authority."[38] This "barami" is not hereditary and cannot be given or passed on to anyone. Rather, barami is "earned" and is built over a long period of time through hard work and dedication. Barami is a marker of legitimacy and authority that can be used to enhance someone's power. The king is regarded as having a lot of barami, which makes his actions and words powerful moral suasion that can shape behaviors and outcomes in the political arena. This is why a royal blessing is so critical to the success of many of the unelected prime ministers such as Prem and Anand. In times of conflict, many political elites look to the king for a solution and royal appointments. This power and authority the king derives from his barami as opposed to the fact that he is the king per se.

The moral and political dominance of the monarchical institution presents a set of unique challenges to the development of democracy in Thailand. First, the power and authority of the monarchy, at times, competes with that of formal democratic institutions. The fact that the monarchy successfully intervened to stop two major episodes of bloodshed in Thai history, where state agencies and other democratic bodies failed, is testament to the strength of the palace vis-à-vis other institutions. To leave the task of conflict management to the monarchy may serve to alleviate ad-hoc crisis situations, but in the long run the political system needs to develop and strengthen its own mechanisms of conflict management. As the greatest strength of the monarchy has rested on the personage of King Bhumibol, future succession may leave both the monarchy and the country vulnerable to conflicts.

Second, the king's moral suasion can be a more powerful marker of legitimacy than any power derived from constitutional or parliamentarian positions. This is particularly true because of the deep reverence toward the king among the majority of Thai society, which further contributes to the power of the king's words and actions. As Suwannathat-Pian (2003, 192) argues:

It is evident that Bhumibol's socio-political strength comes from the unconditional devotion of his subjects who are willing to support and be guided by him because they have been convinced that his interest for their well-being is a genuine mission that Bhumibol has embraced since he took the reign . . . that Bhumibol has been able to defy ruling military juntas, parliaments and even constitutions with impunity is by itself proof of his unshaken bond he has cultivated with his people.

This "informal" power of the monarchical institution can shape and change political outcomes in times of crisis.

Lastly, some groups have manipulated the power of the monarchy for their own political gain. They use the monarchy as a "front" to achieve their ends, knowing full well that the monarchy cannot always respond to political matters. In fact, the most powerful way to discredit someone is to accuse him of defaming the monarchy. Even the rumor of being alleged to have done so can go a long way in tarnishing that person's reputation, which sometimes leads to dismissal and even temporary exile. Sulak Sivaraksa, a well-known public intellectual, a prominent leader of a number of key NGOs, *and* a self-confessed royalist,[39] was accused by General Suchinda[40] after the 1991 coup of lèse-majesté. Sulak, who was forced into exile for four years, was targeted because he was a popular challenger to the coup government. Such examples of abuse of the monarchical institution have occurred throughout Thai history. The Yellow Shirts will use "royalism" as a key driving force for mobilization as well as a legitimization of their movement.

While these factors make coups more likely in Thailand, compared to other Third Wave democracies, democracy in Thailand does not always break down. The Black May Uprising and its implications dramatically changed Thai politics in ways that have fundamental impacts on future coups d'état as well as the emergence of mass-based politics. First, Black May significantly weakened the military's position in the political arena. This is particularly true when considering the power of the military vis-à-vis the public, career politicians, and the monarchy. The second and related point is that the cost of coups d'état as mechanisms for regime change dramatically increase for the military. Third, the uprising set in motion the process of political liberalization, driven by reformist elites who have gained political prominence following Black May.

Black May also contains its contradictions as it confirms a long-standing nondemocratic tendency within the Thai polity. The uprising was *not* in opposition to the coup d'état per se, but rather an opposition to the military staying on in power. Moreover, the public support for royally appointed prime ministers underscores the monumental power of the monarchical institution as well as illustrating public acceptance of political leadership that does not come from the democratic process. These tendencies among the public are not new in Thai political history and thus demonstrate continuity, rather than change, in this respect.

Contesting Visions of Accountability

Black May set in motion a broader-based reform movement centered on reducing corruption and improving accountability. However, there was serious disagreement over what accountability meant, for whom, and to what end. I argue that tensions emerged among three different notions of accountability, (1) horizontal, (2) vertical, and (3) moral accountability, with the former two dimensions of democratic accountability while the latter is aligned with authoritarianism. While the resulting political reforms implemented after Black May represented a compromise among these three notions of accountability, they were heavily influenced by the moral notion of accountability. As Rodan and Hughes argue, the moral approaches to promote accountability can end up undermining democratic reforms.[41] In the Thai case, the sources of moral accountability are drawn from nondemocratic sources, with the monarchy at the pillar. These moral, but inherently antidemocratic, undertones of the reforms clashed with other democratic dimensions of the reforms, eventually paving the way for the emergence of a mass antidemocratic movement a decade later.

Horizontal accountability and vertical accountability are conceptions of accountability that sit within the broader concerns of improving democratic accountability. Advocates for improving horizontal accountability in a democratic polity are fundamentally concerned with holding those in political office answerable to the public. Reforms that are designed to safeguard democratic institutions and citizens against the concentration of executive power or the potential for executive abuse of power are meant to strengthen horizontal democratic accountability. On the other hand, vertical accountability is concerned with inclusiveness in a democracy: how we can design a democratic system that maximizes inclusion and power-sharing as well as reducing political inequality. But both horizontal accountability and vertical accountability can be advanced at the expense of each other. For champions of a majoritarian vision of democracy, where the voices of the majority population matter most, promoting vertical accountability, not curbing it through executive constraints, is paramount. Conversely, others may worry about the potential for the executive to abuse power if insufficient measures to constrain it exist. The Thai case demonstrates how this uneasy tension between the two notions of democratic accountability manifest themselves throughout the reform process.

But the post–Black May reform efforts were also influenced by the moral notions of accountability, which espouse attachment to conservative political sources of power. Moral accountability, as a distinct notion of accountability, does not mean that other types of accountability ideologies do not have moral bases, but that it may also draw on nondemocratic sources of authority.[42] In Thailand, the moral ideologies that guided the reform efforts and subsequent antidemocratic movements were based on unaccountable traditional sources of power—namely, the monarchy and Buddhism. As the subsequent paragraphs will demonstrate, advocates of the moral accountability ideology sought to exert its influence over those seeking to champion democratic notions of accountability. Ultimately, the tensions that existed between horizontal and vertical accountability, on the one hand, and moral versus democratic accountability, on the other, became exacerbated following the election of Thaksin Shinawatra, which symbolized the victory of vertical accountability at the expense of other accountability ideologies.

The key areas of the 1990s political reforms in Thailand were motivated by concerns regarding accountability in these three dimensions: (1) checks and balances on the executive abuse of power and the military (horizontal), (2) greater political participation from the masses (vertical), and (3) reducing corruption and attracting good people to politics (moral). This process of reform remained largely elite-driven despite a concerted effort to include the voices of the people in the process.[43] The reformist elites constituted a loose and varied coalition of academics, activists, professionals, bureaucrats, and public intellectuals. It is important to view them as "elites" for despite the fact that some have deep roots in society at large (i.e., activists), they remained at the top of the hierarchy of their networks and often represented their own personal opinion rather than the interests of their groups. Also, their participation in the reform process was much more pronounced than that of their networks; this signified the rather elitist nature of the reform.

The reformists took charge of the reform process under the leadership of a highly respected public intellectual who subscribed to the *moral* accountability ideology, Professor Prawes Wasi, to create a political system

TABLE 3.2. Reformist approaches to three accountability ideologies and the subsequent reforms enacted in the 1997 constitution

Accountability ideologies	Key problems	Reform outcomes	Key reformists (selected)
Moral accountability	Morality and ethics of political office holders	1. Single-member district replaces bloc voting 2. Funding for party development 3. Restrict party switching (must be member of party for 90 days before election) 4. PR list second tier voting 5. More oversight on campaign donations 6. 5% threshold	Prawes Wasi,* Theerayuth Boonmee,* Chamlong Srimuang,* Khien Teerawit, Kaewsan Athipoh, Prasong Soonsiri, Kanin Boonsuwan, Likhit Dheravegin
Horizontal accountability	Poor checks and balances on executive power	1. Creation of legislative ordinary session 2. Smaller cabinet size 3. MPs cannot be cabinet members at the same time 4. Creation of new independent bodies to increase checks and balances (Election Commission, National Human Rights Commission, Office of Ombudsman, Constitutional Court, National Anti-Corruption Commission)	Anand Panyarachoon, Amorn Raksasat, Uthai Pimjaichon, Bawornsak Uwanno, Somkid Lertpaitoon, Kanit na Nakorn, Pongthep Thepkanchana, Chai-anan Samudvanij*
Vertical accountability	Inclusiveness Political inequality	1. Public hearings with state officials 2. Petition to dismiss MPs, ministers (50,000 signatures) 3. Community rights/ conservation of traditional culture 4. Autonomy to local government 5. Direct election of Senate 6. Compulsory voting 7. Prime minister must come from the lower house	Suchit Boonbongkarn, Somsak Kosaisuk,* Prateep Ungsongtham,* Weng Tojirakarn,* Bamroong Kayotha,* Saneh Jamrik*

* Not part of the 99-person Constitutional Drafting Committee (1996) but noted as having some influence in the discourse of constitutional drafting

that would be ruled by "good people." While there was some broad agreement as to what is "wrong" with the Thai polity, there was no consensus as to what exactly needed reforming. The reformists' ideas for reforms could be categorized into three domains of accountability: moral, horizontal, and vertical. The moral ideologists were reformists who believed the "people" were what was really wrong with the Thai political system. They questioned the morality and ethics of the political elites and purported that unless their behavior could change for the better, no amount of constitutional or electoral engineering could increase Thailand's political stability. These immoral and corrupt political elites were going to find loopholes to circumvent new institutions to continue their clientelistic, corrupt, and nepotistic ways. Unless the behavior of political elites were to change, no "real" reform could occur. Democracy must rest on moral and ethical foundations, otherwise it would not work, according to the morality reformists. Key problems that needed reforming in the Thai polity, according to this group of reformists, were poor-quality politicians, vote buying and selling, patron–client relations, and a lack of general moral ethics among the political elites.

The biggest proponent of this approach was none other than Prawes Wasi, who advocated for Buddhist moral principles and ethics as a key to building a better society. In his earlier writing (Wasi 1990), he lays out his thoughts on what democracy should be in Thailand:

> Democracy and dharma[44] need to go together so that democracy would be more righteous. . . . If everyone lives by moral and ethical principles, then they would be better people . . . they would not be interested in politics just to seek power or benefit themselves. . . . Dharma-based democracy will help political parties to recruit good people into politics, which will improve the quality and morality of democracy.[45]

Two decades later, Prawes's famous "triangle that moves a mountain" (สามเหลี่ยมเขยื้อนภูเขา) theory, which he promoted widely among prorefom academics, politicians, and activists, underscores his earlier pessimism about the lack of morality among politicians. Since politicians will never be "good" or "honest," according to Prawes, they must be pressured to reform by other groups in society, namely the empowered citizenry and those with knowledge (academics).[46] Some of the supporters of this approach take a royalist stance by using King Bhumibol's words and teaching as a yardstick for how people should behave. Prasong Soonsiri, veteran politician dubbed the "CIA of Thailand" for his long tenure at the National Security Council, said: "Where politicians seek power for themselves and their cronies, that country will not likely prosper. Politicians know they should be good people but they don't want to be. . . . They should adhere to the king's [Bhumibol] advice and follow his teaching."[47]

Influenced by the moral reformists, strengthening horizontal accountability was a priority for another set of reformists made up largely of lawyers and political science academics. They believed that if the right institutions were put in place, they would exert sufficient constraints on political officeholders to curb executive abuse of power and corruption. Bawornsak Uwanno, a law professor and constitutional drafter, saw in a new constitution the solution to the malaise of Thai politics. He pointed to three key problems: (a) representative democracy was highly problematic; (b) political affairs were writ large with corruption, and lacking in ethics or legitimacy; and (c) parliament lacked stability, the prime minister lacked leadership skills, and both government and parliament were ineffective.[48] A new constitution would make the political realm an arena for the people; make the political and bureaucratic systems honest and legitimate by empowering citizens at all levels; and increase the government's stability and capability by both ensuring that the prime minister has leadership qualities and enhancing parliamentary effectiveness.[49] Likewise, Pongthep Thepkanchana, another constitutional drafter who subsequently served in both Thaksin's and Yingluck's governments, argued that the independent bodies created by the 1997 constitution are at the heart of good governance. "These institutions are needed to create mechanisms of transparent checks and balances."[50]

Champions of horizontal accountability had good reason to be optimistic. After all, out of Thailand's eighteen constitutions since 1932, only three very short-lived constitutions (1946, 1949, and 1974) had any elements of democratic accountability. But these, as a result, were quickly torn up by the various military juntas that came to power.[51] The majority of the constitutions were written to allow authoritarian regimes to remain in power, not provide rights and protection for citizens under the law. Field Marshal Sarit, who staged a coup in 1958, took nearly ten years to write up the 1968 constitution: a foil that served to keep him in power. "For the past 77 years Thai constitutions have failed to serve as rules and social contracts. . . . Thailand is unable to establish a regime that uses the rule of law to solve conflicts and always relies on coups d'état," claimed law professor and student leader of the Black May uprising, Parinya Thewanaruemitkul.[52]

Advocates of vertical accountability, supported largely by reformist elites drawn from civil society organizations, viewed existing sociopolitical structures as major impediments to a more participatory and just society. Pervasive and growing gaps between the rich and the poor, a lack of access to resources, a lack of social mobility, and a foreshortened future all made the majority of Thais feel powerless, according to proponents of vertical accountability. They saw measures to empower citizens and opportunities for their meaningful participation in the political process as key to fixing the broken political system. Raewadee Prasertchareonsuk, head of the Coordinating Committee of NGO Networks, argued that a true democracy must have the people, especially the poor and the disadvantaged, at its center.[53] Rights, liberty, and equality must be given to the people in order for any structural reforms to be sustainable, adds Raewadee.[54] Somkiat Pongpaibul, a propoor activist who later became one of PAD's top leaders, contended that Thailand needed "new politics" that was not a politics of representation, but a politics for the people.[55] This "civic politics" would open doors for people at the grassroots level to participate in politics and have their voices heard beyond the mere act of voting. Thailand really needed participatory, not representative, democracy, adds Somkiat.[56]

The resulting 1997 constitution was an extraordinary but contentious compromise across all three dimensions of accountability. First, provisions were made to increase public participation in political life and to empower ordinary citizens with new rights as a means to guard against the abuse of state power. A total of fifty-one new rights were extended to Thai citizens by virtue of this new constitution.[57] Examples include the right to hold public hearings (Article 59); community rights to preserve natural resources (Article 56); the right to submit a petition for consideration of legislation (Article 170); and increased devolution of state power to local governments (Articles 282–90). Boonlert Changyai, one of the 1997 Constitution drafters, argued that these social rights constituted a flagship of the constitution because they had been so poorly dealt with in the past.[58]

Second, the 1997 constitution sought to build a political environment conducive to moral governance. The drafters' conception of "good governance" followed along the same lines as King Bhumibol's notion of promoting "good" people to rule. In order to reduce incentives for corrupt politicians to stay in politics, or to reduce the extent of vote buying and money politics, a number of articles were drawn up to bring about moral politics with the effective aim of helping to improve good governance. The upper house, for instance, would be directly elected for the first time by the populace (Article 315). However, candidates would not be allowed to campaign to dissuade political parties from intervening. This unprecedented measure was intended to reduce the influence of the "old elites" since the upper house had long been dominated by retired generals, bureaucrats, and public intellectuals. Samudavanija calls this "the informal political party" or the "legislative arms" of the bureaucracy (Samudavanija 1989, 333–34). It was hoped that a popularly elected Senate would make the National Assembly more democratic and that the elected enators would be less likely to be corrupt.

To attract better-quality candidates to enter politics, the drafters put in place measures to overhaul the entire electoral system. The previous system of bloc voting, which Hicken (2006) argues creates incentives for more corruption as candidates from the same parties are forced to compete with one another, was done away with. The new electoral system introduced a mixed member system of single-member districts at one tier and closed-list proportional representation at a second tier. Single-member districts would reduce intraparty competition, while closed-list proportional representation would create stronger incentives for party identification and reduce vote-buying opportunities. The combined effect of these measures was to help reduce the number of parties, force parties to develop a national agenda and broad appeals, and strengthen the overall party system. With these significant changes, the drafters hoped that gone were the days of personalistic campaigning, an endless number of parties, and a lack of party roots in society. To enhance government efficacy and stability and to dissuade party switching, new rules required politicians to hold membership with a political party for at least ninety days before an election. The prime minister must also be drawn from the body of MPs; and if an MP wanted to be in a cabinet, he would have to resign his seat.

A major concern for the horizontal accountability reformists was the abuse of power by political elites and state agencies. To curb power abuse, new independent institutions[59] were created to provide checks and balances against the administrative branch of powers. A Constitutional Court was established (Article 255) to ensure that the rights afforded by the 1997 constitution would be protected. The Ombudsman position was created (Article 196) to keep abuses of the state and government in check. The National Human Rights Commission was created (Article 199) to allow for the protection of human rights. The National Anti-Corruption Commission was established (Article 297) to reduce and deter corruption: namely, that of political leaders. The National Human Rights Commission was notable because it had the power to prosecute those in political positions, remove someone from office, and enforce the declaration of assets for politicians—all powers that did not exist in previous constitutions.

The last notable change that the constitution sought to effect was a stronger executive. Given the history of weak and unstable coalition governments in the past, the constitutional drafters wanted to lengthen the government's term and empower the prime minister to govern more effectively. As such, the prime minister could dissolve parliament and call new elections within sixty days (although he cannot do so during a no confidence motion). This, in combination with the ninety-day party membership requirement, would make it very difficult for MPs to defect from a party or a coalition party to cause government collapse. Moreover, the prime minister would have the power to remove and appoint cabinet ministers at will (Article 217)[60] and no less than two-fifths of the lower house would be required to call a no confidence motion on the prime minister (Article 185).

While supporters heralded the success of the 1997 constitutional engineering, the so-called People's Constitution contained illiberal and conservative elements that did not necessarily facilitate democratic development. This was partly because of the heavy influence of the reformists' moral accountability ideologies whose overemphasis on "good people" reflected a deep-seated bias against elected politicians, whom they saw as "bad." Moreover, those not elected, like Prem or Anand, were considered to be better alternatives. Another conservative and elitist example was Article 107, which required MP candidates to have, at minimum, a bachelor's degree. Such a requirement was wholly out of touch with reality given that only 5 percent of the Thai population had completed tertiary education in 2000.[61] In effect, the degree prerequisite discriminated against the majority of the population by preserving the position of MP for the educated few.[62] This requirement also reflected the reformists' idea of what "good" and "capable" politicians should be. Better-educated people were thought to be needed to govern the country.

Many of the new provisions of civil and community rights promulgated in the 1997 constitution were seen as ineffectual without legislative guarantees. One of the flaws of the 1997 constitution was that "many of the rights guaranteed under the constitution cannot take effect without legislation."[63] This generated much contention with the people's sector, which demanded more legislation to implement these rights provisions in the constitution. Bamrung Kayotha of the Assembly of the Poor contended that many of the constitutional provisions that were greatly needed by the poor were likely to be of no use due to the lack of further legislation. "The state tries to prevent the constitution from taking effect. Issues like community rights, protection of traditional way of life, conflict over access to land and resources are all very important to the poor. If they don't become legislative acts, they would be of little use to the poor."[64]

The draft constitution also elicited some strong opposition from the public. The so-called People's Constitution was not as popular as many people had assumed. Waves of protest between the supporters of the draft—"the Green Group"—and their counterparts erupted weeks before the parliamentary vote. Some 30,000 village chiefs or *kamnans*, mostly from the North and the Northeast, were protesting against the draft.[65] Another royalist group that called itself "Those Who Love Their Monarch" (กลุ่ม ผู้รักเจ้า) was among the oppositional voices that argued that the new constitution sought to change the regime from a constitutional monarchy to a republic.[66] Meanwhile, some 3,000 supporters, drawn from the Student Federation of Thailand, prodemocracy groups, labor unions, and NGO groups, gathered to support the draft. Pipob Thongchai, a senior NGO activist who later became one of PAD's top leaders, was among the supporters. "We need to put pressure on the politicians so that they back down and let the draft through."[67] At some point they shouted former Prime Minister Anand's name as he joined the proconstitution movement.[68]

The 1997 constitution had a real deficit in mechanisms that might work toward increasing vertical accountability, most critically between the state and its citizens. It did not emphasize good governance because it did not create mechanisms necessary to hold the ruling class and civil servants accountable to the citizens. The way that the constitution was written suggested that it was the public who should shoulder the initial costs of creating good governance.[69] For instance, those who wanted to push through legislation needed to obtain 50,000 signatures. Moreover, they had to pay for such a process in order to petition parliament. Those who sought transparency or access to public service data likewise had to pay for the process of obtaining such data. The 1997 constitution discussed good governance only superficially—namely on issues of transparency and participation. Poor people, particularly, would be hard-pressed to produce either sufficient documentation or the financial resources necessary to file a petition. The defeat of those reformists who believed in improving vertical accountability—many NGO activists—provided the grounds for their involvement and leadership in the PAD movement later on.[70]

Conclusion

I argue in this chapter that the political reforms in the post–Black May period exemplify a contestation over the meaning of accountability. While the reformist elites agreed that reforms were needed to make the Thai polity more open and more democratic, there was serious disagreement over how to go about it. The 1997 People's Constitution and other associated political reforms represent a compromise across the three domains of accountability—moral, horizontal, and vertical. Yet the dominance of moral accountability proponents meant that the reforms of the 1990s were not grounded in democratic or liberal principles, but rather in traditional sources of authority. Understanding the illiberal, undemocratic, and conservative elements within the 1997 Constitution is crucial to help make sense of the subsequent emergence of antidemocratic movements whose leaders were drawn from the same group of reformists.

Despite frequent government changes in the 1990s, an increasingly mobilized society, and the most severe economic crisis in contemporary times, an antidemocratic movement did not emerge in Thailand during the 1990s. Why not? First, there was an alternation of power and significant uncertainty over the makeup of the government. Political leaders felt included in the political arena, and all considered they held a fair chance of securing a place in government. The military was allowed full control of its budget, and no one meddled with its internal structure. Political parties had a fair chance of either winning the next election or of being part of a multiparty coalition government. Between 1992 and 2001, small, medium, and large parties rotated power, amalgamated, or opposed one another. Factions were fluid: they joined a new party when they pleased, and there was no "fixed" political arrangement. Since parties were neither rooted in society nor had much programmatic appeal, party switching was not a costly action for politicians to take. There were effectively no "forever" friends or foes in this political arena. Losing an election was not a detrimental event because parties knew they could wait their turn to take power next time. Given that a government lasted on average, just eighteen months, that wait was never long.

Second, the society became more open and inclusive in the aftermath of the Black May Uprising. The opening up of the society was exemplified partly by a greater degree of activism and a massive expansion of the civil society sector. Civil society organizations were able to gain concessions from the central government, and even held political elites responsible for their action at the time (Pathmanand 2001a). Moreover, the Thai political system became more devolved in part due to the decentralization of the early 1990s that saw the creation of subnational governments in order to meet local demands.

Lastly, an executive could be dislodged from power, and a government replaced, in multiple ways. The mechanism for power alternation was not crippled or rendered ineffective. A coalition partner or even a faction could defect from a governing coalition, resulting in dissolution of the House of Representatives and a new election. Because coalition governments in the 1990s were so weak and fragmented, opposition groups, be it in formal or informal democratic channels, felt they could influence the course of politics in one way or another. The Chuan government (1997–2000) tried to cling to power for as long as possible despite frequent and intense protests, as well as much internal bickering with the coalition partners, but it eventually succumbed to a House dissolution. In sum, both formal and informal channels to channel grievances for both elites and the mass were open, and no organized group felt shut out by the system.

FOUR

The Origins of the Yellow Shirts

The 1990s was not just an important period of political reforms, it was also the time of great turmoil. Thailand was also hit especially hard by the 1997 Asian Financial Crisis—which sent its currency into free fall, caused millions of people to lose their jobs, and led to incessant street protests. Not even at its weakest, though, did Thailand witness mass antidemocratic mobilization. Instead, the People's Alliance for Democracy was born at a time of political stability, economic growth, and expansive civil society: all three major conditions that should make democracy work. Why and how?

The People's Alliance for Democracy started out as a prodemocracy movement but evolved into an antidemocratic one. This chapter examines the first stage of the PAD's transformation: becoming an anti-incumbent movement. It discusses how democratic institutions become blocked, and in so doing, exclude the participation of key groups and actors in the polity. Initially, the PAD began as separate and diverse antigovernment opposition groups—many of which were ideologically opposed to one another. As the number of opposition groups grew and their protest activities intensified, the former made the decision to unite under the banner of the PAD, and to wear yellow shirts in symbolic allegiance to King Bhumibhol. Uniting as a PAD movement was strategic: leaders of the opposition groups recognized the difficulty of gaining leverage against the uncompromising incumbent without presenting a strong and united front. As a number of the PAD's demands continued to go unmet, the movement leaders made another strategic choice: to oppose democracy. Chapter 5 will cover in detail how the PAD took an antidemocratic turn.

To clarify, adopting antidemocratic tactics was not a *natural* outcome of the process of institutional blockage; but it was a strategic option that was most likely to succeed. Their chosen strategy directly affected whether the process of institutional blockage would continue—or not. As such, both the *sequence* and *timing* of this process affects the outcome. When opposition groups feel cut off from access to power both in the present and foreseeable future, they appeal to nondemocratic, alternative sources of power to reverse or, at a minimum, halt this process of institutional blockage. And it is when these nondemocratic institutions responded to the opposition forces that we see a complete democratic collapse.

An examination of the Thaksin government also reveals how its marginalization of opposition voices was perceived as a threat to democratic accountability. Both the political dominance of the Thaksin government *and* his increasingly illiberal rule had made, for his opposition, constraints on the executive very difficult. As I will show in detail, each opposition group that mobilized against Thaksin had at once been adversely affected by his policies *and* experienced political intimidation and harassment. The closing down of opposition space coupled with encroachments on fundamental democratic freedoms underscored the nature of institutional blockage during the Thaksin era.

While much of the focus of this research is on the PAD movement, I will also discuss the broader Yellow Shirts movement of which the PAD was part. The Yellow Shirts encompassed three major groups. The engine of the movement was a loose network of alliances, this being the PAD. Supporting the movement, albeit indirectly, were sections of the armed forces and key individuals close to the king. I discuss these broader networks and the PAD by referring to them collectively as the Yellow Shirts but am careful to distinguish among the three. This chapter will break down the key groups and actors within the PAD and will also discuss their key allies as part of the broader Yellow Shirt movement. The PAD set the stage for a coup d'état, while the armed forces launched the coup with support from those close to the monarchy. These three components were, I argue, crucial to the successful overthrow of a democratically elected government. The emergence of this antidemocratic mobilization and the breakdown of democracy was regarded, from the perspective of numerous 1990s reformists, as an extension of the reform process shaped by proponents of the moral accountability ideologists—those who believe in political reforms centered on morality, Buddhism, and ethics. Viewed in this light, many PAD protesters believed that supporting a military coup and the eventual overthrow of the Thaksin government *was* democratic. A coup was merely a means to "recalibrate" the political system in order to attract moral and ethical leaders capable of providing good governance to the nation.

The first section of this chapter offers a background analysis to the emergence of the People's Alliance for Democracy. Following the 1990s political reforms, significant in that these ushered in the first-ever constitution written by "the people," Thailand entered a period of extreme instability: the economy collapsed, millions became unemployed, civil society was mobilized with incessant protests, and yet we observe no antidemocratic movements. Instead, Thailand saw democracy as the answer to its political, economic, and social woes, and voted in the most popularly elected prime minister in the country's history: Thaksin Shinawatra. The second section chronicles the meteoric rise of Thaksin and his party, Thai Rak Thai (TRT). It outlines a number of policies that made Thaksin such a popular leader. The second section additionally chronicles the emergence of the anti-Thaksin opposition, examining key groups, their grievances, and their opposition activities. The third section outlines major civil society networks that later become the key drivers of the PAD, recounting their beginnings as prodemocracy activist groups that ended up supporting a military coup. The institutional blockage theoretical framework is empirically applied throughout this chapter to demonstrate its operationalization in the Thai case.

The 1990s: Economic Collapse and Civil Society Growth

The 1990s were not only a period of great political reforms, the decade also bore witness to Thailand's economic collapse in the aftermath of the 1997 Asian Financial Crisis and its significant expansion of the civil society sector. In many ways, democracy had the best chance of collapsing in the 1990s: the country was embroiled in its worst economic crisis, millions had spilled onto the streets in protest, millions more lost their jobs, and the numbers of NGOs and civic groups in Thailand had risen to levels not seen before. Thailand in effect was bankrupt, civil society was mobilized, and it had a ready and willing military to step in to restore order should it be called upon. But that call never came. There was no antidemocratic mobilization. Instead, there was only a series of anti-incumbent protests—these subsequently led to leadership change, but not to democratic collapse. Indeed, the very same people who would later become leaders of the antidemocratic PAD and PDRC movements were at this moment in the streets protesting against government corruption and the handling of the financial crisis—yet they never took the antidemocratic turn.

Prior to the economic collapse, the majority of business figures steered clear of direct involvement in politics. A major impediment to business leaders entering into politics was the existing patronage-based politics that is at once time-consuming and resource-intensive (Prasirtsuk 2009). One has to build local networks with key vote-canvassers over time to generate electoral support. For these reasons, provincial bosses (political mafias) have long held an advantage in the political arena. Another barrier to entry for business leaders is their likely unwillingness to have their finances probed as politicians often do. Not that the Thai system does not have lax rules about scrutinizing politicians' assets, but the 1997 Constitution ordained stricter guidelines for asset declaration for those seeking political office. Nonetheless, the 1997 crisis prompted a number of key business figures to become fully involved in politics. Ironically, if being connected to politicians helped to propel the crash of 1997, what major Thai firms learned instead was that the only way to survive was to *increase*, not decrease, their ties to politics. A number of business leaders who survived the economic crash concluded that the only way to protect their business interests would be to run the country themselves. More importantly, as Prasirtsuk (2009) argues, as globalization and the push for economic liberalization intensify, key business firms, especially those dependent upon government concessions, become wary of leaving their fate in the hands of non-business-savvy politicians and bureaucrats.

Thaksin Shinawatra, who made his fortune from telecommunication concessions, explained his decision to found a new party, Thai Rak Thai, in 1998: To bring Thailand into the new era requires leadership that understands sales strategies so we can compete in the world economy. Business elites have the advantage over career politicians because they understand the complex nature of business. (Pisitsethakarn 2004, 36). Figure 4.1 shows that in the wake of the Asian Financial Crisis, candidates from the business sector outnumbered career politicians. In the 1996 general election, business leaders accounted for 29 percent of MPs, while career politicians accounted for 59 percent. By 2005, the number of career politicians running for parliament dropped to 17 percent in the party-list system, and 23 percent in single member districts. As for their business counterparts, these figures rose to 28 percent and 27 percent, respectively.

First, as more businessmen entered into politics to defend their business interests, more opportunities arose for rent-seeking. Most major business conglomerates in Thailand are family-run and largely by Sino-Thais. While a few are publicly traded, the founding families of the remaining

Persons

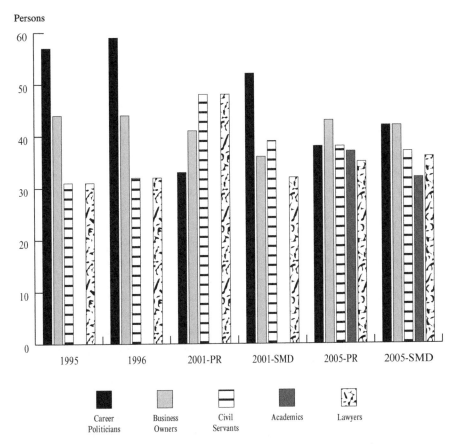

Figure 4.1. Professions of candidates in national elections (1995–2005)

companies manage to maintain large shares of ownership (Nikomborirak and Tangkitvanich 1999). This makes rent-seeking easier when some of the family members become politicians. Second, opportunities for rents are not concentrated in certain political figures but diversified among many political actors. This means that private rents can be sought through various positions in the political arena, be it in the cabinet, the lower house, or the upper house. Imai's (2006, 241) detailed study of politically connected firms in Thailand between 2001 and 2005 shows that political participation of family members yields private rents. Moreover, these economic benefits are largest when family members are cabinet ministers. Third, the new electoral system introduced by the 1997 Constitution made it easier for business elites to enter politics as party-list candidates. Since in Thailand, members of parliament are elected through a closed-list proportional system, influential business families who are financiers of certain parties could become party-list candidates without having to have established local networks and patronage like their nonbusiness counterparts in a given constituency. This explains why there were more businessmen in the party-list system than single-member district ones in both the 2001 and 2005 elections.

This proliferation of "crony capitalism" stands in stark contrast to the intentions of the political reforms in the 1990s. It is precisely these "conflicts of interest" between family businesses and politics that the reformists sought to rectify both through the 1997 Constitution and through other economic reforms. There are a number of provisions built into the 1997 Constitution that are specifically designed to prevent conflicts of interest, such as not allowing ministers to hold shares in public companies (Article 209); not allowing members of the National Assembly to be granted concessions from the state (Articles 110, 128, 208); and that anyone in political positions must declare their assets and liabilities before taking office (Klein 1998). But because business conglomerates in Thailand are family run, upon joining politics, members simply transfer their shares to their spouses or relatives. To illustrate but one such case, the wife of Warathep Rathanakorn, a Peau Thai MP, transferred both her and her husband's shares of their family-run tour businesses to her mother prior to him taking office.[1] Kanlaya Sopohonpanich, a member of the banking tycoon Sophonpanich family, transferred shares worth 300 million baht to her children and their spouses prior to taking office during the Abhisit Vejjajiva administration.[2]

The superrich entered Thai politics in full throttle when they formed the Thai Rak Thai party in 1999. Although it is not uncommon for the wealthy to finance or be involved in politics (table 4.1), what is completely unprecedented, in the case of the TRT, is the extent of wealth concentration in the party. The *Bangkok Post* reports that the ten richest families, owning between them in excess of 40 percent of market capitalization on the Thai Stock Exchange, have close ties to the Thaksin government.[3] Many of the rich within the TRT party made their wealth as concessionaires or through long-standing close ties to political elites. This raises the potential for conflicts of interest when they hold positions that allow them to make national policies and agendas that could directly influence their business interests. When concessionaires hold a political position, particularly in policy making, there is a real danger of this leading to monopolization, as a leading economist of the think tank Thailand Development Research Institute observes: "When monopolization occurs as a product of the political process, it can lead to less competition as those with political power legislate or have access to state resources in ways that hamper competition."[4]

The period of the 1990s also saw the greatest expansion of the civil society sector with the number of registered nonprofit organizations rising nearly 700 percent between 1997 and 2007.[5] Civil society organizations really began to proliferate in the 1990s as a result of a more open, democratic, and inclusive political environment. Veteran NGO leader and activist Pipob Thongchai, who later became one of the leaders of the PAD movement, saw the growing NGO sector as critical to curbing the abuse of state power by politicians and to fighting against crony capitalists (Prasertkul 2005, 158). The 1997 Constitution also provides hope for a more open and people-oriented politics for civil society organizations—many

TABLE 4.1. Professions of candidates in national elections (1995–2005)

Family	Party	Position	Net Worth (USD)
Shinawatra	Thai Rak Thai	Founder, Thaksin (PM)	$1.3 billion
Chiarawanon	Thai Rak Thai	Founding member, party list MP (Veerachai Veeramethikul)	$1.4 billion
Bodharamik	Thai Rak Thai	Deputy head, party list MP, cabinet minister (Adisai Bodharamik)	$248 million (son, Pitch Bodharamik)
Maleenont	Thai Rak Thai	Deputy head, party list MP, and cabinet minister (Pracha Maleenont)	$380 million
Sophonpanich	Democrat	Party advisor, MP, cabinet minister (Kanlaya Sophonpanich)	$440 million
Chirativath	Democrat	Financier	$485 million
Sirivadhanapakdi	Thai Rak Thai	Close ties to cabinet ministers (Chaiyoth Sasomsab and Wiruth Techapaibul)	$3 billion
Asavabhokin	Thai Rak Thai	Financier	$540 million
Yoovidhya	Democrat	Financier (ties to Bhirombhakdi and Banthadtan families—both influential in the Democrat Party)	$2.2 billion
Mahakijsiri	Thai Rak Thai	Deputy head and party list MP (Prayuth Mahakijsiri)	$365 million
Jungrungroengkij	Thai Rak Thai	Party secretary, party list MP, and cabinet minister (Suriya Jungrungroengkij)	$420 million
Bhirombhakdi	Democrat	MP candidate, minister's secretary (Jitpat Bhirombhakdi)	$500 million

of which believed in the need for greater vertical accountability and moral accountability in the Thai polity. A more mobilized society combined with consecutively weak governments did not, however, give rise to an antidemocratic movement. Rather, what we see in Thailand during this rather turbulent period are proreform movements following the Black May Uprising and anti-incumbent mobilization after the 1997 crash. In 1998, a backlash against austerity measures resulted in a wave of discontent that had economic nationalism in its sights. Some sections of the business and academic communities mobilized to oppose eleven bills introduced into parliament by the Chuan Leekpai government that they dubbed "11 bills to sell off the nation." The opposition alliance was loosely referred to as the "People's Alliance to Save the Nation" (พันธมิตรกู้ชาติ), composed of some forty-five organizations, including those leading the Black May uprising that aimed at opposing IMF reform packages. This alliance drew support from the State Enterprise Workers' Relations Confederation, the Confederation of Democracy, the Assembly of Lawyers, and the Retail and Wholesale Trade Association, to name but a few. The opposition came out in protest against globalization, against the IMF, against the free trade agreements, and so on and so forth. Moreover, Thailand's largest civil society organization, the Assembly of the Poor, having staged a ninety-nine day rally (its longest) in 1997, won "unprecedented concessions" from the government.[6]

This protest wave of nationalist mobilization pushed for parliament dissolution and several policy changes, as opposed to an attempt to overthrow the democratic regime altogether. This took place despite the fact that many of the very same figures behind the antigovernment and anti-IMF mobilization would, only a few years later, be instrumental in the emergence of the PAD movement. The Alliance sought to maximize the greater access to power provided by the 1997 Constitution to stop the passage of the "11 bills." They did so by submitting a petition to table the proposed bills. At the same time, the Alliance also staged mass rallies in opposition to the Chuan government.[7] By 1999, more protests from activists, academics, students, and state enterprises had taken place, calling for Chuan's resignation and the dissolution of the House. Throughout this entire period, the Chuan government reshuffled the cabinet three times in the hope of surviving a no confidence motion despite rising public discontent. Yet the government was besieged by internal scandals and threats of defection, and it eventually succumbed to a collapse when the House was dissolved in November 2000.

Antidemocratic mobilization did not arise during this period, despite dire economic conditions, highly contentious politics, and an actively mobilized mass base for two reasons. First, when political conflict reached an impasse, the conflict was able to be resolved within the formal democratic institutions. In the 1990s this often meant that governments tended to dissolve the House in the face of a crisis, whether the latter originated from within the coalition government itself or externally from societal pressure. Given the fluid nature of the party system, a new election is the least bad option for most parties. Since there were several successive coalition governments in the 1990s, major parties of all sizes felt they had a fair chance of again forming a government if they could make the right deals. Second, the channels for opposition to be heard were not blocked or rendered ineffective in ways that prevent the opposition from having a voice. Opposition parties could threaten a motion of no confidence if they gained support from two-fifths of the parliament. Opposition movements on the streets, such as the Assembly of the Poor, were able to make some inroads with the policymakers. In essence, the democratic system was still working to channel grievances and provide access to power for the opposition.

The Paradox of a Functioning Democracy

The deaths of Thailand's democracy in 2006 and 2014 paradoxically occurred at a time when democracy, supposedly, was working well: Thailand elected an extremely popular leader who became the first prime minister to ever serve a full term. His unprecedented electoral victory in 2001—the first election to be held since the 1997 Constitution had come into effect—was astonishing, even for his skeptics. No other party had ever won more than one-third of the seats in national elections since the 1990s. As a new political party, Thai Rak Thai (TRT) was able to garner 49.6 percent of the seats in parliament—two seats shy of an absolute majority. TRT would eventually go on to win an absolute majority in the subsequent election of 2005, and become the first ever party to win two consecutive elections. Scholars have sought to explain the astonishing rise and success of the TRT. Phongpaichit and Baker (2004) attribute Thaksin's wealth and huge business and government connections to his party's success. Others have pointed to institutional changes, such as a new constitution and electoral system rules (Ockey 2003; Hewison 2004; Hicken 2006; Pongsudhirak 2008). What were the sources of opposition to the Thaksin government, particularly given its immense popularity? I answer this question in two respects. First, I identify the nature of the opposition's emergence; and, second, I capture the ways in which the opposition framed its discontent. As I later argue, these elements both helped to propel anti-incumbent mobilization. What is crucial to emphasize here is that being blocked from channeling their grievances both through formal and informal institutions is what turned the PAD *antidemocratic*.

Part of Thaksin's popular appeal to the Thai people was without doubt his propoor policies. As Sinpeng and Kuhonta (2012) pinpoint, the use of meaningful policies to drive election campaigns was surprising given that most support for Thai political parties is garnered largely through their patronage networks and not through programmatic policies. Before running in the 2001 national election, Thaksin toured the country to talk with various NGOs, activist groups, and people in rural areas[8] to assess their needs and problems.[9] The "dual-track policy," as it was referred to by the Thaksin administration, was an effort to maintain stable economic growth: a slowdown in exports due to slackening external demand would be met with a boost in domestic demand through government policy measures. Conversely, domestic demand stimulation would be held back when exports picked up. Thaksin's economic team[10] strongly believed in the need to overhaul the economic structure to prevent the economy from succumb-

TABLE 4.2. Thaksin's key propoor policies

Program	Description
30 Baht Healthcare	Aimed to create universal healthcare by offering a 30-baht fee (US$1) for each visit to a healthcare unit regardless of procedure
One Tambon One Product (OTOP)	Promote local products and indigenous knowledge through state subsidies. Encourage Thai producers to export their goods.
One Million Village Fund	One million baht (US$33,000) given to each village nationwide as development fund to be managed by the community itself
Debt Moratorium for Farmers	Debt relief for farmers for at least 3 years, no interest
SME Subsidies	Government subsidies to aid small and medium-size enterprises (investment, development, and export promotion)
Farmers' Subsidies	Debt restructuring for farmers, co-operative development, debt relief with private banks
People's Bank	Target low-income families who want to borrow but lack credit; aimed to keep them away from loan sharks
Low-income Housing	Government housing for low-income citizens nationwide.
Education loan	Students from low-income families can take government loans for education to be paid back at low interest

ing to another crisis similar to that of 1997. Thaksin asked: "How is it that Thailand is wealthier overall but [its] people are poorer? We're too dependent on exports and foreign investment . . . and such growth increases inequality."[11] "We've long neglected the gap between urban and rural and between industrial and agricultural sectors," argued Somkid Jatusripitak,[12] one of the architects of the TRT's policies.[13]

The socioeconomic context for the TRT's rise to power and its championing of propoor policies was extremely important. While the TRT's economic policy aimed to reduce the income gap and raise overall growth through a combination of exports and increased domestic consumption, one must not forget that the party was driven by some of the country's wealthiest individuals. Yet the fact that these powerful businessmen had a strong mandate to run the national economy, some argue, was tantamount to allowing them to capture state power to control and manage national resources (Phongpaichit and Baker 2004, 97). This "political capture" of the business elites could be a double-edge sword. On the one hand, the country's economy is in the hands of a (supposed) highly capable group of people who understand what is required for Thailand to compete in the global market. On the other hand, they could use their state power and access to resources to benefit their businesses. Tejapira (2006) argues that the Thaksin government was made up of "crony capitalists," who "combined aggressive neo-liberalization with capitalist cronyism and absolutist counter-reform politics with populist social policy to radically transform the existing patterns of power relationships and elite resource allocation." Yet Thaksin defended his propoor policies as "policies for the development of human capital" and not as populist. He argued that Thailand suffers from three diseases: poverty, corruption, and drugs.[14]

Unlike many leaders before him, Thaksin in fact followed through with most of the policy announcements that he had made in the lead-up to the election. Many of Thaksin's policies were widely welcomed, both at home and abroad. His supporters are quick to point out that no other prime minister had given them anything "tangible," nor did they ever keep their campaign promises. Even long after Thaksin was ousted from power, his supporters proclaimed him the best leader Thailand had ever had. A taxi driver from Payao province explained why Thaksin was his "hero":[15]

When Thaksin was in power, it was so easy to make money. . . . Whatever Thaksin promises, he follows through. Like the 30-baht healthcare, I used it right away. My son has low platelet count—medicine costs 10,000 baht a pop. Without the 30-baht program, he would not have survived it. This current prime minister, Abhisit, he promised free schooling. But it's a lie. They only give 490 baht per child, which doesn't even cover the cost of a uniform. I have to take out a loan to put my kids through school. Thaksin would never let that happen.[16]

Another key factor for Thaksin's success was his charisma and likeability. He presented himself as an approachable person, one who understood the needs of the poor. Being from Chiang Mai Province in northern Thailand, Thaksin was able to portray himself as a self-made man from the provinces, whose hard work had helped to propel his success. "I don't need to be a prime minister. I'm already rich enough . . . why bother? But I volunteer to help the country. I don't gain anything from trying to combat corruption . . . only to put myself and my family in trouble," claimed Thaksin.[17] Thaksin's seemingly down-to-earth nature and approachability struck a chord with many people from the provinces. When Thaksin was under investigation for falsely reporting his shareholdings in his first year in office, some 50,000 people in Khon Kaen Province held a massive ceremony to brush away "bad omens" so that he might be acquitted.[18] His popularity with people, particularly those in the North and Northeastern provinces, which later became his electoral stronghold, was unmatched by the many leaders who had preceded him.

Thaksin's brilliant marketing schemes served to strengthen his leadership. He pioneered the weekly "Prime Minister Thaksin Talks to His Citizens" (นายกทักษิณคุยกับประชาชน) radio shows, where he established a rapport with listeners by discussing what he or the TRT had done recently. Not only did he try to reach out to people living in the provinces, his radio shows also sought to counter the largely military-dominated radio airwaves (McCargo 2000). For instance, Thaksin was the first prime minister to set up "mobile cabinet meetings." In these, cabinet minister meetings were rotated throughout various provinces around the country instead of always being held in the capital city, as was the norm. These marketing maneuvers were clever ways for Thaksin and the TRT to not only better market themselves but also to expand their influence and presence. "They want to show the electorate that it's not enough they elected TRT and Thaksin on election day, but the voters need to be reassured that their government is doing their job. They can build long-term relationships with citizens this way," argued Pipon Udorn during a seminar on "Thai Politics of Marketing vs. Marketing of Thai Politics" (Kasertsiri 2009).

The Nascent Opposition and Institutional Blockage

Yet Thaksin was a man shrouded in controversy and corruption allegations. While his supporters admired his policies, his charismatic leadership, and his can-do attitude, his opposition loathed him for the same reasons. When Thaksin was campaigning for his first election as head of the TRT, members of the National Anti-Corruption Commission, an independent body created through the 1997 Constitution, voted almost unanimously that, while deputy prime minister under the government of Chavalit Yong-chaiyudh in 1997, he and his wife had been guilty of falsely declaring their assets by transferring their shares to their housemaids and drivers, and of insider trading and securities price manipulation. Since this was considered a "political case" the matter was referred to the Constitutional Court; the Court narrowly struck it down by 8–7 votes. His critics cried foul that this "miracle" was only possible because Thaksin bribed officials to influence their vote.[19] This corruption allegation was the first among many that plagued the Thaksin government throughout its first and second terms (figure 4.3). Thaksin was not the first corrupt prime minister that Thailand had had, but his scale of corruption, his opponents claimed, far outstripped that of his predecessors.[20]

Skeptics who had been wary of the influx of the "superrich" into Thaksin's cabinet only found cause for further critique. Ukrist Pathmanand authored a piece in *Matichon Weekly*, just weeks after Thaksin took up the prime ministership, about the "total monopolization of telecommunications and mass communications business"—warning not to trust politicians with vested interests.[21] Thaksin's own family business, AIS, Thanin Chianravanont's (finance minister advisor) Telecom Asia,[22] and Adisai Bodharamik's (cabinet minister) Jasmine and TT&T account for most of the shares in telecommunications providers in Thailand. By late 2001, aca-

TABLE 4.3. Selected corruption allegations during Thaksin administration

Case	Amount (Baht)
Shin Corporation sales tax evasion	73 billion
CTX bomb scanner purchase	35.8 million
Computer auction	900 million
Rubber purchase	1.4 billion
Electricity concession	4 billion
Solar home project	7.9 billion
Car park bribery	300 million
Ample rich investment	16 billion

demics had begun to protest what they believed was a "major conflict of interest" when the Thaksin government sought to convert telecom concession fees into excise charges (which they would eventually succeed in doing in 2003). Researchers at the Thailand Development Research Institute published reports arguing that the move would not only reinforce existing telecom monopolies, but would make them billions at the expense of the state and the Thai people. "This is a blatant example of conflict of interest as well as policy-based corruption," the institute report claimed.[23] Thaksin's close allies also admitted to his corrupt ways. One close aide, who chose to remain anonymous, revealed: "Thaksin is no democrat. He's a businessman. He's a man of 'grey'—not white or black."[24]

As a highly successful businessman, Thaksin had a tendency to monopolize control and was not particularly open to dissenting voices, even from his own people.[25] His CEO-style management was viewed by some as abrasive, controlling, and dictatorial.[26] Thaksin shuffled cabinet ministers often, regardless of their performance, so that no one felt secure in their position. For example, he shuffled Pongthep Thepkanchana, a minister of justice (a US-trained lawyer and a drafter of the 1997 Constitution), to the Ministry of Education and then switched him back to the Ministry of Justice. An interview with an unnamed former minister during Thaksin's second term also revealed that Thaksin did not like any cabinet minister taking credit for his or her work. A *Matichon Weekly* article entitled "Thaksin Does Everything, His People Become Mute" mocked Thaksin for being controlling to the point that his inferiors (including ministers) dared not openly disagree with him. His former deputy government spokesperson, Jakrapob Penkhae, agrees that Thaksin had his faults: "I am with Thai Rak Thai because Thaksin has plans to bring progress to Thailand. But his way of getting things done may not be legitimate. . . . another of his faults is that he is too focused on what he wants to do and is not open to alternatives, especially from the opposition" (Matichon 2008b).

Mechanisms for opposition through formal democratic channels

TABLE 4.4. Seat share of Thai Rak Thai vs. opposition parties (2002–2006)

	Government (% of seat shares)	Opposition (seat shares)
Thaksin 1 (2001–2005)*	Thai Rak Thai 57 (inc. KWM, SRT) Chart Thai 8	Democrat Party 26
Thaksin 2 (2005–2006)	Thai Rak Thai 75	Democrat Party 19

* Following party mergers occurring between 2001 and 2002

include lobbying, bargaining, participating in the policy-making process, engaging the media, and using personal connections to influence government policies. If the government blocks the opposition's access to power within democratic channels, this is considered formal institutional blockage. Note that opposition forces can come from *both* outside and inside formal democratic channels. Opposition within the formal democratic institutions might include opposition members of parliament (MPs), opposition senators, or independent bodies that would normally serve the purpose of placing checks on the executive. Opposition external to the formal institutions but inside the democratic polity includes interest groups, pressure groups, and labor unions. In the following paragraphs, I demonstrate how the process of institutional blockage occurred in Thailand when opposition to Thaksin mounted between 2002 and 2005 and eventually became the PAD.

Parliament

Opposition in parliament was rendered completely ineffective on two grounds: (1) executive unaccountability; and (2) declining electoral competitiveness. First, parliamentary means for the opposition to hold the executive accountable were rendered ineffective. The 1997 Constitution required two-fifths of MPs to launch a no confidence motion against the prime minister—something that the main opposition party, the Democrats, was never able to do throughout the Thaksin administration. Thaksin was successful at consolidating political power by absorbing coalition parties into the TRT,[27] which meant that the threat of coalition defection was significantly reduced. In essence, the TRT had a majority in parliament—something unprecedented in parliamentary politics in Thailand.[28] One of the most effective tools for parliamentarian opposition—the no confidence motion—was rendered useless. Things turned for the worse for the Democrats in Thaksin's second term as its seats amounted to merely 19 percent of the total seat share, compared to the TRT's mammoth 75 percent (table 4.4).

Not only was it difficult to put constraints on the executive, the ruling government allowed little opportunity for question time. The Speaker sometimes had to close business early because parliament lacked a quorum, and five times between 2002 and 2004 House sessions were effectively halted following head counts. As Uthai Pimjaichon, House Speaker during the TRT government, revealed: "Thaksin doesn't value parliamentary sessions. Even important issues like budgetary meetings, sometimes he was absent. . . . I don't need to mention how [many times] he did not answer questioning periods. . . . Sometimes he chose to go see people in the villages, who would give him praise, as opposed to showing up to parliament" (Pinthong 2004, 76). Eventually the TRT whip proposed a salary raise for MPs to entice them to attend meetings (McCargo and Pathmanand 2005, 106). Wittaya Kaewparadai, Democrat MP and former minister, commented:

> Parliamentary mechanisms for checking the executive were crippled. The 1997 Constitution created such a strong executive and Thaksin knew it. We in the opposition couldn't launch the no confidence motion on Thaksin. So many times parliamentary sessions had to be cancelled because not enough MPs showed up. Thaksin did not respect parliamentary procedures. The upper house couldn't do anything either. This is a total parliamentary tyranny. . . . Since formal parliamentary channels were closed off, we had to pursue extraparliamentary ones.[29]

While not rare in parliamentary democracies with majority governments, this blockage drove anti-incumbent mobilization from within the formal democratic institutions. The Democrat Party (DP), which had become the only viable, permanent opposition party,[30] could not win elections. This made national elections in Thailand no longer competitive. The Democrats' last election win in which they were able to form a government dated back to 1992, following the Black May uprising. Since then the Democrats had only been part of a coalition government or the opposition. But the rise of the TRT and its later electoral dominance rendered the Democrats as the only main opposition in town. Other small and medium parties, such as Chart Thai, Chart Pattana, and Kwam Wang Mai, were either absorbed by the TRT (in the case of Kwam Wang Mai) or remained fluid enough that they still had the option of joining either the TRT or the opposition. In essence, the rise of the TRT meant that the Democrats had become the de facto opposition party. Since it could not win elections while the TRT or other Thaksin-aligned parties still existed, its only chance of being in government would be through extraconstitutional means, or through a collapse of the TRT government.

The frustration of the opposition party prompted its members to join forces with anti-Thaksin groups. Democrat MPs began to frequent PAD rallies, some even going on stage to demonstrate their support for the movement. Democrat MPs who went on the PAD stage included Kasit

Piromya, Somkiat Pongpaibul, Kulaya Soponpanich, Anchalee Thepbutch, and Kraisak Choonhawan. Kaewparadai confirmed this during an interview: "The Democrat Party considered the PAD as an ally. . . . indeed some of our members joined PAD and engaged in their activities. Some went on stage, others donated food and money. . . . What the PAD leaders said on stage resonated very much with how we felt in parliament. We saw eye to eye on a number of issues."[31] The biggest contribution the Democrat Party made to the PAD movement was to provide mass support. In fact, Democrat Party leaders admitted mobilizing their mass base to attend PAD rallies—most notably the infamous 193-Day Protest in the postcoup period. While figures varied, according to party estimates the Democrat Party forces most likely accounted for about half of the total PAD mass base. "Democrat Party members, mostly from the southern region of Thailand, mobilized the mass to join PAD rallies."[32]

Senate

Some senators felt that the upper house could not provide the checks and balances to the lower house, as was envisioned by the 1997 Constitution. In fact, the first ever elected Senate was plagued by both corrupt elections and the fact that many elected senators were from families and friends of the ruling party, raising serious concerns over nepotism and conflict of interest.[33] The Senate election in 2000 was held five times. In the first round, 78 of the 200 candidates elected were not approved by Thailand's Election Commission due to concerns over electoral misconduct. This resulted in an additional thirty-five by-elections. Such by-elections were to be repeated for four more rounds until all 200 senators were signed off on by the Election Commission. Some elected senators later resigned from the upper house to run for a position in the lower house, which was a clear indication that they remained very much part of the political party system.[34] Another senator was found to have bribed a fellow senator (Klaew Norapathi from Khon Kaen) with cash and Buddha amulets in exchange for his committee's withdrawal. The last nail in the coffin of the 2000–2006 affairs of the upper house was the first ever "fight" in the history of Thailand's National Assembly: Bangkok senator Prathin Santhiprasop's brazen punching of Maehongson senator Adul Wanchaithanawong during the debate over the Tak Bai Incident.

A more politicized and progovernment Senate also meant it could not act as an effective institution to constrain the executive branch. First, senators could never reach the required three-fifths to submit a motion for general debate and request that cabinet ministers explain important matters on state affairs. Somkiat On-wimol, Supanburi senator, questioned Thaksin during a seminar: "Is it true that you, Prime Minister, and Thai Rak Thai intervened in the affairs of the upper house by buying off senators?"[35] Nakornsawan senator Prasit Pithunkijja voiced similar concerns: "Don't think that the Senate is fully independent—not all 200 of us— because some have vested interests. . . . I don't believe we [the Senate] will ever have the necessary three-fifths vote to remove anyone from political office."[36] Second, the upper house's committee work was no more effective.

The opposition to Thaksin's government that had formed inside the upper house as early as 2002 massively escalated following the Tak Bai Incident in 2004.[37] Some senators formed an alliance with the opposition party, the Democrats, to question Thaksin during a joint parliament-Senate session following the Tak Bai Incident.[38] However, when Thaksin turned up, he explained his side of the story for half an hour and then left without allowing senators to question him, despite a number of senators raising their hands.[39] "This is not a press conference. We, as senators, are elected to represent the Thai people. Why did the prime minister come and not let us do our job and question him?," asked Senator Sompong Srakrawee angrily.[40] Senator Jermsak Pinthong, one of the most outspoken critics of Thaksin and himself a 1997 Constitution drafter, led the opposition movement inside the upper house against the Thaksin government, with support from senators drawn largely from academia and NGOs.[41]

Independent Institutions

Independent institutions were created following the 1997 Constitution to provide more checks and balances in the political system and to reduce the abuse of state power by political elites.[42] The fact that Thaksin surprisingly escaped the verdict of the Constitutional Court in 2001 cast a long shadow of doubt with regard to the impartiality of the newly created independent bodies. Over the course of Thai Rak Thai rule, there were numerous allegations of Thaksin's interference in independent bodies. "The current [Thaksin] government has influence over every single institution; be it parliament, Senate, independent bodies, and the media," warned academic Sangkit Piriyarangsan.[43] By 2005, as talks over potential constitutional amendments surged, some sections of the judicial system went so far as to suggest the complete dissolution of all independent bodies, since they were neither impartial nor independent.[44] "These institutions were created to provide checks and balances to the political institutions; but not only were

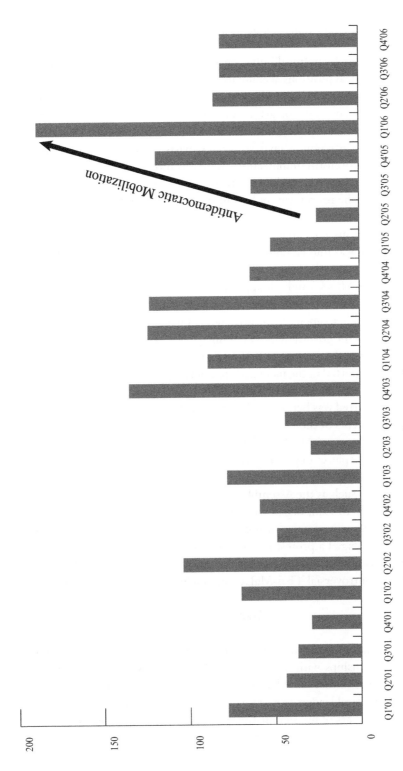

Figure 4.2. Protest events as reported in fourteen newspapers (2001–2006)

they dominated by political influence, they also lacked the capacity to hold those in political positions accountable," lamented a judge.[45]

As the opposition inside the formal democratic institutions was finding that their channels for grievances were blocked and becoming futile, groups in the informal institutional realms met with the same fate. While in the 1990s academics, civil society, activists, and other groups were engaged in proreform mobilization, there was little of that during the rule of the TRT before it turned into anti-incumbent mobilization. This was in part because the proreform mobilization had already taken place over the course of the prior decade, and so the reformists were less willing to push for more reforms since much of this should have happened when the 1997 Constitution was implemented. It was also partly because some of the key reformists felt they had their own lobbies for change within formal institutions. The "shock" and "disappointment" that followed brought many of the reformists into the whirlwind, which forcefully mobilized various groups into an anti-incumbent movement. They took to the streets.

The Thaksin government saw a flurry of protest activities during its administration. Between 2001 and 2006, there were more than 1,850 protest events reported in the media. More than 60 percent of these were organized by NGOs. The biggest and most continuous spike in the number of protests reported was between mid-2005 and the end of the first quarter of 2006. Opponents of the Thaksin government had begun to engage in protest politics in 2002. Much of the opposition movement was directly targeting specific pieces of government policy. Protest activities started slowly in 2001 but effectively gained momentum in 2002, when a number of large rural NGOs, such as the Assembly of the Poor and the Small-Scale Farmers' Assembly of Isan, began to demand governmental responsiveness to their problems—a promise of the 2001 election campaign. The Assembly of the Poor staged a protest that lasted more than sixty days in late 2002. During this time it demanded that the government reconsider its plan to build the controversial Thai-Malaysian pipeline and the Pak Mun Dam.

Civil Society

Thaksin sought to sideline civil society organizations in order to establish direct relationships with the poor. Initially there was immense optimism that Thaksin's victory would usher in a new era of democratic politics, one in which political leaders would finally be responsive to the people's sector. In the early years of his administration, Thaksin showed signs of commitment to the people's sector, either by personally talking to demonstrators or by sending his personal aides or cabinet members to hear their claims, be it the Assembly of the Poor, anti-power-plant groups from Bo Nok, or antipipeline groups. Yet, for Thaksin, it was more important to establish direct relationships with the people, instead of working through NGOs. Professor Saneh Jamrik, a well-known academic within the human rights NGO community, agrees: "When Thaksin became prime minister initially we [the NGOs] were all hopeful; he was a wealthy man who wanted to help the poor . . . but as time passed he's not what we thought and even said bad things about us, saying we sound like a broken record. Now Thaksin would deal with the poor himself without having to work through us or Anand. So, we are disappointed."[46]

The broad discontent against Thaksin from the civil society sector was first shaped by the general feeling of marginalization. Underneath this broad resentment were deep disagreements with Thaksin's policies and his unwillingness to negotiate with NGOs and labor unions. Four key constituencies represented the most vocal of the opposition groups, among whose civil society organizations rose up in protest against the Thaksin government: (1) state enterprise workers; (2) teachers' unions; (3) media activists; and (4) grassroots networks against megaprojects. As opposition from the people's sector continued, it became clear that many of the NGOs were ideologically against the TRT party platforms. Table 4.5 shows some of the key dimensions of the NGO opposition to Thaksin's policies.

Two key issues underscored much of the grassroots discontent toward Thaksin and his government: (1) executive abuse of power, and (2) economic redistribution to the poor. The growing lack of effective constraints on the executive—particularly on Thaksin—was the most contentious issue for the people's sector. This "policy-based corruption" (*Khor rup chan cheung nayobai*), defined as large-scale corruption committed by those in the highest political positions determining national policy, allowed the ruling party elites to abuse power for personal gain. Policy-based corruption was rife within Thai Rak Thai because, according to critics, many of the TRT cabinet members were elite businessmen who themselves possessed monopolies or semimonopolies in their industry (McCargo and Pathmanand 2005). By being at the highest level of government, their businesses continued to enjoy far greater monopolies due to their very status as policymakers. After he came to power, Thaksin's own businesses in telecommunications—Shin Corp, AIS, and Jasmine—posted impressive profits.[47] Within a few years of Thaksin coming to power, AIS became the largest mobile phone provider in Thailand. Thaksin also exercised his executive decree power—power reserved for emergency situations only—

which enabled him to block future competition in the mobile phone service industry (Phongpaichit and Baker 2004, 209–10).

The most explosive example of executive abuse of power, according to his critics, was the sale of Shin Corporation to Singapore-based Temasek Holdings in 2006—the biggest stock market trade in Thailand's history. The sale outraged such vast numbers of people that it became one of the biggest rallying points for the opposition movement; it quite literally drove hundreds of thousands to join protests on the streets. The biggest point of contention was the fact that the sale was completed exactly two days after the passage of a new telecommunications bill that allowed foreign ownership of Thai companies to increase from 25 to 50 percent. More significantly, the deal was exempted from capital gains taxes since, prior to the sale, Thaksin had opportunely amended the law regarding foreign investment in the telecommunications sector. Supinya Klanarong, who led the media opposition against the TRT, declared: "Thaksin has prepared for this deal for quite some time. This trade is not transparent—no one can actually explain the entire process."[48] Thaksin never offered a full explanation for the Shin Corporation sale. He merely stated that his son had sold the shares, but he was unable to explain why the tax was not paid on the sale.

Thaksin's successful welfare policies instigated the loss of popular support and credibility for NGOs.[49] Thaksin's propoor policies were not wel-

TABLE 4.5. Civil society organizations that led major protests (2001–2005)

2001	Small-Scale Farmers' Assembly of Isan
2002	Assembly of the Poor, Small-Scale Farmers' Assembly of Isan, Buddhism Protection Centre of Thailand, Network Against the Trans Thai-Malaysia Pipeline, Association of Tambon Administrative Organization, Campaign for Popular Democracy, Assembly of the Poor (Pak Mun Dam Division)
2003	Network Against the Trans Thai-Malaysia Pipeline, Assembly of the Poor (Pak Mun Dam Division), Campaign for Popular Democracy, Muslim Organizations of 5 Southern Border Provinces, State Enterprise Workers' Relations Confederation, Southern Network of Land Reform for the Poor, Ram Kamhaeng University Student Assembly
2004	State Enterprise Workers' Relations Confederation, Provincial Electricity Authority, Metropolitan Water Authority, EGAT, State Railway Union of Thailand, Students of Luangta Mahabua Group, Tak Bai Incident, Network Against the Privatization of EGAT, Entertainment Industry Association (Bangkok), People's Alliance for Democracy
2005	State Enterprise Workers' Relations Confederation, Four Region Slum Network, Network of the HIV Positive, Anti-FTA Network, Assembly of the Poor, Network Against the Privatization of EGAT, Student Federation of Thailand, Network Against Education Transfer, Farmers' Debt Network, Network of Agricultural Non-Governmental Organizations of Thailand, *Thailand Weekly* (Sonthi)

comed by a large share of the NGO sector because they drove a wedge between the people and this sector as a result of state intervention. These populist policies were not intended to transform the structure of poverty in Thailand, according to NGO critics, but were instead meant to weaken the ties between the people and civil society, all the while strengthening the state's power. Opposition NGOs further argued that some of the economic redistribution programs made poor people more dependent on the state instead of empowering them.[50] They allowed the state to not only expand its presence and influence in rural Thailand but also reduced the right of communities to mobilize in favor of alternative initiatives.[51] NGOs were forced to compete with the state for allegiance from the lower class on similar issues. Never before in such a way had NGOs lost their credibility, their support, their leverage vis-à-vis the state, and their standing in political space (Winichakul 2010).

There was also a sense of betrayal among some NGO groups about how Thaksin manipulated their ideas for his own benefit. Before running for election in 2001, Thaksin consulted widely with a number of NGO groups, especially with rural NGOs. They felt that Thaksin's propoor policies had incorporated many of the ideas of their various groups without giving them due credit. As Prapas explained, "Thaksin's redistribution policy took its shape gradually, incorporating many elements from civil society groups and various societal factors, so that when we looked at the success of Thaksin's populist policies, we had to recognize the success of various communities and villagers for their input" (cited in Prapas Pintobtang 2007, 145). Yet, following the implementation of the propoor policies, the NGO sector had serious doubts about the actual intention of these policies.[52] His critics were convinced that TRT used these policies as a tool to benefit the party electorally, for these policies did not aim to create justice for the poor.[53] Sulak Sivaraksa, a well-known figure in the nonprofit sector, condemned populist policies for turning citizens into "consumers" and in the process stripping away their power to be self-reliant (Sivaraksa 2002). Likewise, Sansit Chanpoon, leader of the Network of the Chee River Basin Community (which was negatively affected by the construction of a dam in Roi-Et Province), claimed that Thaksin did not understand the problems of the poor: "Thaksin came to Roi-Et to show that he was serious about solving our problem. . . . he began giving away free buffaloes, cows, land, cheap housing, etc., but he did not see the root cause of the poverty: the dam. The dam construction has caused flooding for five years now and we all got considerably poorer."[54] NGOs feared that economic redistribution policies hurt the prospects for human development because they did not empower the people.[55] Thaksin, in the eyes of many NGOs, lacked the right incentives to help the poor. "I agree with some of Thaksin's policies," claimed Bamrung Kayotha, a well-known activist. "But he doesn't have the right principles to guide him. For example, the Village Fund, instead of decentralizing power to the local level, he just threw a pile of money at the villagers. That's not community development through empowerment of the people. That's throwing money at a problem."[56] There was deep resentment and skepticism among the propoor NGO leaders that Thaksin lacked the experience, foresight, and patience to deal with complicated issues such as poverty.

The Thaksin government's tough stance and hostile attitude toward some of the civil society organizations further created a rift between the people's sector and the government, which bred distrust and hostility. Toward the end of 2002, Thaksin displayed obvious frustration with the lingering demonstrations of the Assembly of the Poor, Small-Scale Farmers' Assembly, and Pak Mun Dam activists, and he sought to discredit the public credibility of NGOs. He accused NGOs of "taking money from foreigners" and "inciting violence."[57] Thaksin told the Pak Mun Dam communities: "I want to consult with the people who experience problems directly. I don't want to discuss with NGOs, which act like their advisors. . . . NGOs are like salesmen . . . they make commissions off poor people."[58] Even some of Thaksin's own supporters recognized his flaws in dealing with the people's sector. Sombat Boon-Ngam Anong, founder of the Red Sunday Group, admitted:

> I don't particularly like Thaksin and have been critical of him in the past—he's too dictatorial. Thai Rak Thai's version of democracy lacks participation. It's what I call "wholesale democracy." He [Thaksin] won't let the people suggest ways to solve problems. You tell him you have a problem in something. He tells you, no problem, I'll take care of it. He won't let others help him think through problems. No feedback mechanism. And if anyone disagrees with him, he gets very defensive. He does not understand why public intellectuals exist. He closes up space for independent thinking. He works too fast, if you try to intervene, he gets really upset. This tends to create enemies.[59]

A group of eight NGO leaders felt that they were unnecessarily "harassed" by the government because they were under investigation by the Anti-Money Laundering Office without justifiable cause. Banjong

Nasae, a well-known activist in fishermen's rights from the south and among those investigated, complained that this was a tactic of intimidation utilized by the government. Further, the fact that the Anti-Money Laundering Office agreed to undertake the investigation without giving any reason for it meant that supposedly "independent" bodies were being used as a tool by the government. The cabinet motion on April 23, 2002, which gave state authorities more power to deal with claims made by citizens, prompted more than 1,000 protesters from more than 300 NGOs to take to the streets. They saw the new motion as yet another extension of state power abuse, as Senator Nirand Pitakwatchara explained: "What the government is doing is worrisome and is destroying opportunities to solve poverty and violence in those communities. What the NGOs proposed to the prime minister were actual facts from the ground, which reflected the poverty and inability to secure resources on the ground. . . . Such [a cabinet] motion only exacerbated this problem."[60]

For a country that, in the past, used to pride itself for having one of the freest presses in Southeast Asia, the TRT government had, for some, significantly shrunk the space for independent thinking. Toward the end of Thaksin's first term opposition had begun to grow, particularly from media activists in the people's sector. Other news outlets were under pressure to produce positive news for the government. The first sign of Thaksin's open war with opposition media occurred when the National Anti-Corruption Commission abruptly began investigating members of the executive board of the independent Nation Multi-media Group, *Thai Post* newspapers, and Naewna newspapers—all of which were openly critical of the Thaksin government.[61] The government claimed that "someone

TABLE 4.6. Selected PAD networks by sector

Sector	Organizations
Media	Manager Media Group, the *Nation*, *Thai Post*, *Naewna*
Nationalists	Network for the Protection of Electricity and Water for the Citizens, Alliance of Teachers for Saving the Nation 4 Regions, Saving the Nation Club
Labor	State Enterprise Workers' Relations Confederation, Provincial Electricity Authority, Thai Airways, TOT
NGO	Student Federation of Thailand, Four Region Slum Network, Network for Senior Doctors, Center for the Protection and Restoration of Local Community Rights, Network of HIV Positive in Northern Region
Farmers	Federation of Farmers in Northern Region, Assembly of the Poor, Farmers' Group
Royalists	The Royalty (Ratchanikul), Club for Truth and Transparency, the Noble Women Group, the Sakdina

asked us to look into their financial accounts" but gave no justifiable cause for this investigation.[62] Then Assumption University (ABAC) poll was threatened, and attempts were made to rid UBC cable TV Channel 8 of political news. Other media outlets began to worry that their own financial accounts would be investigated by the National Anti-Corruption Commission without cause. By early 2003, the Thai Journalists' Association made a public statement condemning the government for its crackdown on media independence through the abuse of state power, personal wealth and connections, and intimidation.[63] Between 2004 and 2005, Reporters Without Borders registered a dramatic spike in the degree of press repression—a trend that continued into the postcoup period. By early 2006, many media NGOs, such as the Thai Journalists' Association, had joined forces with the PAD in protest of the Thaksin government's growing encroachment on media freedom.

The most dramatic, and arguably the worst, move made by Thaksin in his attempt to suppress opposition voices was the cancellation of a popular talk show, *Thailand Weekly*. Sonthi Limthongkul, owner of the multimedia Manager Media Group and a one-time supporter of the TRT, began to expose the TRT government through his talk show that was broadcast on state TV Channel 9 in late 2005. As the show's popularity surged,[64] the government ordered a reduction in *Thailand Weekly's* airtime from five days to one day per week. By Sonthi's own account, the trigger for his campaign to oust Thaksin came when his show was abruptly canceled altogether.[65] Instead of silencing Sonthi, dropping his show prompted the rapid rise of what became known as the "Sonthi phenomenon." He and his Manager Media crew began to broadcast *Thailand Weekly Mobile*, first at a public university, then at parks until eventually hundreds of thousands were turning out and tuning in to listen to what Sonthi had to say.[66] His ability to draw large crowds at rallies and many more on TV and radio via a diversity of (his own) media channels made him a strong candidate for leadership of the PAD. As such, when the PAD was born, leaders of many other opposition groups all agreed that Sonthi would be the top leader.[67] Moreover, Sonthi was able to raise substantial funding for the PAD cause. Chamlong Srimuang, one of the PAD's key leaders, first made an announcement asking for donations on September 1, 2006; within two weeks, opposition-run ASTV had received more than 15 million baht.[68] It was especially important for an opposition movement to have its own media outlet to create and expand its membership base, as well as avoid any government censorship. "Sonthi is the most important leader of the PAD top ranks," admitted Suriyasai Katasila, a member of the PAD secretariat. "He owns the media and he gets to frame the movement the way he sees fit . . . and he has the funds."[69]

One of the largest and earliest oppositions to Thaksin and his government similarly came from state enterprise workers. Under the leadership of Somsak Kosaisuk, chairman of the State Enterprise Workers' Relations Confederation and later one of the top five PAD leaders, antigovernment protest had been gathering force since 2002. He was able to prompt tens of thousands of supporters to turn up to protests—many of whom were workers themselves. The single most important issue for the labor side of the opposition was TRT's plan for state enterprise privatization. Somsak was head of the Electricity Generating Authority Thailand (EGAT) workers union and had long fought against any plan to privatize it. Somsak was such a prominent labor leader that he was one of the movers and shakers of the economic restructuring plans following the Asian Financial Crisis. He outlined, together with other activists, a list of state enterprises that could never be privatized, including the EGAT. In 2003, Thaksin himself vowed that no privatization would be allowed under the new restructuring legislation put forth by the TRT. Yet Thaksin backflipped, and in seeking to privatize EGAT, enacted the exact opposite of those promises. This move prompted some of the largest protests against Thaksin in the precoup era. On several occasions, EGAT threatened to cut off electricity should the government continue with its privatization plan. Other state enterprise unions followed suit. Between 2002 and 2006, unions such as the Provincial Electricity Authority, the Metropolitan Water Authority, and the State Railway Union of Thailand joined in the antigovernment protests.

Beginning in 2005, teachers spanning the whole country also staged a number of mass rallies against the government's plan to transfer control of state schools to local authorities. Teachers argued that the government did not understand the problems that teachers faced; they were concerned that their profession would fall prey to corrupt local politics once it was transferred to local authorities.[70] Thanarat Samok-nae, leader of the Network against School Transfer to Local Administration, discussed the reason for joining the PAD:

> The cabinet motion to transfer the school system claimed it was based on approval and agreement on behalf of teachers. We cannot accept this. . . . Imagine transferring the entire education system into the hands of local elected officials; we would lose integrity and quality and we do not feel certain it'd be good for our nation. The education system is the foundation of our country's stability. . . . The

government must stop this. They can take any other infrastructure but not the education system. They need to leave the system to [those of] us who are teachers and know what is best.[71]

The nationwide mass teacher protests, totaling at one point some 150,000 individuals in the street, greatly strengthened the opposition movement to the Thaksin government. The teachers' union protests generally helped also to draw more supporters to the PAD due to their effective protest campaigns. These involved protesters spilling their blood to demonstrate contempt, boycotting AIS phones, and the threat of a nationwide teachers' strike. Again, leaders of the "teachers against the school transfer" were able to frame the issue as one of a threat to national security and to the fabric of the nation. This carried a powerful message to the conservative-minded, who represented the bulk of PAD supporters. The ability of teacher leaders to build a network across seventy-six provinces also meant that they were able to stage protests in numerous provinces across the country—further heightening the stakes between the government and the opposition forces.

Two Buddhist organizations emerged as the backbone of the PAD movement from the very onset. These were Santi Asoke and Luang Ta Mahabua Group. Members of Santi Asoke, or Asoke Group, were devout followers of Bodhiraksa (the organization's founder, who lived a very modest lifestyle), were vegetarians,[72] consumed organic products, and ate once a day. Santi Asoke had always been political. Bodhiraksa and his followers began engaging in national-level politics with the establishment of the Palang Tham party, led by Santi Asoke's very own Chamlong. Initially, the party was filled with Santi Asoke members but they were slowly replaced by career politicians, including Thaksin in the mid-'90s. Santi Asoke established Dharma Forces (Kongthap Tham), a political unit of Santi Asoke to support its political aspirations and to largely organize political activities, such as demonstrations and petitions. Dharma Forces were crucial to the success of the PAD movement. It began opposing the Thaksin government openly in 2005 when it protested against Thaksin's policy of allowing some of Thailand's largest liquor producers to be listed on the Thai Stock Exchange. "In fact," revealed Sam Din, a key leader of Dharma Forces, "we began opposing Thaksin towards the end of his first term, be it his politics, his policies, and now this alcohol issue and cronyism. . . . we feel betrayed because we have known him to be supportive of Chamlong as he began his political career with Palang Dharma Party (headed by Chamlong). . . . Chamlong used to give him advice all the time when he first took office. We had no choice but to act."[73] As soon as Chamlong decided to escalate his opposition to Thaksin he brought Dharma Forces in to join the PAD, while he himself became one of the PAD's top five leaders.

Santi Asoke's Dharma Forces was indispensable to the PAD movement for two reasons. First, it brought some of the most organized, highly disciplined manpower to the movement. Asoke members were those who had given their lives to Santi Asoke, had given up everything as laymen, and strictly followed the lifestyle prescribed by Bodhiraksa. As such, when their leader, Chamlong, gave orders, they followed these strictly. Yolsiri Damchua, a long-time Asoke member and active member of the Dharma Forces, revealed: "Santi Asoke group is the main 'servant' of the PAD movement. During protests, we had a meeting every day at 7 a.m., we take care of the orderliness and cleanliness of the protest sites, we provided food, water and sanitation; we provided security; donations—you name it. We made it possible for other PAD members to be able to stay at rally sites."[74] Their highly disciplined nature and unwavering loyalty to Bodhiraksa and Chamlong made them powerful organizers of the PAD movement. Dharma Forces also had a permanent force. This meant that if their leaders decided to join a protest or mobilize against something, there was no shortage of supporters from Santi Asoke. Unlike other civil society groups, whose members waxed and waned over the protest period, Dharma Forces always supplied a steady number of people whom the PAD could rely on. Second, Santi Asoke made the PAD movement "more holy" or more allied to Buddhism. This religious spin on the PAD was crucial to the framing of their campaigns. One of the tenets of the PAD ideology was its belief in dharma, dharmic democracy, and righteousness. The preaching of Bodhiraksa and Chamlong on these issues not only provided common ground between other PAD members and Dharma Forces, it significantly helped to reinforce and consolidate the opposition movement and its message.

Luang Ta Mahabua was another important group inside the PAD, most crucial to the initial efforts to mobilize forces to oppose Thaksin. In the precoup stage, Sonthi Limthongkul had a close relationship with Luang Ta, so there was a deeper connection with the ASTV forces. However, Luang Ta was fiercely against Thaksin's plan to list alcohol beverage companies on the stock exchange. Luang Ta and Thaksin had some degree of personal relationship and Luang Ta admitted to using his followers to help Thaksin in the lead-up to his first election victory. Luang Ta had thousands of devout followers, many of whom turned out to protest against Thaksin, under the name of the "Luang Ta Mahabua Students Association." They therefore provided a reliable source of supporters to the overall PAD movement and further solidified Buddhism as one of the key aspects of the PAD's opposition to Thaksin.

A number of academics, public intellectuals, and students began to adhere to the mobilization movement. The Student Federation of Thailand reached an agreement to join forces to "save the nation" on February 4, 2006. Katchawan Chaiyabut, the Student Federation's secretary, went on stage to proclaim its stance and call for the prime minister's resignation. The Ramkamhaeng University Student Assembly also joined the movement soon after. The other student bodies from Thammasat, Chulalongkorn, and elsewhere joined forces. Many of the student groups felt that Thaksin had abused loopholes in the Constitution, abused the law, and used his overwhelming majority in parliament for his own and his cronies' benefit. This was policy-based corruption. They called for yet another major political reform—one that would lead to real and tangible reforms. Academics from Chulalongkorn University, the National Institute of Development Administration, and the like began to submit petitions or write open letters in support of other academics' opposition to the Thaksin government. These academics proclaimed that there were a number of serious violations committed by Thaksin.[75]

The royalists were a small but powerful and influential section of the PAD movement.[76] There were two key types of royalists. The first type included individuals and groups who had royal lineage. They were drawn to the PAD mainly because they were convinced that Thaksin presented a real threat to the Thai monarchy, their heritage. Groups like the "Royalty" (Ratchanikul), the "High Society Group," and the "Noble Women Group" formed to defend the monarchy and to support Sonthi's opposition to Thaksin. Many of these royalists were high-ranking bureaucrats and, significantly, many of them already despised the many bureaucratic reforms TRT had undertaken. Another group of royalist supporters included pro-monarchy, conservative groups and individuals. Some of these people had worked on various royal projects and had been their long-time supporters. They believed in the king's philosophy and joined the PAD to defend the monarchy. The Club for Truth and Transparency, for instance, was a group of promonarchy individuals who believed that Thaksin had plans to subvert the monarchical system and turn Thailand into a republic. These royalist groups would come to define the PAD movement.

Opposition Alliance Formation

Anti-Thaksin opposition groups, which had separately protested against the government, eventually formed a collective alliance in early 2006 in an attempt to drive out Thaksin once and for all. The People's Alliance for

Democracy was an anti-Thaksin movement[77] that brought together a broad range of groups whose interests had been adversely affected by the Thaksin regime. Despite the diversity of the groups that allied themselves under the rubric of PAD, the nature of PAD's core was exemplified in their five top leaders: (1) Sonthi Limthongkul represented the fight against Thaksin's crackdown on the media; (2) Chamlong Srimuang symbolized the fight against Thaksin's money politics; (3) Pipob Thongchai exemplified an opposition to Thaksin's political reforms; (4) Somkiat Pongpaibul represented a force against Thaksin's reform of the bureaucracy; and (5) Somsak Kosaisuk exemplified forces against Thaksin's plan to privatize state enterprises (Songthai 2008, 99). Indeed, the precoup PAD anti-Thaksin rallies were largely supported by networks of NGOs, state enterprises, and trade/labor unions. Somsak, for instance, was the leader of the State Enterprise Workers' Relations Confederation, which represented over 200,000 workers. Similarly, Pipob was a highly respected NGO leader and head of the Campaign for Popular Democracy, which drew support from a large nationwide network of NGOs. Drawing on the networks of the core leaders themselves and other non-NGO anti-Thaksin groups, such as the 40 Senators Group, university academics, Luang Ta Mahabua Students, high-ranking civil servants, students, and opposition parties,[78] the PAD came together to form an alliance in February 2006—just months before the September coup.

The PAD self-identified as a "largely middle-class urbanized" movement.[79] Chaiwat Sinsuwong, one of the PAD's top leaders and former Palang Tham MP, concurred: "The majority of PAD supporters are middle class, although we have some lower-class folks too. Many had followed Sonthi's TV show 'Thailand Weekly' and joined the protests of their own accord. But people who attended rallies often had money."[80] The urban middle class from all across the country constituted the bulk of the PAD movement support base. They were drawn to the anti-Thaksin movement largely on account of their political and ideological dispositions. The PAD supporters believed in the monarchy as the utmost important institution in Thailand. Their reverence toward King Bhumibol, affinity with and emotional attachment to the monarchical institution, helped to propel their opposition to Thaksin (Bowie 1997, 82). But it was also for a practical reason: manipulating the issue of the monarchy was an effective tool for mobilization. A PAD leader revealed: "We [PAD leaders] use the monarchy for forming an alliance. . . . A broad-based movement like the PAD needs a common ground. . . . We know the monarchy doesn't really like us because we troubled the king. But we need to mobilize people, to draw in the masses. So, we had to do it [use the monarchy]."[81]

Because the government restricted the number of access points to chan-

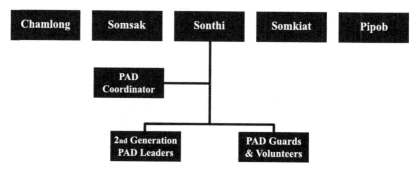

Figure 4.3. The PAD leadership structure

nel demands from the public, opposition and resistance built up among the many affected groups. In need of outlets to express their demands and opinions, these groups held separate rallies before ultimately coming together in an alliance against the Thaksin government.

The PAD comprised two levels of networks: (1) the most active and committed supporters, some with a vertical relationship to the leadership; and (2) transient supporters, with a horizontal relationships to the leadership. While all the opposition groups formed networks and relationships with one another under the umbrella of the PAD, differences were apparent in the type of relations and the degrees of separation from the PAD's core leadership. Moreover, over the course of the PAD's three-stage mobilization, the structure of the PAD network was far from static. Indeed, while over time some of the groups remained as core supporters, others left, while still others rejoined. The dynamic nature of the PAD structure had serious consequences for the size of its membership, which waxed and waned over time.

The core leadership of the PAD was divided into three parts. The first we can identify as the first generation leadership, which was composed of five leaders drawn from a variety of groups. Sonthi Limthongkul represented the ASTV/Manager Media portion of the PAD, which was among the largest. The membership of the ASTV was particularly useful to mobilize thousands of protesters at every major rally. In fact, more of Sonthi's followers subscribed to ASTV or were regular consumers of Manager Media. The second group was under the de facto leadership of Chamlong Srimuang, which, apart from drawing the devout Santi Asoke members and numbering into the thousands as well, also elicited support from those who liked Chamlong. Chamlong was an extremely popular Bangkok governor in the 1990s and among the top leaders of the Black May uprising. Somkiat

Pongpaibul and Pipob Thongchai were representatives of the NGO sector. While numerous in terms of the number of organizations that joined the PAD, in absolute terms the number of supporters that these NGOs brought into the movement was not large. For instance, the Network of 30 Organizations against Corruption had thirty members, each with its own membership, but they may have collectively sent just one or two of the Network's representatives to a PAD protest rally at any particular time. The overall support of NGOs inside the PAD was thus less visible from the perspective of rally attendance. The same was true of the labor unions, under the leadership of Somsak Kosaisuk. Somsak was a chairman of the State Enterprise Workers' Relations Confederation, an umbrella interest group that represents state enterprise workers. He was asked to join the leadership of the rank and file because of the labor portion of the PAD movement that he represented; but the number of workers that actually attended PAD rallies was not a true representation of their overall support. Again, few leaders of the labor groups were sent to attend, while the remainder (and majority) stayed behind due to their inability to miss work to join the long rallies.

The first generation of leaders made major decisions with regard to the movement (figure 4.3). The structure of the PAD was centralized in this respect—albeit with five leaders, not one. They met regularly and voted on issues such as rallies, protest strategy, legal actions, or the position to adopt toward the opposition and government. The name, the People's Alliance for Democracy, was adopted following Suriyasai's suggestion (Katasila 2007). Based on fieldwork interviews, these leaders divulged that the decision to take action did not take the strict form of unanimity or a majority vote. Rather, all leaders tried to find grounds that would be acceptable to all. Often prior to each major rally or major action taken by the PAD, the leaders issued a press release via Manager Media outlets. The leadership was not set apart from its members: it spent significant amounts of time with the PAD members, particularly during rallies. During quiet times, these leaders appeared frequently on PAD media outlets, be it on ASTV or other non-ASTV media, and writing in Manager Media's various publications. During rallies, they spent much of their time with fellow protesters, speaking on stage, and making the rounds of mingling with the PAD members.

Of note was the fact that all of the PAD first generation leaders had significant experience in mass mobilization and in organizing protest activities. Those representing NGOs and the labor section of the PAD, in particular, had a number of decades-long experience in "street politics."

They had the know-how to organize protests, and this particularly came in handy when conducting protest strategies. They deeply understood the logistics of protest activities, knowing what worked and what might not. Prior to the PAD's official establishment, each of the core leaders had in fact mounted their own protest against the Thaksin government. For instance, Sonthi's *Thailand Weekly Mobile* drew thousands of supporters to his weekly shows. Somsak himself had staged numerous protests against the privatization of state enterprises between 2003 and 2005. The PAD movement, in some respects, was the conglomeration of multiple opposition movements against Thaksin into one major, unified movement.

The second part of the core PAD leadership was composed of the PAD coordinators. They had responsibility for the day-to-day running of the PAD movement. The coordinators also formed the link between the core leaders and other groups inside the PAD. Suriyasai Katasila, Chachawal Chartsuthichai, Panthep Pongpuapan, and Prapan Koonmee, for example, were key coordinators of the PAD. They often partook in the decision-making process along with the first generation of leaders, particularly on the question of press releases and media relations.

Another important part of the PAD structure was the movement's security apparatus. This was composed of three major elements: (1) PAD Volunteer Guards; (2) Dharma Forces; and (3) Srivichai Warriors. The PAD Volunteer Guards (PVG) were recruited largely from protest attendants, but also from state enterprises and NGOs that represented the core of the PAD movement. Kittichai Saisa-ad was the main leader of the PVG. The EGAT, the Waterworks Authority, and the like sent in their people as volunteers. According to guards, the PVG went through rigorous recruitment processes. There was a Center for Public Safety inside PAD that did background checks and required trial periods for all guards. Additionally, because there were instances of ill-intentioned persons impersonating as PAD guards, every few weeks they would change the badge for the guards: guards without the appropriate badge would not be given access to the PVG. The most organized security apparatus for the PAD was during the third stage of mobilization—the 158-day rally—in which Chamlong insisted on using the Dharma Forces only. In addition, the recruitment of Srivichai Warriors was under the leadership of Damrong Yotarak, a southerner in charge of a PAD subgroup, Pak Panang PAD. Damrong recruited men from other PAD subgroups in Thailand's south to form the Srivichai Warriors. The hijacking of a train headed to Bangkok from the south resulted in the group making a name for itself; they subsequently became front-liners for various occupation activities such as the Suvanabhumi Airport (Thailand's largest, and a significant regional aviation hub), Government House, and various other major arteries in the capital. They also acted as guards for the five core leaders of PAD.

The second generation of the PAD leadership was composed of second-in-command leaders. Officially there were only three leaders: Sirichai Mai-ngam, Sawit Kaewwan, and Samran Rodpetch. There were also five additional spokespersons for the PAD: Prapan Koonmee, Sarocha Pornudomsak, Anchalee Paireerak, Kamolporn Worakul, and Saranyoo Wongkrajang. These individuals were either all close associates of the First Generation leaders or heads of powerful PAD allies. Unofficially, there were many more Second Generation PAD leaders who frequented the PAD stage and ASTV and were respected as the "elders" of the PAD, but they did not assume the official title of Second Generation leaders. They provided leadership support to the First Generation leaders and at times helped make major decisions related to the overall direction of the movement. Some of these Second Generation leaders were the right-hand men of their First Generation counterparts, so their relationship predated the PAD movement. Trust is a major issue, particularly when it comes to being responsible for mass protests.

Conclusion

This chapter examines the Thaksin regime and the emergence of the People's Alliance for Democracy as an antidemocratic movement. It illustrates the development of the PAD formation, which went through stages of opposition mobilization. This chapter addresses the first two stages: formal and informal institutional blockage, and opposition alliance formation. The first stage took place in the 1990s, a proreform phase, when a number of key figures (who would later become PAD leaders) engaged in the reform process. Following the government of Thaksin and his Thai Rak Thai party, opposition groups began to form to oppose a number of TRT policies as well as Thaksin himself. This stage of opposition politics is considered as an anti-incumbent mobilization when opposition forces sought to pressure Thaksin to resign. Then, the last stage of opposition movement occurs—antidemocratic mobilization—when all other strategies have failed.

An examination of the Thaksin government also reveals a number of key issues that drove both the actual and perceived institutional blockages. At one level, the strength of the Thaksin government served to marginalize the voices of the opposition. At another level, however, the actions and behavior of Thaksin and his government created the perception of exclusion among the opposition. Over the six years of Thaksin's dominance, numerous triggering events occurred to fuel the opposition discourse for anti-incumbent dissent. What constituted the PAD opposition to Thaksin, I argue, is based on both substantive *and* constructed discourse. In other words, while Thaksin and his party sought to block a number of institutional channels for dissenting voices, the opposition also intentionally constructed this discourse to further its own case for opposition. Embedded within the early anti-Thaksin discourses were conservative, royalist, nationalist, and antidemocratic elements that eventually evolved to form the identity of the PAD movement. At the heart of the PAD's characteristics lies its different conception of democracy.

Beyond class structure, what defined this conflict and what accounted for why the PAD was, broadly speaking, a "conservative-royalist movement" was the PAD's vision of the nature of the state and its relation to society. This was clearly a political and ideological conflict. The PAD saw the Thai state as being composed of what Thais understand to be the traditional sources of power: the monarchy, the military, and the bureaucracy. The military and the bureaucracy have the duty to protect and safeguard the monarchical institution. All three units work to uphold the system of "constitutional monarchy" whereby the monarchy continues to be the ultimate source of moral authority and righteousness. The democratic institutions, such as the lower (House of Representatives) and upper (the Senate) chambers of parliament, ought to accept such a hierarchy and work hand in hand to preserve this constitutional monarchy. Electoral democracy is an important aspect of the polity, but it is deeply flawed due to ongoing corruption and money politics. As such, reforming the polity to halt the progression of this very corrupt form of "democratic" politics is necessary for Thailand to move forward. The middle class must become enlightened in order to educate others about what is right or wrong so that once the majority of the populace understands this, then they will choose good leaders to lead the country. Only then can Thailand become fully democratic.

FIVE

Democratic Breakdown

This chapter outlines the process of antidemocratization of the PAD movement and the eventual overthrow of the Thaksin government. The PAD started out as a movement seeking more accountability, particularly from the executive, yet ended up supporting a military coup. How did this happen? I argue here that the institutional blockages facing the PAD, both in the formal and informal democratic institutions, forced the movement to turn toward nondemocratic institutions. The antidemocratic turn happened gradually and was a strategic decision made by the movement's leadership, which became increasingly influenced by royalist and Buddhist groups, whose moral ideologies and authoritarian tendencies lent support to antidemocratic strategies to remove Thaksin. Becoming an antidemocratic movement was a means to an end, but it also reflected latent undemocratic tendencies among the leadership and support base of the movement. When opposition actors and groups felt they were shut out of accessing power now and in the foreseeable future, they appealed to nondemocratic alternative sources of power to reverse or, at a minimum, halt this process of institutional blockage. In essence, the strategic interactions between the opposition forces and Thaksin mattered to the former's perception of "blockage." Thaksin took a number of steps during the critical moments in the lead-up to the 2006 coup to not only cement the opposition's perception of permanent exclusion from access to power but he also underscored on multiple occasions the government's lack of credible commitment. These two key conditions helped to further drive the PAD movement to mobilize around nondemocratic sources of power to help break the political deadlock.

The next section outlines the anatomy of the 2006 military coup d'état. I advance a claim here that the coup was not a purely elitist overthrow of an elected government. Rather, the alliance between the People's Alliance for Democracy and other groups opposed to the Thaksin regime was crucial to the success of the 2006 coup. The PAD afforded the basis for legitimacy to the coup by signaling strong mass support for military intervention that would overthrow the government. To illustrate the importance of popular support for extraconstitutional interventions, I provide empirical evidence such as public opinion polls and an analysis of the PAD discourse to demonstrate popular backing for the coup. Nondemocratic actors moved against Thaksin on the condition of "sufficient popular support." To substantiate this claim that the 2006 coup hinged upon the perceived popular support of the military, I later examine the absence of another military intervention at the end of 2008, following the world's longest street demonstration. Popular support for the movement was dwindling, while public opinion in favor of another coup d'état had become progressively negative. The military leaders likewise admitted to "making a mistake" in relation to their 2006 coup. All of this suggests that an elite-centric explanation, which centers on the internal power struggles of elites alone, is insufficient to explain the democratic collapse of 2006. The last section offers a detailed examination of the discourse and ideology of the PAD movement. Understanding the PAD's disposition toward antidemocratic attitudes tells us much about how its members previous experiences of democracy had adversely affected them.

Antidemocratization

The PAD movement began to transform itself from an anti-incumbent movement into an antidemocratic one following a series of political deadlocks that occurred in early 2006. Up until early 2006, the PAD remained at the stage of antigovernment mobilization, but as its demands continued to go unmet and its voices continued to be ignored by the political leadership, the movement needed to find a way to "amp up their game." The perception of "permanent exclusion" and "desperation" was a result of strategic calculations as well as outcomes from a series of failed negotiations with Thaksin. When the opposition did not get what it wanted, or Thaksin refused to negotiate, that perception of desperation escalated. The shift toward becoming an antidemocratic movement was also an inward-looking strategic move to save the movement or risk losing momentum and support. For the PAD, being an antidemocratic movement was unplanned—something that would not ring true for its successor movement, the PDRC. But it was the first major decision made for this once prodemocracy movement—one that succeeded. Significantly, its success set a precedent for what would later become the PDRC. This section will also illustrate that the nondemocratic norms and beliefs, which had been residual to the movement during its anti-incumbent stage, would subsequently take center stage.

To elaborate, the process of antidemocratization occurs in two parallel steps. On the one hand, the strategic interactions between the opposition and Thaksin eventually convinced the former that (a) their other strategies have failed; (b) their future is foreshortened; and (c) they are likely to be excluded from access to power. This perception of "permanent exclusion" and "desperation" is a result of strategic calculations as well as outcomes from a series of interactions with Thaksin. When the opposition does not get what it wants, the feeling of desperation escalates. Note that because the later stage of the movement's antidemocratization is largely driven by emotions and perception, perceptions of actions by the opposition matter as much as the actions themselves.

Three things constitute an "antidemocratic" mobilization: (1) appealing to nondemocratic sources of power; (2) supporting extraconstitutional interventions to dislodge a democratically elected government; and (3) demanding an end to elections. The precoup period of PAD mobilization was marked in large part by its appeal to powerful nondemocratic institutions. Its demand to overthrow the democratic system occurred in the later stage of the movement's mobilization (postcoup) as the PAD's identity evolved; specifically, when it became the People's Democratic Reform Committee. While the PAD reached out to nondemocratic institutions, namely the military and the monarchy, the latter's responses and reactions to the PAD's appeals served to directly and indirectly empower the opposition movement. The military's conflict with the Thaksin government, in particular, provided hope to the PAD movement that an intervention from the "men in uniform" could break this political deadlock.

By early 2016, a political deadlock between the Thaksin government and the PAD protesters emerged. From the antigovernment side, demands for Thaksin to step down after months of long drawn-out and escalating protests went unheeded. Thaksin and his supporters felt that Thaksin has no reason to resign: he had just won the country's biggest electoral victory in history in early 2005. With such a mandate, Thaksin felt he did not need to compromise with the opposition. The opposition felt they needed to find other strategies to break the deadlock and mobilize more support for Thaksin's resignation. This was when the PAD leaders began to contemplate taking an antidemocratic turn. Becoming antidemocratic was a contentious decision even among the top five leaders of the PAD movement, with NGO leaders being the most opposed to the strategy. The power dissymmetry among the movement's leaders became evident. With media mogul Sonthi Limthongkul and Buddhist sect leader Chamlong Srimuang the more powerful of its leaders, the PAD made demands for extraconstitutional interventions from the monarchy and then the military—this paved the way for a coup d'état in September 2006.

The PAD leaders began to appeal for royal interventions as a strategy to bolster momentum and mobilize additional public support. The PAD leaders exposed what they strongly believed was Thaksin's plan to subvert the monarchy and transform Thailand into a republic. This was called the "Finland Plan." PAD leaders argued that Thaksin's strategy was to (1) create a one-party system; (2) weaken the bureaucratic system so that it would serve the politicians unconditionally; (3) privatize state property; (4) ensure that the monarchy was merely a national symbol; and (5) turn the party system into a cadre party under the guise of a mass party.[1] "Thaksin had succeeded in overtaking the Thai economy and political arenas with his money and capitalist ways, now he would take on the most important institution in Thailand—the monarchy," PAD leader Sonthi Limthongkul claimed.[2] A Bangkok senator went on a PAD stage and claimed to confirm the existence of the Finland Plan. This drew thousands of supporters to the PAD rallies to drive away Thaksin.[3] Some of the PAD supporters were outraged that Thaksin was allegedly both disloyal and disrespectful to the king. They launched a powerful campaign called "Save the Nation" to illustrate that in overthrowing this man they would be both doing the nation a favor and saving the monarchy. A coup would indeed be the only way to save democracy in order to rebuild a new one, which would uphold the ideals of "constitutional monarchy" (Nakornthap 2011, 10).

One of the most powerful appeals to the monarchy was the call for a royally appointed prime minister. Royal decree, in particular, the right for the king to appoint a leader set forth by Article 7 of the 1997 Constitution, was among the most widely discussed, and admittedly controversial, issues within the NGO community. Sonthi Limthongkul, through his televised talk show, *Thailand Weekly*, which mobilized opposition to Thaksin and Thai Rak Thai government, was responsible for the construction of this discourse. In late 2005, Sonthi had his audience (over 10,000 people) take an oath:

Your Majesty, from the situation in Thailand right now it is evident that a crisis is looming . . . the kind of crisis that cannot be solved within the existing political system. The issue of a royal decree has been discussed so widely—something so unprecedented. This is no accident. Whenever the country has a political leader who has no morality, that's when the people look to you, your Majesty. . . . the union between the king and his people, which has historically been our principal rule of law of constitutional monarchy is being challenged by the new capitalist monopoly. . . . we the people will not reject the government as long as the government still represents the people, as long as the government holds on to dharma, as long as the government still keeps its promise, to you, your Majesty . . . but the current situation requires change. . . . The new political structure has to have a royally appointed person to lead . . . of course we will have a referendum on this.

Then Sonthi asked the entire audience to say aloud the following: "I, [name], Your Majesty, will fight to the best of my ability and through peaceful means and constitutionally, in order to return royal decree so that your majesty can appoint a new leader to embark on political reforms in order to sustain the system of constitutional monarchy . . . to provide happiness to all the people."[4]

In reflecting on why the civil society groups inside the PAD supported the antidemocratic turn, the PAD's leaders admitted to being "strategically forced" to go in that direction. As Suriyasai reveals in a candid interview:

We [Committee for Popular Democracy] came to a breaking point in March [2006] when the situation was at a dead end. The majority of support for PAD already wanted Article 7 [the right for the king to appoint a leader]. We kept pressing on, hoping to break Thaksin . . . perhaps he would concede, but he did not. . . . I know some of the NGOs opposed this, a few even left PAD. . . . But there was a rumor that Pipob and I worked for the leftists inside Thaksin's government . . . that we were anti-royalist, that's why we were holding out on Article 7. . . . we needed to maintain our mass, our support and this would not be our last fight. We knew that if we didn't go ahead with Article 7, we would need to back down and we would be accused of leaving our supporters. We couldn't do it, so we finally agreed. (Katasila 2007, 229–32)

The PAD's appeals to the monarchy—Thailand's most powerful institution—and their instrumental use of it as their symbol both united the various groups inside the alliance and helped to propel popular support. The monarchy strikes a chord for many Thais, since the majority of Thais had only lived under the reign of one king. Royalism and nationalism have become intertwined in the consciousness of many Thai people and the two concepts are inseparable. For example, when the opposition claims that Thaksin is selling out the nation due to his plans to privatize many state enterprises, such acts can just as equally be construed as an offense to the monarchy. "Today there's a person who disrespected the king. He wants to sell off our nation. He wants to take this land which our ancestors have built, and give it to another country. . . . The King has never neglected his nation, so how could we neglect our King, our nation," said a frequent PAD demonstrator.[5]

Thaksin understood the political importance of the military despite its weaker political role following the Black May uprising. As such, he sought to engage with the military through co-optation (McCargo and Pathmanand 2005). While a number of retired generals staffed Thaksin's first administration, Thaksin also built up a loyal support base inside the military by placing within several officers, just as he was, who were Class 10 graduates of the Armed Forces Academics Preparatory School. Despite this, the relationship between the military top brass and Thaksin began to sour in 2005 when former prime minister Prem Tinasulanond openly criticized Thaksin's government. Prem was one of the most respected individuals both in the army and within the palace circle. Prem served as president of the Privy Council, a position appointed by the king. His vast personal networks in key institutions ensured that he maintained significant political clout despite not being actively involved in politics. In March 2006, just months before the coup, Prem told reporters that the situation had reached a complete deadlock and that a solution needed to be pursued.[6] In the weeks following, Prem had been reportedly speaking at various military establishments criticizing Thaksin and his government.[7] Prem later emerged as the key figure behind the 2006 coup.

The PAD movement appealed to the military to "step in" on numerous occasions, particularly as the situation escalated in 2006. Sonthi and Chamlong were the biggest proponents of military intervention among the PAD's top leaders.[8] For Sonthi, he always saw the military as the defender of the Thai nation and, most of all, the monarchy. On his account, it is the "duty" of the military to act to save the nation: "We need to rely on the military now to solve the crisis in our society."[9] Chamlong, who himself had worked for Prem when Prem was prime minister, spoke out in support of "a coup for the people," reportedly telling a number of military officers "not to be afraid."[10] "I'm happy the military staged a coup," Sonthi said. "General Sonthi [Bonnyaratklin], I feel for him, he never thought he'd be a coup leader . . . but because he was surrounded by those who respected General Prem, he saw what was wrong with the Thaksin regime" (Sithisaman 2011, 285).

The height of the crisis and political deadlock that marked the months preceding the September coup were critical to shaping the strategies of both pro- and anti-Thaksin forces. Ultimately, my central claim here is that the coup was not inevitable. The coup was a *choice* made by the military elites based on the unfolding of events. There was a point in time during this entire ordeal that room for "negotiation" between the opposition forces and Thaksin may have been conceivable. During the few months prior to the coup, the opposition forces, particularly the PAD, showed signs of fatigue and waning, while Thaksin was suffering a significant loss of political support, most notably from the TRT party itself. This "precarious" phase of the tug-of-war between Thaksin and his "adversaries" gave out signals that some sort of compromise or deal between these forces might have been reached. In the end, however, neither side would make concessions that might be perceived as acceptable. Suriyasai discussed this period in detail:

> I think the PAD did what they could to prevent the coup d'état. . . . Thaksin should have at least announced his resignation from power to preserve the system and the constitution. This [the coup] is what the PAD has always warned him about. I was absolutely certain that as long as Thaksin remained center stage in politics, we would reach a complete dead end. If Thaksin wouldn't back down, the PAD couldn't back down either. None of us could back down and we passed the point of any compromise or reconciliation, which means some sort of extra-constitutional power would have to intervene. . . . Thaksin essentially staged a "coup" on himself before the military launched another one. . . . As such I'm not surprised 89–90% of Thai people agreed with the coup and the subsequent Surayuth government. I don't blame the coup leaders for doing what they did. They prevented bloodshed. (Katasila 2007, 211)

Thaksin was facing the greatest opposition from both the opposition forces and his own party: a situation inconceivable only a year earlier (2005) when TRT won a landslide majority. The massive corruption scandals and endless antigovernment protests significantly weakened the authority and legitimacy of the embattled prime minister. It was at that point that Thaksin decided to break the political deadlock by dissolving parliament. Notably, he did not resign as the opposition party wished. This transpired just two days before a major protest planned for late February by the PAD. Thaksin offered the following reason on February 24, 2006: "As many of you know there were efforts to overthrow the government by some political groups that the government has tolerated and provided explanations for the many accusations . . . but the majority of the people continued to support the government and asked us to fight. What the government has done has received much attention from the rest of the world, but it elicited political instability. . . . I cannot accept mob politics . . . so I figured that the best way out of this conflict is to return the power back to the people."[11]

However, some critics argued that Thaksin took advantage of the situation knowing full well that an election would be a sure win for his party. Thaksin had dissolved parliament, the opposition insisted, to avoid the no confidence motion. Thaksin had earlier promised the opposition in the House and the Senate, as well as those on the streets, that he would "explain" all of the corruption allegations by allowing parliament to question him over the most controversial issue of his administration: the tax evasion following the Shin Corporation sales. It would have been the first time that Thaksin "unblocked" channels for the opposition inside the formal democratic institutions by allowing this no confidence motion. Thaksin even promised to allow ten days of questioning so that other issues such as political reforms could be discussed.[12] The House–Senate joint session was scheduled to take place on March 6, 2006. The opposition's dream shattered completely when Thaksin dissolved parliament on February 29, just days after promising a more transparent leadership.

The lower house dissolution allowed Thaksin to retract three key promises that, if followed through, would have, I argue, changed the course of opposition–government strategic interactions in ways that might possibly have prevented his downfall. First, he refused to be questioned by the National Assembly—an opportunity to not only engage with the growing opposition but also with his own supporters on the most controversial corruption scandal to date. Second, he broke his promise to the opposition *and* his own party that he would not dissolve parliament. Third, he had earlier stated that he would never step down from his role of prime minister. But following an audience with the king, he did step down, remaining only as caretaker prime minister. This last development should have been good news for the opposition, but because a new election had been called for October 2006 following the Election Commission's annulment of the April election, the opposition was more than convinced that Thaksin would be returned as prime minister and their "life would be over." Thaksin had never, in the eyes of the opposition, provided them with any credible commitment.

When Thaksin dissolved parliament, he more than convinced the opposition, from both formal and informal institutions, that he lacked any form of credible commitment to make future deals with the opposition. In November 2005, Thaksin informed his own ministers that he would "never resign or dissolve parliament" as his government was facing daily escalating protest activities. "Don't worry. I'm definitely not dissolving parliament or resigning. . . . We'll have an election in April 2009. Now let's do our job the best we can," Thaksin reportedly told his cabinet ministers.[13] Once he had dissolved parliament, effectively to avoid being questioned, the opposition was more than outraged. "Thaksin did not want to face the growing opposition who called for his resignation . . . ," the *Thai Post* reported. "He has lost all credibility, ethics or any sort of legitimacy to govern. After five years of corruption, and this last one where his family made off with 73.3 billion baht without paying any taxes, he completely broke all mechanisms for accountability and lost all credibility."[14]

The historic election on April 2, 2006 was like none other in Thailand. Once announced, the election date allowed parties just thirty-seven days to prepare, which put smaller and less-established parties at a disadvantage. From the day Thaksin dissolved parliament, key opposition parties (the Democrats, Chart Thai, and Mahachon) met on several occasions to think over how best to deal with the sudden and short-notice election. Leaders of the parties then held a joint press conference to declare that the House dissolution and upcoming April election lacked legitimacy, that they unanimously sought a boycott, and that they would not be fielding candidates.[15] The Thai Rak Thai party was also hollowing out, with members beginning to abandon ship.[16] Others in the cabinet, such as highly respected veteran politicians Bawornsak Uwanno and Wisanu Krue-Ngam, also left, causing internal rifts inside the TRT government.

P-Net, an important election watchdog, manifested its full support of the call for Thaksin's resignation; it even resigned from its duty to observe the April 2006 election. The PAD also held major rallies to call for Thaksin's resignation. Some sixty law academics from fourteen institutions wrote an open letter to the head of the Election Commission of Thailand calling for it to revoke Thaksin's right to stand for election; they believed that on several occasions he had violated electoral rules. Another network of some 500 academics gave a press conference entitled "To the People who are the Sovereign, please vote on April 2 by selecting 'Vote No.'" Parinya Thewana-ruemitkul (2006), representative of the group and former Black May upris-ing leader, saw Thaksin as the malaise of Thai politics whereby his resigna-tion was the only way out of the current political deadlock. On March 11, 2006, Premsak Piayura resigned as a party-list candidate of the TRT in the middle of the campaign; as a result, TRT no longer had the requisite 100 candidates for the party list. Despite this, the election went ahead.

The April 2006 election was one of the most bizarre elections in con-temporary democratic times. Out of the 400 constituencies available, only 247 of them put forward TRT candidates; and in thirty-eight constitu-encies, the candidates who received the most votes still did not attain 20 percent of the votes. In Bangkok, twenty-six out of thirty-six constituencies had more "No Votes" than votes for listed candidates. Some polling sta-tions saw more invalid ballots than the No Vote ones. A Bangkok exit poll also showed 42 percent of respondents in the capital chose purposefully not to vote.[17] If an election was supposed to solve the political deadlock, or at least bring the heat down a notch, it would not be *this* election. More than 70 percent of respondents in the ABAC poll believed that the politi-cal crisis would not improve after the election.[18] "Even the most optimistic of Thais," reported the BBC, "had to admit that Sunday's elections were unlikely to resolve the ongoing political conflicts."[19]

Thaksin took the much-boycotted election as a good sign for his party to secure an even stronger mandate. Irrespective that TRT was ostensibly the only party running in the election, of the unusually high invalid and No Vote ballots, and of the hundreds of thousands of protesters in the lead-up to the election, Thaksin remained undeterred. "I've passed the test to prove my popularity," proclaimed Thaksin, upon announcing that his party had won over 50 percent of the vote, his self-declared benchmark for continu-ing in power.[20] While Thaksin was clearly buying time until he could plan his next moves, the opposition was more than convinced that he would not step down, nor commit to any effort for "reconciliation" as he claimed he would. Effectively, any "promise" made by Thaksin to the opposition forces could not be taken seriously.

Thaksin only conceded to some opposition demands following an audience with King Bhumibol. Just a day after the election results showed Thai Rak Thai to have received sixteen million votes nationwide, Thaksin refused to take up another term as a prime minister. In a televised press conference, he explained: "If we only fight each other then the country is the one that will lose. That is what the King said in 1992 [Black May uprising]. . . . This year is a holy year. His Majesty's 60 years on the throne will be celebrated. . . . I want to see us Thais united. . . . We need to work together for the country and for King Bhumibol."[21]

The PAD movement received a major boost of legitimacy following King Bhumibol's speech to members of the judiciary on April 25, criticizing the election results:

> As for the [April 2, 2006] election, [Thaksin] who did not even get 20 percent and that person was running for election by himself . . . this is not a legitimate election. . . . What Thai Rak Thai did was an act done to gain power to govern the country that was unconstitutional—a danger to national stability and illegal or contradicts the moral ethics of the people, contradicts democratic principles, blatantly violates the law and thus should not be able to maintain its standing as a political party for the sake of Thailand's overall political system.[22]

The king's speech prompted the courts and independent bodies to reconsider their actions toward the Thaksin government. The Election Commission declared the April 2006 election to be in violation of electoral laws. Three members of the ECT were jailed for misconduct.[23] Yet Thaksin balked at his own promise to stay on as caretaker prime minister only, and reassumed full leadership in May, just weeks after the election was annulled. At this stage, a clash between the opposition and government forces now seemed inevitable. The opposition movement continued to press ahead as it held a nationwide assembly to find ways to "overthrow Thaksin" before Thailand could embark on any future reform. Thaksin stood his ground and vowed not to back down. Thaksin's final remarks before his overthrow in September confirmed what the opposition has believed all along: he would neither resign, back down, compromise, nor reconcile: "Extraconstitutional institutions, and individuals who derive their *barami* from nonconstitutional sources are interfering in the working of independent bodies. . . . People don't follow the [democratic] rules. They don't like the outcome, so they try to use nondemocratic means to change the situation. This is totally unacceptable."[24]

The Collapse of Democracy

The PAD was a unique movement for Thailand because it was the first time that a broad-based movement such as this contributed to the overthrow of a democratically elected regime. This raises two questions: (1) Why did the military have to engage a social movement to stage a coup? (2) Is the PAD, or more generally a popular movement, necessary for the success of the coup? This book advances the following claims in answering these questions. First, the military needed to involve a broad-based movement to legitimize its action of overthrowing the Thaksin government. Second, while the 2006 coup was not the first coup to be launched against an elected government, it was the first time in history that the coup overthrew a *very popular* elected government. This leads us to the second question about the necessity of the movement in creating conditions favorable for such an extraconstitutional move. I argue that the PAD was necessary to the success of the 2006 coup because it lent public support and legitimacy to the coup plotters. The coup makers themselves admitted that the opposition forces against the Thaksin government signaled the need for some kind of extraordinary intervention.[25]

Supporters of the coup, many of whom were PAD members, would argue that the coup was necessary to restore democracy. For them, Thaksin was not a legitimate leader, despite being elected. They believed he had the capability to continue to fool millions of supporters to vote for him in every election, and that there was no other way to be rid of him but to overthrow his government. In the words of a PAD leader: "a military coup requires popular support to succeed. If we [PAD] are able to show the powers that be that we have a lot of supporters, then we hope the military would know what to do. The military are there to serve the people. They must stand by the people" (Sithisaman 2011, 69). In the very few interviews that General Sonthi Boonyaratkin accorded about the coup, he always emphasized the importance of "popular opposition" against Thaksin as the barometer for military intervention.[26] "The people are cheering us [the military] on to stage a coup . . . what happened was what the people wanted," said General Sonthi in a televised interview five years after the coup.[27] The only people who were publicly calling for a military intervention were those in the PAD movement.

The 2006 coup was intended to break up Thaksin's political and electoral influence. A series of well-crafted plans to dismantle Thaksin's financial and political dominance was immediately carried out as the junta dislodged him. The so-called 4-step-ladder plan called for (1) dislodging Thaksin from power; (2) confiscating his assets; (3) dissolving his party and eliminating his political influence; and (4) putting the opposition back in power.[28] For the next several years, this plan was carried through to the letter. General Sonthi Boonyaratklin, a coup leader, outlined his reasons for the coup:

I received calls for the coup from many people. Soldiers are obliged to protect national security, safeguard the nation and uphold loyalty to the monarchy. The military cannot tolerate any leader who lacks or has limited loyalty to the king. Under the previous government, widespread corruption was evident. . . . Independent organizations failed to function; the administrative mechanisms as per the 1997 Constitution were stalled. . . . There was no functioning legislative body, and the judiciary could not function. There appeared to be no way out. This was before factoring in the social divisions. The country could not survive under the circumstances, and the coup was deemed necessary. . . . I believe a little interruption is acceptable in order to enable everyone to move forward once again. . . . I suspect many Thais still lack a proper understanding of democracy.[29]

Wassana Nanuam, a well-known Thai journalist reporting exclusively on military affairs, writes in her best-selling book *Lub Luang Prang* [Secret, Deception and, Disguise], which reveals the story behind the September coup d'état, that this was a coup different from all others in the past. "It's a strange coup because it's not just the military officers alone . . . but also civilians, bureaucrats and social group like the People's Alliance for Democracy that made this coup."[30] One of the generals close to the military coup leaders, General Saprang Kallayanamit, had close relations with PAD's top leaders Sonthi and Chamlong. It is widely believed that General Saprang was the source of the PAD's intelligence that Chamlong often refers to as "sources from a general" when he spoke on the PAD stage.[31] This relationship, the coup leaders claimed, may have influenced the course of the coup.[32]

TABLE 5.1. Poll data on the coup and coup government (2006)

Pollsters	Questions
Suan Dusit poll (September 20, 2006)	Do you agree with the coup? 1. Yes 84% 2. No 16%
ABAC poll (September 22, 2006)	How do you feel after the coup? 1. Politics will be calm again 83% 2. Improved economy 67% 3. Worried 37%
ABAC poll (September 23, 2006)	How do you feel about the role of the military? 1. The military are dependable 92% 2. Unpleasant 8%

Source: ABAC poll and Suan Dusit poll.

The coup of 2006 and the direct army rule over the country between 2006 and 2007 marked a return of the army to politics in a way not seen for over a decade. The last coup launched by the army was in 1991, in which popular protest against the coup government led to its leader resigning from power less than a year after the putsch. Since then, the army appears to have retreated from politics, and rumors of a coup—usually a "constant" in Thai politics—were not taken seriously by either the public or politicians. Thaksin himself brushed off numerous warnings by close aides of any possible extraconstitutional overthrow of his government. General Sonthi personally warned Thaksin that a coup would be launched against him. In retrospect, Thaksin admitted that he thought "no one would dare launch a coup in this twenty-first century" (Nanuam 2010, 41). The 2006 coup reinstated the military to the political arena after more than a decade of being sidelined. Having a politically powerful military significantly increases the risk of threats to the stability of government should the latter not toe the army line or seek to intervene with the army hierarchy, especially by displacing its chief (Nanuam 2010, 48).

Another major implication of the 2006 coup was the partisanship of the army. The "4-stepped" ladder did not reach its ultimate objective: to rid Thaksin from political power. Thaksin-allied parties won the next two subsequent elections: in 2007 and 2011. Although the army continually claimed it respected the wishes of the people and likewise the election results, the fact that they tried to directly influence electoral outcomes or to openly reveal their political positions is testament to the lack of political neutrality for an institution so powerful in both the political arena and society. During the 2011 national election campaign, poll after poll showed that the Thaksin-backed Peau Thai party would win. Army chief General Prayuth Chan O-cha made a televised announcement—something usually done only when the army declares a coup—that the Thai people should "choose only good people to run the country and people who would protect the monarchical institution."[33] His predecessor, General Anupong Paochinda, made similar statements.[34]

The escalating crisis prompted a number of key political figures to look for signaling from the palace. Under the active guidance of Prem, the coup leaders were able to garner the necessary legitimacy from within the military institution itself to launch the coup. The *barami* and power of Prem in shaping the course of politics was made far more evident when he handpicked retired General Surayuth Chulanond, known widely as his favorite, to serve as the prime minister of the coup government. Surayuth would later become a member of the Privy Council—an institution that acts as a proxy for the monarchy.[35] As the king addressed the illegitimate nature of the April 2006 elections, the Constitution Court immediately moved to annul the election results—throwing Thaksin and his TRT party completely off course. This was the first in a series of interventions by the courts to resolve the political deadlock that had occurred following the 2006 coup (Dressel 2010). Thaksin's audience with the king prompted him to step down as prime minister following the April 2006 election, albeit temporarily.

The PAD's antidemocratic and anti-incumbent mobilization was thus instrumental to the successful coup d'état on September 19, 2006. The PAD mass base provided what the coup plotters needed to launch a coup: political legitimacy. Although previous coups were carried out without consideration of the public's response, the Black May uprising incident and subsequent political reforms in the 1990s to reduce the role of direct military intervention in politics made public support key to the success of a coup. The public's overt support for the coup took many by surprise. Ordinary citizens and some organized Yellow Shirt groupings greeted the soldiers with flowers, food, and asked for photographs. Not only was this a bloodless coup, it was seemingly a popular one.[36] Both the Suan Dusit and ABAC polls reported overwhelming support for the coup d'état. Eighty-four percent of respondents nationwide, according to the Suan Dusit poll, agreed with the military intervention, while the ABAC poll reported favorable views toward the role of the military (see table 5.2). As General Sonthi admitted, "I did not invite anyone to be part of the coup plotting, but many people volunteered on their own terms. It was not exactly like they were part of the plotting operation, but they were supporters who kept encouraging us to stage a coup finally" (Nanuam 2010, 48). "When it was all done," General Sonthi added, "we were greeted with so much popular support—from the flowers they put on our guns and tanks, to chanting me as their white knight and hero—I was so touched and relieved" (Nanuam 2010, 17).

TABLE 5.2. A survey of PAD attitudes

	Agree (%)	Disagree (%)
Vote buying and selling is a problem of Thai democracy	84	14
Bringing in good people to govern will solve the problems of Thai democracy	89	7
Do you agree with having a royally appointed prime minister (Article 7)?	74	16
Thaksin regime is dangerous to Thailand's constitutional monarchy	98	1

Source: Based on 503–31 respondents and adapted from Chareonsin-olarn, 2008.

There was much internal disagreement among even the top five leaders of the PAD with regard to the coup. Collectively they issued an official press statement that they did not endorse the September 2006 coup;
individually, though, some leaders were very procoup. Sonthi was the
biggest supporter of extraconstitutional channels to resolve political conflicts; these included military intervention, judicial intervention, and royal
prerogative. Pipob, on the other hand, was the coup's biggest opponent.[37]
Suriyasai argued that a coup could be justified if an elected government
had lost its political legitimacy (Katasila 2009): "True that Thaksin was
legitimately elected, but once in power he lost his legitimacy through corruption, cronyism and abuse of power."[38] For Suriyasai, the mounting cases
of corruption were not the key reason for why he so strongly opposed
Thaksin. Rather, the prime minister's patent refusal to be held accountable either by the authorities or the people prompted him to support an
alternative power transition mechanism. "Thaksin did not allow himself to
be held accountable [by the people]. . . . The coup took place inevitably"
(Katasila 2009, 86). Somsak initially showed ambivalence toward the coup,
but later admitted a coup could be legitimate as long as it took place for
the right reason. "The military top brass was opportunistic with the coup.
I asked Sonthi [Boonyaratklin] why a coup? Why? We talked about political reforms, what kind of democracy we wanted. If the coup could lead to
important reforms, in a good direction, it would be fine. It had to be for the
majority of the people. But if the military staged a coup and did nothing
then it would be worse than bad quality democracy."[39]

The PAD's "New Politics"

To justify its support for antidemocratic solutions to Thai politics, the
PAD movement constructed its new politics discourse, which rested on
strong and politicized nondemocratic institutions, moral and ethical governance, and elitism. The PAD envisioned a Thailand with a strong and
politicized monarchy, and moral and ethical governance led by the (Buddhist) enlightened elites. These enlightened elites would know what was
right for the country instead of relying on what the PAD believed was the
"rural, gullible mass." When examining PAD's discourse on new politics,
it became increasingly clear how undemocratic some of its core notions
of accountability, governance, and citizenship were—partially reflecting
what the reformists of the moral ideologies sought to achieve in the 1990s
during the decade of the great reforms. These latent ideas of moral and

ethical politics, which were intertwined with royalism and Buddhism, help to explain why there was vocal grassroots support among some sections of the PAD movement before the 2006 coup for antidemocratic actions. Of course, at the leadership level, the antidemocratic mobilization was a strategic move—one that had strong support from the base.

First, the PAD believed in the necessity of a politicized constitutional monarch who would continue to enjoy extraconstitutional power and the political legitimacy to intervene in politics in times of crisis. For the PAD, a constitutional monarch indicated a political system in which the monarch was "above" or "on top of" politics (Winichakul 2013). This suggests that, for the PAD, the monarch was the ultimate legitimacy in Thailand. The king remained the "Father" of the land—the original owner of the land, he who gives sovereignty to his people. In this, I agree with Winichakul (2008), who argues that the prominence of the monarchy was built upon its being superior to corrupt political institutions. The PAD's version of constitutional monarchy preserved the royal institution as the pinnacle of the state. This conception of the constitutional monarchy meant that it remained far more powerful than any elected politician. Viewing a constitutional monarchy in this light, it is not difficult to grasp why the PAD might easily transform itself into an antidemocratic movement. After all, the notion that the monarchy remains at the top of the political hierarchy is fundamentally antithetical to democratic ideals. Even as an arbiter of last resort, a powerful monarchical institution can weaken the actual formal democratic institutions. Such a perception of the monarchy in fact empowers the institution in the minds of the people. A strong palace, in turn, empowers other nondemocratic institutions, such as the Privy Council and the military.

Second, good governance for the PAD meant greater moral and horizontal accountability. The NGO side of the PAD had always fought for a more accountable leadership who would truly represent the people and allowed itself to be answerable. Thaksin's intolerance toward opposition voices, his marginalization of NGO activities, and the crippled checks and balance system inside parliament convinced his critics that he and his government could not possibly govern Thailand justly or fairly. Thaksin's oft-cited statement that "19 million people voted for me so I won't let a mere thousands of protesters get in the way" was exactly why Thaksin had to go: for these PAD supporters, his majority mandate and leadership style prevented him from being fully accountable.

For the majority sections of the PAD—the royalists, Buddhists, and the conservatives—good governance was about morality and ethics. Drawing on a popular discourse generated by King Bhumibol, Thailand needed to reform its political system so that it would attract only "good people." The good people, for the PAD, who should be governing Thailand were individuals like Anand Panyarachoon who had spent their lives dedicated to the public good without wanting anything in return. According to Suwinai Pornwalai, a PAD intellectual and author of *The PAD Party*, "superhuman" are those who are not only good but who also have a good mind beyond being human.[40] These superhumans, for Suwinai, can tell right from wrong and sacrifice themselves for the greater good. Suwinai depicts the PAD movement as a force full of good people who are fighting against the "evil forces" that seek to destroy them.[41] A war, he further argues, is needed to safeguard Thailand's constitutional monarchy from the forces of evil and to bring the entire nation "enlightenment."[42]

Buddhism was a core element of the PAD's conception of moral governance, which its supporters referred to as "dharmic democracy." Dharmic democracy, or Thammatippatai (ธรรมาธิปไตย), is an "ideal" version of democracy, whereby the leader who is elected democratically by the people exercises truthfulness, ethics, and righteousness as a principle of rule.[43] The elected leader must listen to the people and uphold utmost sincerity and honesty in serving the people. Anek Laothamtas adopted this idea when founding a new party, Mahachon, in 2005—a move that was supported by a number of NGO leaders. He indicated that to achieve dharmic democracy, the people who would elect their leader need wisdom and education and to use dharma to guide them when they vote. They ought to think about the interests of the public more than their own.[44] Many PAD leaders drew on the teachings of Buddha when they spoke on stage, especially when referring to decisions on what is good or bad.

For the proponents of moral governance, Thaksin stood in stark contrast to a "good leader": he was corrupt, immoral, selfish, and appeared to be disloyal to the monarchy. For the PAD, "good people" would need to campaign: their good deeds would be apparent to all such that there would be no need to advertise the fact. The PAD's conception of good governance as "good people bringing about a just society" sounds, on the face of it, noble; but it is not only elitist, it is wholly antidemocratic. Who gets to decide who is a good person? Both Prem and Anand were regarded as "good people" who remained nonpartisan, impartial, and in some ways "above politics." They are held in such high regard because both received the blessing of the palace. But neither of them had been elected when they served as prime ministers. Prem's direct involvement in the 2006 coup through his privy councilorship also shows that these "good people" can be detrimental to democratic politics. Anand, who was the biggest proponent of good governance during the reform period in the 1990s, also lent his support to the coup. It is also unrealistic to expect individuals with such "heavenly" qualities to emerge from an electoral process.

To explain the overwhelming electoral support for Thaksin and his Thai Rak Thai party, the PAD announced that his supporters were "gullible, stupid voters." This elitist notion—the third pillar of PAD's new politics in which those who voted for Thaksin and his clans were considered too dumb to understand their actions and were likely to sell their vote to the highest bidder—was pervasive within the PAD and PDRC rhetoric. Essentially PAD believed that the majority of Thai electors were neither sufficiently educated nor well informed, and thus were outsmarted as a result by self-serving politicians through money politics. While vote-buying was indeed an issue in Thai politics, the Yellow Shirts placed the blame squarely with crooked politicians, exemplified by Thaksin, his allies, and the naïve voters who supported them.[45] Thaksin's supporters, the PAD claimed, were duped by his handouts (populist policies) and seemingly limitless wealth to the extent that they turned a blind eye to his egregious corruption and danger to the nation (Paireerak 2006, 137). The movement often called Thaksin supporters "buffaloes" or "red buffaloes," which in Thai are derogatory terms that indicate a stupid person. A frequent PAD protester, Chairoj, explained why he joined the PAD:

> People who did not know who Thaksin truly was, is because they watched evening soap and not news or only watched government news. The government would privatize state enterprises and used populist policies to dupe people . . . people were not well-informed. It would be like if you had rented your house to someone and he turned around to sell it, how could you stand that? Politics was the affairs of the people; we must be able to hold our government accountable, not let them steal what belonged to us and then sell it for a profit.[46]

The Yellow Shirts saw themselves as the bulwark of progress and political change in Thai society. As the "enlightened people," the Yellow Shirts understood that a good democracy should be void of vote-buying and corrupt politicians.[47] Unlike the Red Shirts, who supported Thaksin, the Yellow Shirts were more educated, had more access to information, and the moral high ground to adjudicate between right and wrong. "The Red Shirts were blind to the truth. . . . these people were not qualified to determine the nation's direction . . . and elect the nation's leader" (Pornwilai 2010, 135). Kamnoon Sithisaman, a key PAD advisor and former senator, made the case in the Senate for why the Yellow Shirts should lead the way in saving Thailand's democracy:

> They [the Yellow Shirts] wanted to see more for their country. They were the progressive group, the tax-paying group, the middle class and upwards, the business owners, and professionals. They were intelligent—more than us here in the [National] Assembly. They knew what kind of politics would be good and bad; they could see right from wrong. They knew an election alone would not be enough to have good politics. . . . They knew we must get good leaders to govern the country and establish the rule of law.[48]

There is also a practical reason why the middle class defines the PAD movement—cable TV. The PAD was largely mobilized through ASTV cable, which was owned and operated by Sonthi Limthongkul's Manager Media Group. Cable TV was neither cheap nor widespread—cable lines were only available in Thailand's urban areas, making it accessible only to the middle class in these areas. Later, the PAD sought to enlarge its support base to incorporate less well-off sections of the population by handing out ASTV satellite dishes free of charge, but that still would only reach urban pockets of the population. The middle class was also critical to the financing of the PAD movement. Worakul's (2012) survey of the PAD's 193-Day Protest reveals that the sources of PAD funding during its longest rally were derived 70 percent from donations, 20 percent from ASTV revenue streams, and 10 percent from the sale of goods.[49]

PAD leaders admitted, however, that the role of the middle class made the PAD less democratic. Suriyasai, reflecting on the "failure" of the PAD, gives a succinct explanation for why the PAD was antidemocratic:

> The middle class understands democracy from the perspective of a group that has developed and grown from neoliberal economics and political liberalization during authoritarian times. They are very much selfish and are interested only in what would benefit their prosperity. They are self-centered. They don't really care whether the regime is democratic or not. They hardly care about the poor. The biggest challenge for our country today is to figure out how we can create a political system that both the poor and the middle class can benefit from and co-exist. Right now, the poor are concerned

about access to resources, while the middle class are concerned about liberty and stability.[50]

Finally, the Yellow Shirts' mobilization was a response to a failure of representative democracy, one in which people felt excluded from the system and that politicians were not held accountable for their actions. "Wherever there was an election, there was money. And if a candidate spent 10,000 million baht, that person could not represent you. This was a fake democracy," argued a leading public intellectual influential within the NGO community, Prawes Wasi (Pongpaibul 2004). Given that many of PAD's top leaders were long-time activists, they preferred a consensus-based, participatory, and open process of negotiation to a representative/delegative style of governance. "The process of conflict resolution had to be democratic," according to Pipob. "We needed a round-table and representatives from all sections of society—both pro- and anti-Thaksin—but they had to come from the people, not Thaksin's representatives or nominees."[51]

Conclusion

When Thaksin and his Thai Rak Thai party won the 2005 election in a landslide victory, the PAD felt that the days of its anti-incumbent activities were numbered. While they pressed on with their allies to pressure Thaksin to resign from his leadership, the leader's immense popularity rendered the opposition's strategies ineffective. Eventually the PAD appealed to the institution of last resort—the monarchy—for a royal intervention in the political crisis. Simultaneously the movement also pleaded to other powerful nondemocratic institutions—the military and the Privy Council—to step in and help "save the nation." Their call was answered, and the coup d'état succeeded in overthrowing the most popularly elected prime minister in Thailand's history.

This last stage of the process of institutional blockage—the antidemocratization of the PAD movement—was a key turning point in the political conflict. I demonstrate here the importance of an alliance between the PAD and nondemocratic institutions in the breakdown of Thailand's democracy. I show how popular support for extraconstitutional intervention from the PAD was crucial to the timing *and* the success of the coup. Public opinion polls immediately following the coup were also used to demonstrate the strength of popular support. Ultimately, the coup was contingent upon sufficient popular outrage against the incumbent leader as well as the PAD's call for nondemocratic institutions to step in. The coup was not purely an elite overthrow of an elected government. The PAD provided the basis for the coup's legitimacy by signaling strong mass support for military intervention that would overthrow the government. By motivating the military to intervene, the PAD directly reduced the cost of a coup and improved the probability of its success.

The last section examines in great detail the discourse and ideology of the Yellow Shirts, which included both the PAD and the PDRC. Both of these movements were similar in their ideological foundations, values, and aspirations for the future of Thailand's politics. Their entrenched views regarding the necessity of righteous, ethical, inclusive, and elitist politics was shaped by the influences of both the monarchy and Buddhist thought, as well as their lived experiences of past failures of democratic governments. The Yellow Shirts, whose members were drawn largely from the urban middle class, saw themselves as the enlightened guiding force for a more progressive society. Their understanding of democracy was not only based on their righteousness and moral ethics but also on the value of a more consensus-based and participatory form of rule. Their strong opposition to electoral and representative democracy, as well as their firm belief in the gullibility of the rural masses, prompted them to accept nondemocratic means of rule. The solution for the malaise of the Thai polity did not lie in the procedural form of democracy, but rather in the unwavering conviction of allowing "good people" to rule. Paying closer attention to the Yellow Shirts' disposition toward antidemocratic attitudes brings us closer to grasping the underlying reasons why they supported military coups.

PART 2

SIX

Social Media and the New Antidemocrats

The People's Alliance for Democracy played a crucial role in the breakdown of democracy in Thailand in 2006. The postcoup period, between 2008 and 2011, saw the weakening and radicalization of the PAD. I argue that the PAD weakened because the same conditions of institutional blockage that gave rise to an antidemocratic mobilization in both formal and informal institutions were no longer present. The two key mechanisms that would have created the condition of institutional blockage—a perception of permanent exclusion of power and a relative change in access to power—were changed in the postcoup period. For the opposition, the perception of being excluded significantly weakened while there was *positive* change in access to power. Key figures inside the PAD helped to write the 2007 constitution[1] and held powerful positions inside the military-installed government of Surayuth Chulanond.[2] The new constitution was widely seen as an attempt at constitutional engineering to punish Thaksin and avoid creating conditions that would return him to power. Mechanisms that had enabled Thaksin to consolidate power, to avoid his being held to account, and had rendered the opposition ineffective were "corrected" in the 2007 constitution. Party mergers were no longer allowed during parliamentary sessions; family members of existing MPs were disallowed from running for the upper house; the Senate became partially appointed again, and the opposition needed only one-fifth of the votes to launch a no confidence motion against the prime minister. In effect, the 2007 Constitution was designed to check executive abuse of power by those in office and make it difficult for any political party to be elected to a majority—thereby blocking other means for the executive to gain excessive power. The PAD continued to mobilize in the postcoup period, but it never regained the popularity and potency that it once held.

This chapter also examines the role of social media and the emergence of the PAD successor movement, the People's Democratic Reform Committee. Social media was a central and defining feature of the PDRC that was absent from the PAD. Social media in Thailand, which included platforms like Facebook, Twitter, LINE chat application (app), and YouTube, did not become widely available until the mid-2010s—by which time the PAD had already disintegrated. What role did social media play in the antidemocratic mobilization of the PDRC? Through a detailed examination of Facebook data—Thailand's most popular social media platform—this chapter makes three arguments. First, social media facilitates the coordination and mobilization of antidemocratic movements. Second, social media deepens political polarization. Third, social media amplifies antidemocratic voices. Overall, social media has made coups cheaper and more likely by playing a critical role in entrenching political divisions, expanding the reach of nondemocratic voices, and helping to mass produce popular support for a military putsch. My analysis has also produced some positive outcomes for online political participation. Social media has been shown to help bridge the participatory gap by drawing mostly young and hitherto disengaged publics into the political realm through platform engagement. Unfortunately, while social media helped to democratize political participation, it did not fully result in *prodemocratic* participation.

Existing theories on the relationship between social media and democracy have provided cause for both optimism and pessimism. Scholars argue that there are several mechanisms by which the internet can bring about positive political change (Benkler 2006; Trippi 2004; Shirky 2008). Internet usage can potentially (a) increase political participation; (b) activate previously inactive citizens; (c) challenge the politically vested interests of leaders; (d) narrow the gap between political elites and the mass public; and (e) devolve power from traditionally centralized institutions to the periphery. The internet can also flatten out existing social inequality through the creation of a horizontally networked society (Castells 2011). Information and communication technologies provide political opportunities in ways that sharply reduce barriers to civic engagement: if citizens can write their own news, create their own political commentary, and post their views before a worldwide audience, then making a political difference through content creation and online participation becomes relatively simple, cheap, and fast (Chadwick 2007). In a large multicountry survey, Loader, Vromen, and Xenos (2014) find that there is a strong, positive relationship between social media use and political engagement among youths in Australia, the United States, and the United Kingdom. In a continent where voting and political party membership has long been in decline, social media tools provide optimism that more networked European youths can enhance more traditional forms of political participation. While the Arab Spring has spawned a growing scholarship on political participation and social media, debate continues within the fields of political science and communication on exactly what role social media plays in relation to political participation (Segerberg and Bennett 2012; Howard and Hussain 2011; Eltantawy and Wiest 2011). Some scholars argue that people utilizing social media help to drive political participation offline. Tufecki and Wilson (2012) find that protesters in Egypt's Tahrir Square not only learned of the protests via social media, but their social media use made it more likely for them to engage in political protest. Survey data on Facebook users in Chile also shows a strong association between Facebook use and offline protest activity (de Zuniga, Jung and Valenzuela 2012). Similarly, Howard and Hussein (2013, 5) argue that the internet was so important to civil society actors in Arab states because they lacked other forms of political communication and because internet content could be hosted on servers that were beyond the reach of the state. In China, online activism, particularly political protest, thrived online partly because offline political opposition was strongly restricted (Yang 2014).

Yet recent revelations of the extensive Russian interventions in the US 2016 presidential election, and in the 2016 Brexit referendum, laid bare the pervasive and entrenched global networks of actors and firms implicated in manipulating elections through social media with a view to undermining democracy (Galante and Ee 2018). Social media—once believed to be a force for democracy—has directly contributed to flawed elections in nearly fifty countries and to fueling ethnic and religious conflict in dozens more around the world (Woolley and Howard 2017). False information proliferates through social media and is aided in this by machine learning tools such as bots and humans posing as social media influencers (Woolley 2016; Ferrerra et al. 2016). Networked societies such as Thailand that are already polarized by years of political divisions are believed to be particularly vulnerable to the dark side of the internet as fake news, bots, trolls, and influencers can all sow discord and worsen an already brittle political situation. Furthermore, there is growing empirical evidence that social media can create filter bubbles: people selectively consume only information that confirms their preexisting beliefs, thereby creating an echo chamber effect (Iyengar and Hahn 2009; Adamic and Glance 2005). The early optimism that social media could advance democratic values has been seriously dampened and in question due to recent events and to emerging scholarly research on social media and politics.

This chapter is divided into two parts. The first section discusses the post-2006 coup political environment and the decline of the PAD. It also charts the emergence of the People's Democratic Reform Committee and provides a comparative analysis of the PDRC against the backdrop of the PAD. The second section examines the role of social media in propelling the PDRC movement. It investigates how social media contributes to political polarization and addresses its impact on existing regional and economic cleavages. Finally, the chapter also discusses the role of social media in amplifying, as opposed to neutralizing, nondemocratic voices.

The Postcoup Resurgence and the Decline of the PAD

The PAD leadership declared a cessation of activities immediately following the coup of September 19, 2006. After the coup and subsequent military installation of the government with army veteran Surayuth Chulanond at its helm, the PAD ceased its activities. By October of 2006, the PAD had changed its name to "the People's Assembly for Political Reform" to work in parallel with the Council for Democratic Reforms as a shadow wing of the coup government composed of "representatives of the people." The PAD's main task during this postcoup period was to discuss the process of constitutional drafting to ensure that its voices would be heard. For many activists of the 1990s reform period who had subscribed to moral accountability ideologies, they saw the 2006 coup as an extension of a reform process that was yet to be completed. Ironically, a new constitution would be needed to right the wrongs of the 1997 Constitution, particularly concerning its articles that emboldened the power of the executive and provided insufficient checks on his power. Numerous PAD supporters and 1997 constitutional drafters such as Jermsak Pinthong, Klannarong Jantik, and Jaras Suwannamala took part in drafting this second one. To increase the legitimacy of a new constitution put together at the behest of a military-backed government, a first-ever referendum was held despite many areas of the country being under emergency decree. Fifty-eight percent voted in favor of the new constitution and a new election was called. Unfortunately for the PAD and its allies, Thai Rak Thai's successor party, Palang Prachachon Party (PPP), won and formed a new government.

The postcoup period, between 2008 and 2011, saw the weakening and radicalization of the PAD movement. I argue that the PAD weakened because the same conditions of institutional blockage both in the formal and informal institutions that gave rise to an antidemocratic mobilization were no longer present. Institutions were not blocked in the same ways they were in the lead-up to the 2006 coup due to much greater inclusion of the opposition both in the formal and informal democratic institutions. The perception among government critics of political exclusion was no longer strong nor viable. The PAD movement in the postcoup period was no longer shaped by existing institutional blockages, making it harder for the leaders to construct convincing discourse for mobilization. The result was a much harder point of mobilization to sell, a less convincing griev-ance, and a weakening movement. This coupled with a lack of popular support for a military intervention made this extraconstitutional measure neither desirable nor possible.

Despite the PAD's vehement opposition to the return of Thaksin's polit-ical dominance via a proxy party, PPP, formal institutions were not blocked. First, the new 2007 constitution was authored by some of the PAD's stron-gest supporters in an attempt to correct the mechanisms that overempha-sized vertical accountability at the expense of horizontal or moral account-ability.[3] Specifically, these changed mechanisms include party mergers no longer being allowed during parliamentary sessions; family members of existing MPs no longer being permitted to run for the upper house; and the Senate becoming half elected, half appointed. Furthermore, opposition in parliament would only need one-fifth of the votes to launch a no con-fidence motion against the prime minister. Second, the PPP did not have an absolute majority in parliament nor did it want one. The PPP managed to gain 233 out of 480 seats, which accounted for 48.5 percent of the seats. This was close to what TRT had obtained in the 2001 election. In contrast, the Democrat Party—the election runner-up—trailed by nearly 15 percent of the seat share with 164 seats. Samak Sundaravej immediately formed a six-party coalition with five other, mostly small, parties. This was meant to safeguard against any potential coup threat that might arise should the PPP go it alone as a minority government or form a small majority with only one other party. Essentially the PPP did not want a minimal winning coalition, but a maximal one instead. This six-party coalition translated into 316 out of 480 seats, accounting for more than 63 percent of parlia-mentary seats.

The coalition government of Samak was very different from that of Thaksin. For one, Samak did not have the same control over coalition partners as Thaksin did. Samak called his own coalition makeup "ugly" and admitted that his coalition partners gave him little opportunity to lead.[4] "Nobody in the coalition government cares or listens to Samak," academics argued. "They do whatever they want and they often give contradictory statements over government policies. . . . The biggest threat to the stability of this government comes from within."[5] There were also constant rumors of coalition parties defecting from the government. While the Democrats were the only official opposition party during the Samak government, it had no trouble getting one-fifth of the votes to launch a no confidence motion against the prime minister. Less than six months into the PPP-led coalition government (June 2008), Samak and seven ministers were subjected to a three-day grilling by the opposition before surviving a no confidence vote.

The clearest evidence that opposition forces were not blocked in the formal democratic institution is that Samak was eventually removed from power by one of the independent bodies: the Constitutional Court. It was not the case anymore that independent institutions were "crippled" by government interference. In September 2008, a group of twenty-nine senators and the Electoral Commission of Thailand (ECT) filed a petition against Samak for moonlighting as a chef on TV. He was then found guilty of violating Section 182 of the Constitution, which prohibits individuals in political office from being employed elsewhere. Once Samak had been removed from power through the Constitutional Court ruling, his party refused to bring him back as the prime minister.

Somchai Wongsawat, Thaksin's brother-in-law, replaced Samak as the new prime minister; he too was facing an increasingly difficult situation. The seventy-two MPs who were members of the Newin Faction inside the coalition government would not support Somchai's nomination without guarantees of ministerial portfolios.[6] This is reminiscent of the old-style 1990s politics, where coalition partners and factions within the main party would bargain for cabinet posts in exchange for loyalty. In fact, the PPP was growing so divisive on account of many factions wanting to go their own way that Somchai had, at one point, to plead with his fellow MPs not to be "cliquey" and to stay united as a party and not "faction" lest the PPP collapsed.[7] A soft-spoken person, whom Prawes describes a "mild-mannered," Somchai was nothing like Thaksin nor his sharp-tongued predecessor, Samak. Somchai ensured that he maintained a conciliatory attitude toward the "powers that be"—whether that was Privy Councilor Prem, the army chief, the PAD leaders, or even his own party's factional leaders. Somchai visited Prem at his residence to seek "help" and "guidance" in solving the ongoing political conflict that seemed only to deepen n.[8] Eventually PAD protesters encircled government buildings and eventually occupied them.

Following the coup, the Council for Democratic Reforms began placing its people into various independent bodies, beginning with the ECT, the courts, and the anticorruption commission. The 2007 Constitution, in comparison with its 1997 predecessor, gave specific enhanced powers to the judiciary. The Senate would be half elected and half appointed, in contrast to the previously fully elected Senate. This meant that the PAD-aligned elites could vie for seats in the Senate, thereby keeping checks on the PPP. Judges who supported the PAD or military were also appointed to search for committee members for other independent institutions. The new judiciary began to act partially in favor of the yellow-shirted opposition. Following the 2007 election, the ECT found electoral misconduct on the part of Monthien Songpracha, candidate and deputy secretary of the Chart Thai party, and Soonthorn Wilawan, candidate and deputy chief of the Matchimatipatai party. The ECT voted four to one in favor of dissolving Chart Thai and Matchimatipatai. Chart Thai, Matchimatipatai, and PPP were sued for electoral misconduct. Soon after, a PPP MP, Yongyuth Tiyapairat, was given a red card for electoral fraud. Things subsequently went downhill for the PPP when several ministers were stripped of their positions or pressured to resign.[9] Then on December 2, 2008, the Constitutional Court delivered its verdict to dissolve all three parties and revoke for five years the voting rights of the party committee members: PPP (thirty-seven members), Chart Thai (forty-three members), and Matchimatipatai (twenty-nine members).

The opposition party, the Democrats, emerged as the victor when governing coalition parties defected and supported the nomination of its party member, Abhisit Vejjajiva, as the replacement to Prime Minister Somchai. The coalition partners and PPP factions did not have to abandon the government since even after the bans, government MPs still maintained 271 seats out of a possible 480—a total of over 50 percent. But the increasingly untenable situation in parliament prompted mass defections from the governing coalition to form an alliance with the Democrats. With defections from the Newin faction and other coalition partners, Abhisit received 235 parliamentary votes to become prime minister. Many observers believe the new Democrat Party–led government was formed inside the military barracks, while the uniformed men held great sway over the makeup of Abhisit's cabinet.[10] The fall of both PPP-led coalitions were among the most significant victories of the PAD-aligned opposition forces.

While the opposition was gaining ground in various formal democratic institutions, the PAD remobilized to exert even greater pressure against the PPP governments from out in the streets. The alliance between the PAD and key opposition groups from within formal democratic channels (the parliamentary opposition, the Senate, and independent bodies) solidified. This period witnessed both the decline in popularity *and* the growing violence of the PAD movement. This phase of PAD activities officially recommenced on February 25, 2008 when the movement's leadership regrouped and called on its supporters to fight the newly elected Samak government, whom they considered "Thaksin's nominee." The PAD believed Samak was merely a puppet for Thaksin, and that the Palang Prachachon Party was still run by Thaksin from exile. The PAD leaders made a number of demands, all of which centered around their opposition to Thaksin. For instance, the PAD opposed any effort to amend Constitution Articles 237 and 309, amendments that they believed were intended to afford Thaksin amnesty and bring back the banned members of the Thai Rak Thai party. Such claims by the PAD were not far-fetched given that the PPP campaigned on returning the TRT government and bringing "justice" to Thaksin. Moreover, PPP policy was very much that of the TRT, meaning a continuation of state projects that so many organizations within the PAD had fought hard against. The grievances of the PAD precoup seemed to have all but returned under the Samak government, infuriating their leadership and much of their support base.

The first major rally took place in late March 2008 at Thammasat University and drew thousands of supporters from academics, students, media, artists, NGOs, and others nationwide (Katasila 2009, 125). It became clear during this period that the PAD was fighting what it saw as the "Thaksin regime": a system of deep-rooted corruption instigated by the Thaksin administration for his and his allies' benefit. This regime was a threat to the entire nation and the foundation of the Thai state, particularly its beloved monarchy. The PAD movement in this second phase focused on two issues: nationalism and royalism. More so than in the first phase, the identity of the PAD movement was constructed throughout this second period. The first phase of the PAD movement, the largest in size, was a coming together of people and groups who were united only in their opposition to Thaksin and shared little else in common. They came together in this first phase under the campaign of "Saving the Nation" (*koo chart*), most wearing T-shirts emblazoned with "We fight for the King" (*rao soo peau Nai Luang*).

In the second phase of mobilization that followed the ousting of Thaksin, the PAD lost some of its support from the labor movement and NGO community but gained support from the public that had not mobilized the first time around. This led to the period of PAD's longest sustained street mobilization, known as the "193-Day Protest"—the longest protest in contemporary Thai history. In this round of mobilization, the PAD refocused on the issue of the monarchy all the while emphasizing other issues that evoked patriotism. As such, its campaign, entitled "Guarding the Nation" (*yam fao pandin*), indicated the PAD's intention to act as guardians of the nation in protecting both the monarchy and the state from harm and evil, and in seeking to preserve the status quo. This focus on royalism and nationalism was a strategic move on the part of the PAD leaders. Admittedly, claiming that the monarchy was under threat elicited a lot of emotion from the masses, enough to mobilize more people into the streets than any other issue.[11] Prachatai (2008), a Thai online news outlet, reported a rare interview of Princess Sirindhorn with a US newspaper that the Yellow Shirts may have used the issue of the monarchy for their own benefit. "Do they [the leaders] really love the monarchy? I don't know. . . . In fact, I don't even think the monarchy likes the Yellow Shirts very much. The royal family did say the Yellow Shirts cause problems for them."[12]

The PAD and the Democrat Party unofficially united and facilitated one of the longest and most violent mass protests in contemporary Thai history. The 193-Day Protest began soon after Prime Minister Samak Sundaravej of the PPP announced he would seek to amend the 2007 Constitution, which was considered by the PAD to be a "national crisis."[13] After drawn-out rallies that among others included raiding Government House and occupying the country's main airport, the PAD in December 2008 declared its "victory" following the PPP's dissolution by the Constitutional Court. This paved the way for the Democrat Party to cobble together a coalition and ascend to power.[14] This period saw the PAD and the Democrats in a united front: "We turned our eyes blind to the differences among us, and focused on our common goal: to rid Thailand of the Thaksin regime."[15] With their allied political party finally in power, the PAD's popularity dramatically declined as there was no justifiable reason to continue its political crusade.

This period also saw a significant radicalization of the PAD movement, resulting in the occupation of Thailand's Government House and international airport, and subsequent and decline in donations and financial support. The top leaders of the PAD were also arrested on charges of terrorism. The "October 7 Incident" that occurred during the 193-Day Protest became a key turning point for the PAD. It equally marks a day of major casualties of PAD members due to escalating violence and the state's use of force. Today, the PAD commemorates the October 7 Incident as its D-Day or "the Day Police Killed Innocent People"; an annual remembrance day is held to pray for those who lost their lives. During that time the PAD continued to encircle Government House, and protesters occupied all major roads around it. The PAD leaders also announced that their supporters would likewise move to encircle the Parliament Building on October 7. By morning that day, the police had bombarded protesters with over 100 tear gas canisters to carve out an access point for Prime Minister Somchai and his cabinet to enter the parliament. The protesters continued to push on, while another bomb exploded nearby. By the end of the day, the PAD suffered two deaths and 381 were injured; eleven police officers were also injured. At the end of the 193-Day Protest, the death toll had risen to eleven and the number of the injured was more than a thousand. General Chavalit Yongchaiyuth resigned as deputy prime minister and took responsibility for the day's events.

Despite successfully unblocking channels for opposition, the PAD movement displayed signs of weakening as it continued to lose popular support. This becomes even more evident in its third phase of mobilization, which began following the rise of the Democrat-led government. There are multiple factors that contributed to the weakening of the PAD movement. One key factor are the successes of the PAD movement in opening up access to power that had been blocked or rendered ineffective by the Thaksin administration. As the above paragraphs have shown, a number of channels for opposition in both formal and informal institutions were no longer closed off. The perception that the opposition "had no choice" was rapidly dissipating. With the victory and rise to power of a long-time PAD ally, the Democrats, the future looked brighter than ever for those who loathed the Thaksin regime. The honeymoon period between the PAD and the Democrats was over soon after Abhisit came to power. The Democrat Party was, in PAD's view, reneging on its promises made when both had fought together against the Thaksin regime. Resentment began to build up as the PAD felt it was not getting its share of what it wanted, even though it was responsible for Abhisit coming to power. The straw that broke the camel's back, which became the key issue of the third wave of the PAD protest, was the one involving the Thai–Cambodia territorial dispute. The more the radical wing of the PAD (the Buddhist and royalist groups) began to hold antigovernment rallies during the Abhisit administration, the more significantly the mass support of the PAD dwindled. One by one Democrat MPs, who in the past had vocally and proactively supported the PAD, now began to distance themselves from the movement.

When the PAD movement began to hold antigovernment rallies during the Abhisit administration, the mass support for the PAD dwindled. The Democrat–PAD feud weakened the movement and contributed to a number of defections, which branched out to form splinter groups. The Thai Patriot Network, for example, broke away from the PAD because they believed there was a serious situation of conflict of interest with ASTV and that it had sought to benefit from the PAD movement. At the beginning there were seventy-seven organizations in the Thai Patriot Network—all of them were disappointed with ASTV.

Parallel to the antidemocratic mobilization of the Yellow Shirts was the largely prodemocratic mobilization of the Red Shirts. The United Front for Democracy against Dictatorship (UDD), or the Red Shirts, was formed in response to the September 2006 coup and the dismantling of the Thai Rak Thai party. Much of what constituted the grievances of the Reds was political in nature, most notably political disparity and sociocultural inferiority (Sathiniramai 2010, 34–35). The UDD came together as a more organized movement in 2007 composed largely of two groups: pro-Thaksin supporters and anticoup civic groups. The latter was the first to mobilize immediately following the September 2006 coup—protesting what it believed were the country's unacceptable democratic reversal, blatant injustice, and unfairness.[16] Members of the latter did not all favor Thaksin and his policies, but they shared the deep sense of injustice for Thaksin as a result of the coup.[17] The former group, mobilizing chiefly TRT politicians and associates, was loyal to Thaksin and constituted his electoral support base with membership of no less than 5.5 million (Phongpaichit and Baker 2010). The grassroots supporters of Thaksin were mobilized initially by the Veera Muksikapong–Nathawut Saikua–Jatuporn Prompan trio through People's Television talk shows and subsequently through a series of Truth Today rallies between 2008 and 2009. The trigger for the 2010 protest, the largest ever mass protest in contemporary Thai history, came after the Supreme Court seized $1.4 billion of Thaksin's assets. With more than a million Red Shirts on the streets, what was planned as a seven-day rally[18] turned into sixty-four days of protracted protest that ended with a violent crackdown and the deaths of ninety-one people and over 2,000 injured. This was Thailand's worst episode of mass violence in contemporary times. The beleaguered Yellow Shirt–backed Democrat-led government eventually called for a new election. In the 2011 election, the PAD split from the Democrats and among themselves: one faction boycotted the election through its "Vote No" campaign, while the other contested the election under a newly founded political party, the New Politics Party.

The result was disastrous for the Yellow Shirts across the board: both the Democrats and the New Politics Party were decimated at the polls, and the boycott itself garnered less than 3 percent support from the electorate.[19] This was the end of the People's Alliance for Democracy.

The Emergence of the PDRC

As the PAD movement died down, in 2013 the People's Democratic Reform Committee (PDRC) emerged on the back of two years of low-level discontent against Yingluck Shinawatra and what her opponents deemed a continuation of her brother's regime. Since the collapse of the PAD movement, there was an opposition vacuum in desperate need of a justifiable cause and strong leadership. But the anti-Thaksin groups that had emerged between 2011 and 2013 were small and their leaders lacked the charisma and skill needed to mobilize the masses. The opposition in the early days of the Yingluck government was also neither disadvantaged nor desperate: the 2007 Constitution was penned by key figures inside the Yellow Shirts; half of the Senate was staffed with the more conservative Yellow forces; and Yingluck was conciliatory toward the military and opposition forces. The few opposition mobilizations that had appeared, such as Pitak Siam Organization and the Multi-Colored Shirts led by Dr. Tul Sithisom-wongsa, were very small, weak, and disunited. Both Sonthi Limthongkul (former PAD leader) and Suthep Taugsuban (future PDRC leader) were asked to lead the opposition but had refused on the basis that the time was not right.[20] It was not until late 2013 that the PDRC would officially come together after foreseeing again no alternative exit route from the opposition's political exclusion. Ironically, Suthep, the PDRC de facto leader, and his Democrat Party would be the last to join the most powerful unit of the entire movement.

The PDRC and the PAD shared important similarities and differences. First, key networks of the PDRC all constituted part of the PAD networks, but under different names and organizations. The dissolution of the PAD had produced four large networks led by four former PAD leaders: (1) the Student and People Network Thailand Reform; (2) Santi Asoke and the Dharma Forces; (3) the Green Group; and (4) the People's Networks from the 77 Provinces. The Student and People Network Thailand Reform (Koh Poh Toh—STR), known locally as the "Urupong protesters," united some of the smaller opposition groups together and built momentum toward what would become the PDRC. The STR was the newly reformed PAD with a close connection to Sonthi and his ASTV networks. The STR's top leaders were Nithithorn Lamleua, PAD's legal advisor, and Uthai Yodmanee, who was Ramkamhaeng University's student leader and had protested against Thaksin with the PAD. Both leaders revealed a very close relationship to former PAD leaders, particularly Suriyasai and Sonthi, and had borrowed money from PAD figures as well as utilized their kitchen and mobile toilets to cater for staff and protesters present at Urupong junction—their main protest stage.[21] All former PAD leaders appeared multiple times on their stage and publicly endorsed them as opposed to the Democrat-led protests.[22] Chamlong and his Santi Asoke crew were already staging their protests at the Makawan Rangsan Bridge, although their numbers were small. Somkiat Pongpaibul, who led the People's Networks from the 77 Provinces, joined forces with the STR early on, followed closely by Suriyasai's Green Group. The STR staged its first protest on October 10, 2013, with the mass base composed largely of university students, former PAD

TABLE 6.1. Selected media partisanship (2006–2015)

	Yellow/Yellow-Leaning (conservative-royalist)	Red/Red-Leaning (prodemocracy, pro-Thaksin)
Television (broadcast, satellite, cable)	Channel 5 Channel 9 Channel 11 Blue Sky TV* ASTV The Nation	UDD Today* DNN* Voice TV Spring News People Channel* Asia Update PTV* DTV* Peace TV*
Newspapers/Magazines	Phu chatkan (Manager) ASTV Bangkok Post Siamrath Daily News Post Today Thai Post The Nation Naeona Kom chat luek Positioning Magazine	Khao sot Prachathat* Thai Red News* D Magazine* Truth Today* Thong Daeng Magazine* Bangkok Today* Matichon Voice of Thaksin*
New Media (blogs, web message boards, online news)	Kapook News Chao Praya News Thai-ASEAN News Seri Thai Web Board	Ratchaprasong News Same Sky* Thai E-News UDD Red Blog*

Source: Sinpeng and Hemthanon (2019).
* Operations forcibly closed after the 2014 military coup

core supporters, and local residents in the Urupong area. Over the next six weeks, various former PAD networks and their respective leaders officially joined forces with the STR and Sonthi's ASTV media networks, which were helping to popularize the Urupong protests, resulting in greater popular support.[23] However, these early protests against the government protest remained limited and small in number until Suthep and his networks burst onto the scene.

Ideologically, the PDRC was more radical and antidemocratic than the PAD. The PAD's most antidemocratic stance was to endorse the military coup as well as support a stronger and politically involved monarchy. The PDRC went further by mobilizing its supporters to completely boycott the February 2014 election through their "no vote" campaign or to prevent polling stations from effectively operating on election day. In its infamous Reform Before Election campaigns, the PDRC demanded an end to elections in order to set in motion a reform process. Reforms would be put forth by the People's Assembly largely comprising nominated representatives from key occupational associations.[24] This People's Assembly would rewrite electoral and party laws to ensure that only moral and uncorrupted politicians would stand for election, and thus the National Assembly would work only in the people's interests.[25] While various PDRC leaders called for a coup during their speeches,[26] the most telling evidence of the PDRC's support for the military's putsch from 2010 was Suthep's collaboration with General Prayuth Chan o-cha, an army chief during Yingluck's government who went on to became a coup leader and prime minister. In his interview with the *Post Today*, Suthep admitted:

> Before the declaration of martial law, General Prayuth told me that I had worked so hard for so long and now it would be the military's turn to take over. . . . Now that the NCPO [National Council for Peace and Order, the military junta] had taken over the work, mobilization and proposals of the PDRC, they were open to listening to all of our suggestions.[27]

The PDRC protesters celebrated the May 22 announcement that the coup was staged by the military, while a number of ordinary people took to handing out flowers to soldiers standing in key intersections across Bangkok to express their solidarity.[28]

The key trigger for the large-scale antigovernment mobilization and subsequent establishment of the PDRC came in mid-2013 following the government's attempt to pass an amnesty bill regarded by opponents as a ploy to vindicate Thaksin, who was in self-imposed exile since the 2006 coup. More than 100,000 protesters poured onto the streets of Bangkok, some of whom occupied key government agencies, Government House, and telecommunication centers even though the bill had been defeated in the Senate.[29] Demands for Yingluck's resignation failed to subside and break the deadlock; Yingluck dissolved parliament at the end of 2013. All opposition MPs by that time had resigned, with most planning to boycott the subsequent election, an election that Yingluck hoped would break the political deadlock. The PDRC launched a reform effort ahead of the election campaign outlining its demands to indefinitely end electoral democracy to first give the country a chance to rid itself of corrupt politicians. The PDRC soon staged six-month-long protests and rallies throughout the Bangkok area, sabotaging the February 2014 election. When election day finally rolled around, nine provinces in southern Thailand, the Democrats' heartland, had no voting at all, while the overall turnout was 47 percent, the lowest in decades and a far cry from the turnout of 75 percent in the previous two elections. The No Vote movement was believed to have succeeded in keeping ten million Thais at home on election day. Combined with the unusually high number of invalid and No Vote ballots, the PDRC declared its antielection campaign a victory and was quickly followed by a military putsch in May.

Social Media and the Mobilization of the PDRC

The PDRC became the first mass digitally mediated movement in Thailand. Prior to the advent of social media in the 2010s, the Thai media landscape was highly partisan along the Yellow and Red division, the former reflecting the conservative royalist antidemocratic sentiments, while the latter represented prodemocratic and pro-Thaksin forces. These political divisions persisted as social media came on the scene. Both the PAD and the PDRC were media savvy in their own way: the PAD was effectively run by a print media mogul while the PDRC's main mobilization machine was the online sphere. The PAD was reliant on the media networks of Sonthi, owner of the Manager Media Group, which operated cable TV, (print and online) newspapers, magazines, and radio stations. The PDRC took advantage of the growing availability and accessibility of the internet and the popularity of social media to build, run, and mobilize supporters online. Similarly, Thaksin himself was an extremely media-savvy person who used his media business networks to boost his and the UDD's popularity. Yet the

PDRC was able to leverage social media for political mobilization far more effectively than its UDD rival. Part of this success was structural: Thailand was a digitally divided country in the early 2010s when internet access was expanding. According to the 2015 ICT Household Survey, the divide ran along urban–rural and socioeconomic lines: Thais who were urbanized, more educated, and more wealthy were more likely to be active users of social media.[30] These socioeconomic and demographic divides mapped onto the Red Shirt versus Yellow Shirt division: the Yellow Shirts were generally better off and more urbanized than their Red Shirt counterparts. This digital divide partially accounted for why the PDRC was better placed than the UDD to take advantage of social media mobilization.

Social media was important to the PDRC movement generally and to its leader, Suthep Taugsuban, in particular. Social media helped to significantly raise the profile of Suthep as a legitimate contender against the incumbent, Yingluck Shinawatra, who was backed by the red-shirted grassroots support. Suthep became a viable opposition leader because of his sudden popularity online. Here he completely rebranded and resurrected himself in the (new) image of a populist opposition leader. Suthep's rapidly growing online popularity provided ammunition to the beleaguered and disparate antigovernment groups that the opposition could lend forces to after the decline of the PAD. When Suthep, a member of the Democrat Party and the official opposition in the Thai parliament, announced that he, along with eight other MPs, would walk away from formal politics to start a grassroots movement, his Facebook popularity exploded.[31] Within weeks Suthep went from a rather unpopular politician to a beloved "uncle" or *kamnan*[32]—championing the cause of many Thais disenchanted with the incumbent (figure 6.2). His transformation had its beginnings online, through his personal Facebook page,[33] where he diligently documented his meteoric rise as leader of the PDRC.[34] Through it all, Suthep's Facebook profile was akin to that of a rock star: he garnered more than a 5,000 percent increase in "likes" in less than a year. For an "old-timer" who was first elected to office in 1979—decades before the internet became widely available in Thailand—Suthep's resurgence in popularity in cyberspace was both astounding and unprecedented.

Suthep's popularity on Facebook shifted the battle to gain the hearts and minds of Thais from the streets to the online world. Yingluck, whose Facebook profile was similarly popular, also witnessed the sharpest rise in her online activity at a time when she faced the greatest challenge from her opposition, the PDRC. Unlike her adversary, Suthep, social media presence was an integral part of her public profile preceding her political

TABLE 6.2. Timeline of PDRC key protests and events

October 31, 2013	Suthep led the first amnesty bill protest, Samsen train station
November 24, 2013	First mass antigovernment protests led by Suthep
November 25, 2013	Closure of 13 government buildings
November 27, 2013	Closure of government agencies and 14 other ministries
November 29, 2013	Official launch of the People's Democratic Reform Committee
November 30, 2013	Closure of main telecommunication centers and violent clash with the UDD
December 1, 2013	"D Day" 3-day attempt to take over the Government House
December 4, 2013	Lawyers Council of Thailand announced support for the PDRC
December 7, 2013	Multiple university groups joined PDRC protests
December 9 2013	Major protests to take over the Government House
	Thai Airways Union joined the PDRC protests
	Yingluck Shinawatra dissolved parliament
December 14, 2013	Academics formed the PDRC Assembly
December 21, 2013	The Democrat Party announced its boycott of the next election
	PDRC protesters en route to Bangkok from provincial chapters in Krabi, Phuket, Satun, Nakorn Sri Thammarat
December 22, 2013	Professor Seri Wongmontha and associates joined the PDRC
	Chulalongkorn University academics and students joined PDRC protests
December 23, 2013	Local protest in Udon Thani
December 25, 2013	Deadly clashes between STR protesters and government at the Thai-Japanese Sports Stadium
	Election Commission asked for election postponement
December 27, 2013	Press Conference: Bangkok Shutdown Plan
January 13, 2014	Bangkok Shutdown began at 7 major intersections in Bangkok (Ratchaprasong, Patumwan, Lumphini, Silom, Jaengwattana, Lad Phrao, Asoke)
January 17, 2014	PDRC chapters in Nakorn Sri Thammarat and Satun closed down local governments
January 19, 2014	Thai celebrities began to join PDRC protests in large numbers
January 21, 2014	Doctor and nurse groups joined PDRC protests
January 22, 2014	Yingluck government issued an emergency decree
January 26, 2014	Protesters blocked access to 49/50 advanced polling stations in Bangkok and across 10 other provinces in Thailand, mostly in the South
February 1, 2014	Violent preelection protests began at Laksi
February 2, 2014	Election day; election could not be held in 9 southern provinces
February 5, 2014	Court issued warrants for 19 PDRC leaders
February 7, 2014	4-day fundraising rallies for farmers
February 17, 2014	PDRC took over Government House
February 23, 2014	Attacks against PDRC protesters in Bangkok and Trat
February 28, 2014	All protests ceased except for Lumpini Park
March 21, 2014	February election results annulled by the Constitutional Court
May 2, 2014	PDRC-aligned senator became president of the Senate
May 7, 2014	Yingluck ordered removed from office by the Constitutional Court
May 9, 2014	Major protests organized in 6 rounds
May 18, 2014	Suthep announced mass protests beginning on May 19–22
May 20, 2014	Army chief Prayuth Chan o-cha announced marshal law
May 22, 2014	Coup d'état

career. After her party, Pheu Thai, secured a landslide victory in the 2011 election, winning 48 percent of the vote (Nelson 2013), Yingluck became the first female prime minister of Thailand. This generated a fervor on social media, with new "fan pages" being created on Facebook along the likes of "*Ruam kan chia khun ying lak phuea thai*" (Let's cheer for Yingluck Pheu Thai).[35] Her Facebook popularity, however, was starting to wane as Suthep gained ground on social media.

Suthep's interactions with his supporters via his Facebook pages between November 2013 and May 2014 suggest that it was not event driven because his online popularity occurred during both protest and nonprotest times. Each of Suthep's Facebook posts garnered on average more than 100,000 interactions from other net users; on his best day that figure rose to three million.

Interactivity online is a measure of virality: the more one's content is shared, "liked," and commented on, the more popular that content becomes.[36] Further, interactivity also helps to drive web and social media traffic, making Suthep's content more likely to appear on other users' Facebook feeds irrespective of whether that person has "liked" his page or not. The fact that Suthep's Facebook had millions of followers who interacted daily with his content, and in numbers approximating hundreds of thousands, indicated a strong online presence above all other opposition leaders, including the very popular incumbent herself. Suthep, in effect, outdid everyone on social media.

Suthep's social media networks also helped to at once unite the opposition and catapult him to its leadership. The antigovernment rallies were disparate and loosely aligned before Suthep's group emerged.[37] Some of the large opposition groups were drawn from previous PAD networks and were natural allies, such as the Dharma Forces, the People's Networks from the 77 Provinces, and the Green Group. But others were strange bedfellows such as the more right-wing People's Army Against the Thaksin Regime, led largely by former military generals, and the more left-wing Student and People Network Thailand Reform composed mostly of student leaders and activists. Initially, the former PAD networks, which had organized most of the antigovernment protests, renounced the possibility of allying with the Democrats for fear of being seen as partisan.[38] By late November, the STR recognized the strength and expansive reach of Suthep and the Democrat mobilization capacity, which had helped grow and amass significant support. On November 23, all the leaders appeared together on the Urupong stage—officially uniting their forces as one. And on November 29, the PDRC was born with Suthep chosen as the top leader. Suriyasai

Katasila, a former PAD leader and head of the Green Group, revealed that Suthep's resources and social media profile factored into the decision to concede the movement's leadership to him.[39]

Supporters of the PDRC were also more likely to be mobilized to engage in offline activities because of social media than their rival, the UDD. According to the Asia Foundation, which surveyed PDRC and UDD protesters in November 2013, PDRC supporters were much more frequent users of social media than their UDD counterparts in consuming political news and organizing themselves to join offline rallies.[40] To better understand the characteristics and dynamics of PDRC and UDD supporters online and off, I compare results from the Asia Foundation survey with a Facebook analysis of Suthep Taugsuban's and Yingluck Shinawatra's pages from November 2013 to March 2014.[41] The field survey interviewed 315 respondents—154 were PDRC protest participants in five different locations—and the other 161 were UDD supporters who were interviewed at the Rajamangkla Stadium where the UDD held a large rally to counter the PDRC rallies. Yingluck's and Suthep's Facebook pages, respectively, were chosen as the closest proxies to UDD and PDRC support because the movements were most mobilized on Facebook via their leaders (de facto or otherwise) and not on organizational pages, and both pages were of equal size.

The highly polarized media ecosystem, noted by the Red- and Yellow-divided media outlets in figure 6.1, did not dissipate with the advent of social media. Instead of providing "neutral" spaces for public discussions where people of different political beliefs could exchange ideas, social media is shown to have entrenched and contributed to a deepening of the polarization. This chapter is particularly concerned not just with political polarization but also with other societal and economic cleavages that were present in the offline world. Figure 6.2 shows a list of some of the most popular political groups on Facebook in 2015, excluding the PDRC. The social media space was divided largely along the red-shirted and yellow-shirted camps: much of the former were concentrated on the UDD Thailand official page while the Yellow Shirts were more spread out across groups. Moreover, the Yellow Shirts were more numerous than the Red Shirts, both in the number of Yellow Shirt–affiliated groups and in the size of their online support base. Finally, the "Blue" groups, which were neither Red nor Yellow, were the least popular and attracted the smallest support base online. These observations of political groups on Facebook provide some indication of a politically divided social media in Thailand.

To demonstrate how polarization occurs on social media in the Thai

	PDRC	Suthep's Page	UDD	Yingluck's Page
Gender				
Female	50%	51%	48%	44%
Male	49%	49%	51%	56%
Current Residence				
Greater Bangkok	31%	51%	47%	55%
Central	10%	14%	12%	9%
North	8%	6%	14%	16%
Northeast	7%	8%	22%	16%
South	44%	21%	5%	4%
Education				
High school and below	14%	34%	44%	44%
Vocational and bachelor's degree	74%	65%	49%	55%
Master's degree or above	12%	1%	7%	1%
Occupational skills				
High skilled	22%	20%	11%	21%
Low skilled	6%	37%	30%	39%
Government	16%	14%	10%	15%
Entrepreneur / Owner	30%	20%	5%	16%
Other	1%	10%	6%	9%

Figure 6.1. Interaction rate of Suthep and Yingluck's Facebook pages

case, new data from Facebook was collected and analyzed. I performed a "data dump" by extracting all Facebook activities from both pages during the specified time period, a total of over six million data points. I calculated the interaction rates (Facebook shares, likes, and comments) of the public pages of Yingluck Shinawatra and Suthep Taugsuban, and then chose the five busiest days of each page to analyze. I then randomly selected 300 *ano-nymized* comments, which were computed using the software Quintly, for each page for a total of 600 comments. Third, I manually analyzed the pro-files of individuals who had posted comments on Suthep's and Yingluck's pages. I consider "comments" to be an active form of political participation, unlike "sharing" or "liking," which merely requires the unconscious click of a button. Commenting requires the user to actively read the comments above and form a cogent response, and thus represents a more robust indicator of political participation online.

Profile analysis of the randomly selected comments was performed anonymously using both the software Quintly and manual searches of key profile information voluntarily provided by individuals who commented on these pages. Key profile information included (1) gender; (2) current location; (3) birthplace; (4) occupation; and (5) education level. For gender, I note male and female (self-declared gender). Location and birthplace were indicated by province, which were then categorized into five regions: Greater Bangkok, North, Northeast, Central, and South. Taking into account the fact that a large number of Thai people live outside their hometown (and many return to vote on election day), it is imperative that we can analyze the differences in Facebook engagement based on both types of location. For example, a person living in Bangkok whose birthplace is Surat Thani (southern Thailand) may comment positively on Suthep's page because Surat Thani is a PDRC stronghold. Occupation and education levels are important socioeconomic indicators, which I also use as proxies for income, since there is no available income data on a Facebook profile. Occupations are divided into five major categories: (1) high skilled; (2) low skilled; (3) government; (4) entrepreneur/business owner; and (5) other. Educational attainment is divided into three levels: (1) high school; (2) diploma and bachelor's degree; and (3) master's degree and above.

The above analysis also gets to the issue of social cleavages particularly based on regional identities and economic status. The PAD–UDD divisions, as discussed in previous chapters, have been shaped by partisanship, regional identities, and class. Supporters of the PAD and the PDRC were largely from the upper rungs of the middle class, largely urban and more educated, and drawn primarily from the Democrat Party's support base in Bangkok, eastern Thailand, and southern Thailand. The UDD, on the other hand, drew from the lower rungs of the middle class, were less educated, and reflected Thaksin's strongholds in parts of Bangkok, the North, and the Northeast. In terms of demographics, social media users should tend to be from younger age groups given that young adults in general are the primary users of social media; this should be reflected in our survey regardless of political affiliation. If social media could break the regional, political, social, and economic cleavages, we should not see the same divisions reflected online. However, if social media entrenches existing cleavages, then we should see the same patterns observed offline in the online world.

Why do socioeconomic profiles of social media users matter? Understanding the demographic, social, and economic backgrounds, and those online in comparison of those offline, helps to indicate whether social media can reduce or entrench participatory inequality—the unequal level of political participation due to entrenched socioeconomic cleavages. Norris (2001) framed this debate close to two decades ago between two sets of arguments. The mobilization thesis posits that the growing ubiquity of the internet in general invites new groups into politics that were previously disengaged, excluded, or underrepresented. By lowering the costs of participation and offering self-actualizing platforms for engagement, social media motivates previously inactive groups like young people to become involved in politics. The reinforcement thesis, on the contrary, sees the growth in information availability and social media use as having little meaningful impact on the patterns of online political participation. While the political opportunities to engage in politics may widen more than ever, long-standing patterns of inequalities can still persist in domains such as income and education given that engaging in political life online requires additional resources to mobilize individuals beyond simply access (Hargittai and Hsieh 2013). Schlozman, Verba, and Brady (2010) call the internet "weapons of the strong" based on their finding of a powerful and durable association between socioeconomic status and political participation online in their extensive analysis of the 2008 Pew Internet and American Life survey. Thus, internet use only closes the political knowledge and participation gaps among lower socioeconomic status individuals.

The comparison of socioeconomic profiles of political participants online and offline during the 2013–14 large-scale protests in Thailand provides a strong indicator that the participants on Facebook were distinct from protesters on the streets regardless of their political affiliation. Social media, Sinpeng (2017) argues, has the potential to equalize existing structural inequalities in a polity by providing space for political engagement to those who might not be able to participate otherwise. The profile comparison shows that there are remarkable similarities between PDRC and UDD fans online. This, compared with a much wider gap that existed between their street-level participants, shows that the online avenue of political engagement helps to reduce socioeconomic gaps between participants regardless of political affiliation. Sixty percent of PDRC fans and 56 percent of UDD fans on Facebook had completed postsecondary education compared to 86 percent and 50 percent, respectively, for the street protesters, shows that the gap in levels of education in the supporters of the two movements significantly narrows in cyberspace. Similarly, the largest

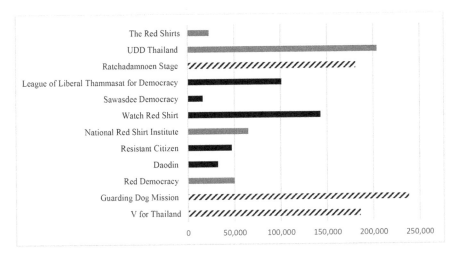

Figure 6.2. Political pages/groups and their number of likes on Facebook (2015)

share of online supporters in both camps had *low-skilled* occupations—a stark contrast from their street protesters where 30 percent of the UDD were low skilled as opposed to a mere 6 percent of the PDRC. Facebook is thus not an arena for the political engagement of the privileged. Rather, in some cases it offers opportunities for participation for the less educated and less skilled in comparison to street protests.

Do the same socioeconomic inequalities observed among the PDRC and UDD street protesters carry over into cyberspace? The findings suggest that the socioeconomic differentials were greater *within* group than across group in the case of the PDRC. While the Facebook political participants in the two movements generally had higher levels of socioeconomic status than the overall population and the control group, the same cannot be concluded between the street-level and online participants. For the UDD, the hypothesis seems to hold: its Facebook fans were slightly more educated and held more skilled occupations than those surveyed at the protest site. In contrast, the opposite is true for the PDRC whose street protesters were significantly more endowed socioeconomically than their supporters on Facebook. A question might arise whether it would be possible that more PDRC participants at protest rallies used social media, which might then lead to a higher proportion of the online participants being better off. The Asia Foundation survey reveals that to be true: 32 percent the PDRC supporters heard about the rallies via smartphone or the internet, while only 5 percent of the UDD supporters did so. Yet, even though more PDRC street protesters used social media than the Red Shirts, it still does not explain why they were better off than their peers on Facebook. Why is this the case? While this chapter cannot provide a more definite answer to this question given the lack of additional empirical data, some tentative arguments can be made. One explanation for the wide margins within the PDRC movement itself is that the locations of the rallies were in central business districts in Bangkok; this may indicate that the street participants were likely to be professionals (i.e., office workers). Moreover, the PDRC rallies might be more resource-intensive, given the six-month protest period across multiple locations in the city. This could mean that those who physically attended protests also helped contribute to the movement's activities at rally sites, potentially meaning they would be wealthier than the PDRC participants on Facebook.

The regional divisions among the support base of the PDRC and UDD do carry forward to the online world. The field survey data shows that supporters of Yingluck Shinawatra approximate her party's electoral strongholds wherein Bangkok, the North, and the Northeast of Thailand are the most important. Similarly, Suthep's electoral base included areas where the Democrat Party was strongest: Bangkok, the Central region, and the Southern region. The Facebook analysis notes a significant overrepresentation of the Bangkokian fan base, with each group comprising more than 50 percent of total fan numbers in this study. Nonetheless, the North and Northeastern regions and the South and Central regions accounted for the second and third source regions, respectively, for the UDD and PDRC. This suggests that regional divides cut across into the online world even though the means of engagement vary. Moreover, the fact that street participants derived from the provinces more than from Bangkok, despite all rallies being held in Bangkok, indicates that the dynamics of mobilization by the two political movements were different in the offline and online spaces. On the streets, movement leaders were likely to depend more on their networks in stronghold areas to recruit and mobilize supporters who would then go to Bangkok and rally. Online, however, it matters far less where their fans came from, and the overrepresentation of Bangkok-based supporters was likely because the protests were in the capital city and people felt more emotionally engaged than if they were from further away.

To measure a degree of polarization, I performed a network analysis of Suthep's and Yingluck's Facebook pages. This inquiry was specifically designed to address the question of whether or not social media can

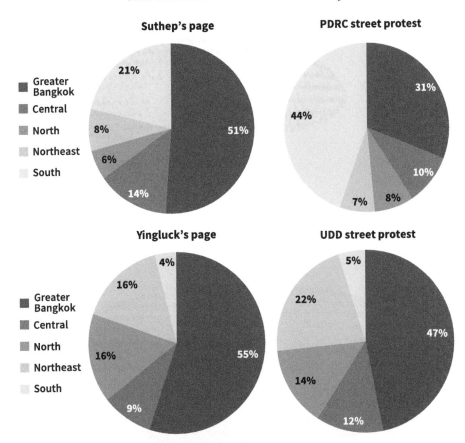

Figure 6.3. Current residence, by region, of PDRC and UDD protesters (street) and Suthep and Yingluck supporters (online)

entrench political divisions. The Facebook posts on December 25, 2013 from each leader's pages were chosen for analysis as a sample of a key post during the 2013–14 protests.[42] Given the large networks of both pages, with in excess of 3,000,000 "likes," it was not feasible to perform a network analysis over the same time frame as the socioeconomic profile data. I used "R" to extract raw data from Facebook posts and conduct an analysis on the networks of "likes," "co-likes" (liking of both pages), comments, and co-comments (commenting on both pages) to infer the extent to which the networks of both pages have cross-over membership. If deep political divisions between the PDRC and UDD exist online as much as offline, we should observe few co-comments and co-likes between members of

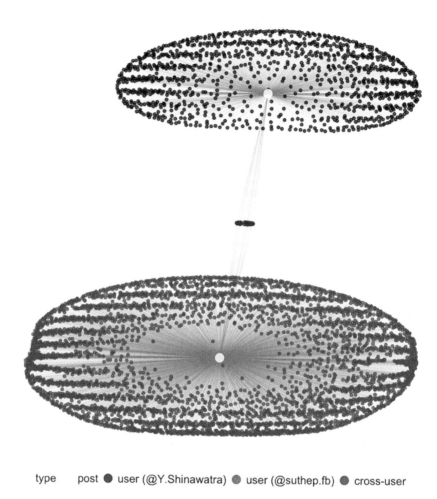

type   post ● user (@Y.Shinawatra) ● user (@suthep.fb) ● cross-user

Figure 6.4. Network visualization of commenters on Suthep's and Yingluck's Facebook pages

the two networks. Content analyses of comments on both Suthep's and Yingluck's pages were performed, drawing on the same data as the profile analysis. Comments were manually analyzed and separated into two large categories: (1) praise/attack; and (2) policy issue. The results are then compared to the motivations of protesters at rally sites from the Asia Foundation Survey. If Facebook represented a mere echo chamber for individuals, we would expect the comments to remain partisan and align with the offline protest movement.

The Facebook network analysis confirms a deep political division between supporters of the PDRC and UDD online. Out of the 41,704 likes on Yingluck's post and the corresponding 48,891 on Suthep's, there were only 236 "co-likes," representing a mere 0.3 percent. Co-likes constitute a measure for Facebook users who like both Suthep's and Yingluck's posts. Similarly, there were 1,163 comments on Yingluck's post and 4,216 on Suthep's but only 28 co-comments. The very low number of co-likes and co-comments indicate how little PDRC and UDD supporters on Facebook interact with each other's networks. These findings suggest that the PDRC and UDD communities act as online "echo chambers"—polarized political groupings that communicate almost exclusively within their respective groups with little crossover to other groups. There is a rich literature in media studies and psychology that notes the prevalence of confirmation bias and selective news exposure on social media that entrenches preexisting views of the political world, thereby creating "filter bubbles" and echo chambers (Knobloch-Westerwick and Johnson 2014; Nikolov et al. 2015). People selectively consume information that conforms to their prior beliefs, and they especially trust information from authoritative sources like politicians and established media outlets that align with their views (Del Vicario et al. 2016). Suthep and Yingluck were both hugely popular on social media and as such attracted a large number of followers who engaged with their content in order to perpetuate these leaders' views as opposed to creating their own. The network visualization in figure 6.4 demonstrates well how PDRC and UDD supporters alike constituted polarized echo chambers, contributing to the further entrenchment of the political divisions in Thai politics.

Additional content analysis of comments from PDRC supporters shows that 90 percent of comments on Suthep's Facebook page during the Bangkok Shutdown protests were supportive of Suthep's posts. This means that the vast majority of Suthep's 2.7 million Facebook "likes" went in tandem with the PDRC ethos, amplifying antidemocratic support for a movement that demanded an end to electoral democracy. Among the issues most prevalent in the comment sections of Suthep's page, praise for his efforts in fighting preelection reforms was the most prominent. Other issues in support of Suthep and the PDRC included (1) opposition to Thaksin and his family; (2) opposition to the amnesty bill; and (3) protection of the monarchy.[43] Moreover, the Facebook comments were highly polarized, as more than 90 percent of comments either supported or opposed the movements—very few were neutral. Such results confirm previous findings in Groemping's (2014) study of partisanship in the Thai 2014 election. Facebook, he argues, played the role of echo chamber rather than a neutral space for deliberation (Groemping 2014). Perhaps such outcomes should have been expected given that these were the public pages of popular movement leaders. But the idea, nonetheless, that social media can create spaces for exchanging ideas, creating new meaning, and regenerating new discourses was not at all evident in these political pages.

The findings in this chapter provide empirical evidence that social media use of political engagement may help narrow the existing socioeconomic structural inequalities in a society by providing the less privileged a space for activism. Despite a significant degree of digital inequality in Thailand, given the mere 40 percent of the population that have access to the internet and the fact that those "wired" tend to be socioeconomically better off than the wider population, we cannot observe a selective bias in the participants of the two political movements on Facebook. Instead, we see that the socioeconomic gap *narrows* in terms of the profiles of those engaged in online politics from what was observed on the streets. The online political participants of the PDRC and UDD were more similar to one another than were their street protesters. The UDD supporters, generally of lower socioeconomic status than their PDRC counterparts, had similar profiles among street-level and Facebook participants: the largest share had secondary education but low-skilled occupations. Most came from Bangkok, the North, or the Northeast, although a majority of online fans were Bangkok-based. The PDRC supporters were exactly the opposite: a vast majority of their street protesters were highly educated and held high-skilled or government jobs, while their online peers were less educated, and many held low-skilled occupations. For both the PDRC and UDD, online political engagement offers opportunities for political activism to those with some education but not skilled jobs.

Moreover, the partisanship of the online UDD and PDRC networks indicates that Facebook would not help to ameliorate the deep polarization in Thailand as a result of a decade long political crisis. Instead, as the content analysis of comments show, Facebook can act to exacerbate the conflict by, on the one hand, bringing a new section of society into political engagement while, on the other, providing an echo chamber for likeminded users rather than constructing a space for deliberation of opposing views. The implication for Thai politics going forward, as Facebook penetration continues to expand, is that the political conflict in Thailand will enlarge rather than dissipate due to a low likelihood of cross-over communication and deliberation of thoughts and ideas.

Conclusion

Social media became a game changer for antidemocratic mobilization in Thailand. After the opening of channels for opposition politics in the post-2006 coup period, the PAD began to suffer a continuous loss of popular support; it was further weakened by the movement's internal squabbles. When another Thaksin-aligned party, Pheu Thai, was elected in 2011, the PAD's decline accelerated, leaving an opposition vacuum in the Thai polity that no viable political opposition movement could fill. The mid-2010s were also marked by a period of heightened connectivity in Thai society in which the number of internet and social media users exploded, particularly in the country's urban and economically advantageous areas where telecommunications infrastructure was available, and whose residents were sufficiently well off to afford smartphones and tablets. The PDRC emerged at this critical juncture: increased marginalization of opposition voices under the Yingluck government, on the one hand, and increased social media connectivity, on the other. However, the dissolution of the PAD had resulted in many small and largely ineffective opposition groups, unable to either unite or mount any kind of credible mobilization. It was not until Suthep Taugsuban, along with several former Democrat Party members, had left parliamentary politics to pursue grassroots street politics that the PDRC was eventually born under his helm. And it was social media that played a critical role in transforming Suthep from an unpopular politician to a beloved protest leader and ultimate leader of an opposition movement that mass-produced millions of supporters online and hundreds of thousands more on the streets. Suthep's transformation into one of the most popular political figures in Thailand took place on Facebook; here, his popularity skyrocketed, despite his having no experience in grassroots protest politics and being a career politician since the 1970s. His online popularity helped unite the disparate and disunited opposition groups and win him its ultimate leadership. The PDRC began its life based on Suthep's social media popularity, and its supporters continued to rely heavily on social media to mobilize online and offline protest campaigns that led eventually to another coup d'état in May 2014.

Findings from an analysis of the social media profile of the PDRC demonstrates equally that social media entrenches social and regional cleavages, deepens political polarization, and amplifies antidemocratic voices. More importantly is that the antidemocratic contributions social media made to the PDRC movement were possible for the sole reason that

Suthep was skilled at social media marketing. Other opposition figures, never having experienced success in garnering online popular support, did not contribute to the movement in the same way due to their lack of reach and depth in online networks and in online popularity to spread their messages. Suthep was the case of a social media "top influencer," making his online impact all the more powerful. Contrary to earlier optimism that social media could be democracy's savior by empowering ordinary people to fight against elites' autocratic tendencies, the PDRC has shown that it was the masses themselves who were propelling the antidemocratic movement. When social media became a tool for public communication, that gap widened, rather than narrowing, existing divisions in society be they social, demographic, regional, or economic. Existing societal cleavages became entrenched because conversations online became polarized and siloed, thereby giving prominence to antidemocratizing voices rather than neutralizing them. On social media, the PDRC became an online echo chamber, where only yellow-shirted supporters communicated, alienating those with differing opinions. Much of the content shared on PDRC pages, numbering in a million data points, over the course of their protest activities of late 2013 to early 2014 showed that the majority of supporters endorsed Suthep's antidemocratic principles of calling a halt to electoral democracy and enhancing the political power of nondemocratic institutions.

This social-media-centric analysis of the PDRC mobilization does not mean that other avenues of mobilization are not important components of a social movement. Suthep became the most powerful opposition leader not only because of his social media popularity but also because he had the networks and resources from the Democrat Party and was himself a wealthy individual. But it was his popularity online that allowed him to gain popular support, grow his support base extensively in a very short period of time, and unite the opposition groups into one formidable movement that eventually paved the way for a military putsch. His large online following also helped fund the PDRC itself, which helped to crowdfund the movement's protest activities.[44] The PDRC better leveraged social media than its UDD counterpart: its fans were more "wired," relied more on social media for news and activities of the movement, and turned out in much higher numbers in offline protests due to what they had seen communicated online. The profile differentiation between the PDRC online and street protesters also shows how distinct the online crowd was from its street-level one, suggesting that those supporting the PDRC online were unlikely to be those who might have been mobilized offline without prior engagement with social media. Social media made it possible for the PDRC's antidemocratic agenda to gain ground with millions of people in a matter of weeks through its online networks. A second military coup in less than a decade, once considered unviable, became plausible and less costly, and this can be attributed partially to the PDRC's dominant political discourse online.

SEVEN

Crowdsourcing Dictatorship

Who supports military dictatorship and why? This chapter uses social media data to analyze support for the antidemocratic mobilization of the People's Democratic Reform Committee (PDRC) and the subsequent military dictatorship, which lasted from 2014 to 2019. Following the 2014 military putsch, which the PDRC saw as a success, the movement had to find a new identity and purpose postcoup. This chapter seeks to understand why people supported the PDRC not just before the coup but also after the military government had been installed. This fills a gap in the literature on regime change, which tends to be focused on explaining support for democratic collapse and remains silent on this support in its aftermath. How do people justify military dictatorships once they have been installed, and why do they support such a regime? The empirical findings from this chapter may present the first-ever evidence of prodictatorship support following a collapse of democracy.

This chapter constructs an original dataset based on fifteen million Facebook data points on all the activities of the five most popular procoup pages in Thailand for a three-year period following the May 2014 coup. I refer to them in this study as the "procoup groups" as they mobilized largely in opposition to an elected government and demanded military intervention to topple such a government. We know less about their online behavior after the coup and whether one could assume their support for the subsequent military government. Social media is not solely a platform for political participation and mobilization. It is a new way to gather political preferences. Recent studies examining the accuracy of data extracted from social media in comparison to traditional public opinion polls reveal social media data to closely approximate polling data (Ceron et al. 2014; Skoric, Liu and Jaidka 2020). Mining social media data is also increasingly being used to measure mass preferences in authoritarian regimes where accurate mechanisms for detecting public opinion are largely absent or seriously flawed (Qiang 2011; Gunitsky 2015). Based on the use of Latent Dirichlet Allocation topic modeling, the findings suggest that the procoup networks of supporters varied greatly in both motivations and support for the dictatorship they had fought for. Contrary to the prevailing notion that a military government would be necessary to "protect the monarchy," royalism was neither the driving force of support across groups nor what united them. Instead, some groups were motivated by their desire for particular policies; others were promilitary for ideological reasons. It was clear that there was a genuine decline in support for the military among the majority of the PDRC supporters with much of their discontent stemming from economic and policy issues. However, prodictatorship support was maintained among the most staunch promilitary groups within the PDRC networks.

By comparing social media data among PDRC key groups during the PDRC mobilization one year prior to the May 2014 coup, the findings suggest important differences in preferences before and after the military putsch. Anti–Red Shirt and antigovernment sentiment, to speak generally, was the most important uniting factor for PDRC's antidemocratic mobilization across all key support groups, not royalism. Other motivating factors varied across groups; but again, royalism was the least prominent feature of all groups' preferences.

The social network analysis of procoup groups during the military dictatorship also demonstrates significant divides across groups. First, the low interaction rate within the prodictatorship networks implies a vertically strong but horizontally weak base in support of the regime. Second, the promilitary supporters were motivated by ideological and not material-based preferences. Third, the mapping of anti- and promilitary communities suggests polarization during the dictatorship period and very little evidence of national reconciliation, this being the primary objective of the military junta. Further, the decline in support of the PDRC under the junta's government instead boded badly for political parties aligned with PDRC leaders in the subsequent March 2019 election: the result was an embarrassing defeat of the PAD/PDRC successor parties.

The chapter is divided into four parts. The first part explains the methodology, outlining justification for the social media data mining tools used. The second part discusses the results from the precoup sentiment analysis of the PDRC. The third part discusses findings from the postcoup analysis of the same groups within the PDRC that were behind the 2014 coup. Social network analysis of procoup networks during the military dictatorship is also analyzed. Lastly, implications of the social media data analysis of PDRC networks before and after the coup are outlined.

Mining Public Opinion Data on Facebook

Thailand serves as a crucial case to examine online sentiment toward a dictatorship not only because it recently experienced a transition from a democracy to a military government. It is significant also because the procoup supporters were largely networked on Facebook through the PDRC movement. Findings from chapter 6 and additional research on the mobilization of the broad procoup PDRC movement demonstrate the central role played by Facebook in expanding and mobilizing popular support for the military putsch (Sinpeng 2017; Groemping and Sinpeng 2018). There is a focus here on the postcoup authoritarian regime precisely because so little is known about the motivations and sentiment among these supposed supporters of the regime. This chapter is especially interested in groups that have been in favor of such regime change for the simple reason that in the climate of an authoritarian regime they are more likely to express their sentiment online than are opposition groups. Facebook is an appropriate site of inquiry especially in cases where the procoup groups are networked online for engagement and mobilization. It means that this social media platform already plays a key role in inducing regime change and should thus remain as an important and relevant site of support for the new authoritarian regime following democratic breakdown.

The key questions addressed in this chapter are the following:

1. What type of discourses are present within the procoup networks before and after the coup?
2. Do the motivations for supporting military dictatorship vary, and if so, how?
3. Are the motivations for supporting military dictatorship following a coup different from or similar to procoup support? If different, how?

Data was collected in two tranches. The first constitutes the precoup data, which includes the top 200 comments of all Facebook posts on the pages of the five most popular procoup groups during the period of May 22, 2013 to May 22, 2014—one year preceding the coup. The second tranche of data was collected between May 23, 2014 and May 23, 2017, constituting a period of three years following the military coup. There is an assumption here that groups that were supportive of military intervention would also be supportive of the successive authoritarian regime. The popularity of these pages was measured by the overall number of "likes" on Facebook (figure 7.1). The public pages of Suthep Thaugsuban, the People's Democratic Reform Committee, V for Thailand, Thailand Informed, and Army Supporter were thus selected.[1] All five of these groups formed part of the PDRC that helped bring down the elected government of Yingluck Shinawatra in the May 2014 coup. Note that groups that were part of the offline PDRC mobilization, such as the STR, are not included here—not because they were insignificant to the procoup networks, but because their pages online were not popular in comparison to others. Again, the main emphasis here is on online sentiment via Facebook, which means that some groups that were crucial offline but not popular online are thus excluded.

Facebook data were extracted directly from Facebook using R, Graph API, and specifically the Rfacebook package developed by Pablo Barbera.[2] The entire dataset contained approximately fifteen million data points, which included all posts by the page administrators, page "likes," comments, replies to comments, "likes" of comments, and shares for the postcoup period. Together these pages generated 3,488 posts, 13.3 million "likes," 585,579 shares, and 718,069 comments. An additional 246,288 comments drawn from the top 200 from the precoup period were also collected to render a comparative analysis between the pre- and postcoup periods. Comments became the focus of the text analysis as "comments"

TABLE 7.1. Key Facebook page statistics (post-coup)

	Suthep Thaugsuban	PDRC	Thailand Informed	V for Thailand	Army Supporter
Original Name (in Thai)	สุเทพ เทือก สุบรรณ	มูลนิธิมวลมหา ประชาชนเพื่อ การปฏิรูป ประเทศไทย	มั่นใจคนไทยเกิน ล้าน ขอบคุณ ทหาร	V for Thailand	คนไทยสนับสนุน กองทัพไทยใน การปกป้องชาติ ศาสน์ กษัตริย์
Posts	459	525	504	1,000	1,000
Likes	11,575,624	286,767	241,395	697,602	449,016
Comments	616,461	8,511	3,905	58,180	31,012
Shares	274,189	16,204	16,339	128,695	150,152

Note: "Likes" are the number of "likes" of posts, comments, and replies, not the page likes; English names of pages are based on the translated names on their Facebook pages and do not reflect the author's own translation
Time frame: May 23, 2014 to May 23, 2017

are considered the most active and nuanced expression of a user's sentiment on Facebook. Unlike "liking" or sharing, comments included texts that could be further analyzed. Following this, a database of the top 200 comments for each post for all five pages was created in a separate file for manual text analysis. Although R was used to extract this data, Python had to be used to analyze the Thai text because the only natural language processing algorithm for Thai is available in Python. The biggest problem with the Thai language in any kind of computational text analysis is word segmentation because the language does not have natural spaces between words like Romance or Germanic languages. The ThaiNLP package offers six algorithms for word segmentation and all six were run to manually examine its accuracy. Algorithms with the highest accuracy were chosen. Stop words were also then removed from the data.

Text analysis was performed both quantitatively and qualitatively in three stages. First, to get a rough sense of important words in the comments section of the Facebook pages, a keyword count package was run on Python. Words were counted by their frequency and then ranked from high to low. A list of the top ten most frequently used words was produced for each page (figure 7.2). The results provide some indicator of potential issues that were heavily discussed in each of the pages. For both Suthep and the PDRC, discussion about Suthep personally—with reference to *kamnan* and "uncle"—dominated. This likely related to his being ordained as a Buddhist monk immediately following the coup. As for V for Thailand, it was difficult to discern exactly what may have dominated the page's discussion, but it could be inferred that it was antigovernment. For Thailand Informed, many of the comments seemed to refer to its followers' nationalistic pride, and for Army Supporter, their love for the army and the monarchy. This keyword count method can inform us on the frequency of term usage, and gives a very rough idea—at times, vaguely so—about the issues that might dominate the page comments. On their own, the word frequencies are insufficient evidence of what might be discussed as they does not compute which certain terms are likely to occur with what others—it merely ranks terms and their frequencies.

To better understand what users of these procoup pages were talking about, including what might be driving the discourse for coup support (precoup) and dictatorship support (postcoup) on Facebook, a more in-depth analysis of comments was needed. To achieve this, I performed topic modeling on the complete set of comment text across the five Facebook pages to examine which "topics" might be fueling the discourse. Topic modeling is a prevalent machine learning method in the natural language processing area. The topic modeling algorithms statistically analyze a big collection of documents (corpus) in order to extract a number of "topics" that represent the document in an abstract way. Each topic is a probability distribution over all words in the vocabulary that shows how likely the words will be used together in a document. Therefore, the "topics" generated by the topic modeling algorithm show words that often occur together, although these may or may not be interpreted as meaningful word clusters by a human reviewer. In this study, the Thai Facebook comments form a corpus for the topic modeling, where each individual comment is treated as a document, and ten topics are extracted using the Latent Dirichlet Allocation topic modeling algorithm[3] using the open source Python machine learning library—Scikit-Learn.[4] Through this approach, the top-thirty most salient terms were computed and the relevance matrix computed to form the ten most likely topics and their probability for term co-occurrence for each page. A list of the top ten topics per page was then produced.

To improve the quality and saliency of topics further, a manual text analysis was performed to make sense of the topics identified through Latent Dirichlet Allocation. For each of the posts made by the page administrator, the 200 most popular comments were extracted using R. The most popular comments were those receiving the highest level of interaction (liking, sharing, commenting, replies). The manual checking allows for more accurate interpretation of topics that are grounded in possible contexts and specific events surrounding the use of certain words. For instance, on the topic of "democracy," there can be a number of different interpretations as to what each page discussion inferred about democracy. The associated

TABLE 7.2. Ten most frequently used words, May 23, 2014 to May 23, 2017

Suthep	amen (สาธุ), uncle (ลุง), kamnan (กำนัน) fight (สู้), together (ด้วยกัน) express gratitude (อนุโมทนา), people (พวกเรา), sir (ท่าน), merit (บุญ), good (ดี)
PDRC	uncle (ลุง), amen (สาธุ), give (ให้), kamnan (กำนัน), may Buddha (ขอพระ), benevolence (พระคุณ), fight (สู้), recover (หาย), prosper (เจริญ), express gratitude (อนุโมทนา)
V for Thailand	มัน (they—vulgar), people (พวกเรา), มึง (you—vulgar) good (ดี), die (ตาย), no way (ไม่ได้), our country (ประเทศเรา), Thai (ไทย) culprit (ตัวการ), this way (แบบนี้)
Thailand Informed	Thai people (คนไทย), thank you (ขอบคุณ), ultimate (สุดยอด), support (กำลังใจ), nation (ชาติ), for what (เพื่ออะไร), protect (คุ้มครอง), country (ประเทศ), citizens (ประชาชน), all/everyone (ทุกคน)
Army Supporter	long live (ทรงพระเจริญ), army (ทหาร), king (พระองค์), lasting (ยิ่งๆ), long live (ยืนนาน), Thai people (คนไทย), only do (ทำแต่), love (รัก), wishing (ขอให้), live well (อยู่ดี)

Note: Excludes stop words.

terms for this topic include "politicians," "election," "vested interests," and "bad." Without manually checking the top comments, one could perhaps infer that V for Thailand, an antidemocratic movement, views elections as illegitimate in Thailand because of corrupt politicians. Through manual verification, one can assign a positive or negative sentiment toward the topic and confirm or unconfirm the topic interpretation. In the case of V, the majority of comments that discussed the issue of democracy referred to the opinion that elections do not equate with democracy—especially in the Thai case where they considered politicians to be bad and not legitimate even when elected.

Understanding PDRC Support for the 2014 Coup

What can millions of Facebook data points tell us about motivations to support the PDRC movement? Opposing the Red Shirts, which the PDRC saw as represented by the incumbent, Yingluck Shinawatra, was the single most important reason for supporting the PDRC. Anti–Red Shirt sentiment was also the only common category of topics, other than royalism, shared by all five pages (figure 7.3). Topic modeling analysis shows that 60 percent of comments posted on Suthep's page could be categorized as anti–Red Shirt, with 52 percent for Army Supporter, 31 percent for Thailand Informed, and 8 percent for the PDRC. Suthep's page was the most popular of all pages, amassing 2.5 million likes just before the coup, and the fact that more than half of all of the top comments on his page were about opposing the Red Shirts speaks volumes to how much hatred the PDRC supporters had toward their adversaries.

Examining more deeply the choice of words most frequently used within the anti–Red Shirt topic, the analysis shows that most of the terms associated with the "Reds" were derogatory and personal. Terms such as "buffalo," "stupid," "no brain," "dog," and "evil" were used to describe the Red Shirts. These keywords have long been used throughout both PAD and PDRC rallies and protests, and corresponded well with the Yellow-Shirt elitist notions outlined in chapter 5 in which they considered themselves as superior, more educated, more moral, and more worthy of being citizens of Thailand and the rightful group to have a say in who should govern. The Red Shirts are, on the other hand, "subhuman," and neither sufficiently educated nor good enough to matter in Thai society. The Red Shirts are immoral and ungrateful and therefore undeserving of being treated as members of Thai society. The PDRC anti–Red Shirts sentiment

Percentage
(%)

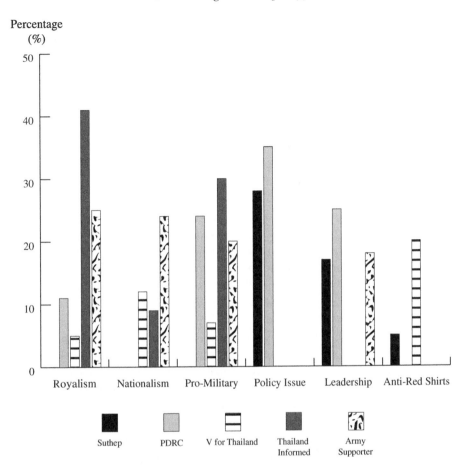

Figure 7.1. Results of topic probability by page during one year preceding the 2014 coup (May 22, 2013 to May 22, 2014)

represents a continuation of the sentiment expressed by the PAD, both at the leadership and grassroot levels.

Royalism is another topic that is shared by all support groups of the PDRC, albeit at a much lower level than anti–Red Shirt topics. This is the most surprising result of the precoup PDRC sentiment analysis since royalism is the very banner that was used to unite all groups opposing the government to form the PDRC. If relying solely on speeches made by the leaders as evidence of what the PDRC support base looked like, we would have likely overestimated the royalist sentiment among PDRC support- ers. This content analysis shows that royalism did not feature prominently across the top five most popular PDRC Facebook groups before the coup.

Figure 7.1 clearly shows that discussion on royalism featured in less than 10 percent of all the top comments on Suthep's and PDRC's pages, as those which constituted the majority of Facebook conversations on the PDRC at the time. A manual check of keywords associated with royalism suggest that most words were associated with King Bhumibol's birthday on December 5, with people posting their happy birthday wishes to the king via Facebook. The manual investigation of keywords also suggests that citing their love for the monarch as a reason for mobilizing with the PDRC was not at all prevalent across any of the popular online PDRC networks.

There is clear divergence across the five Facebook groups on other topics discussed by their supporters. One-third of the comments on Suthep's page and one-quarter on the PDRC Facebook page were about glorifying the leadership of Suthep. This is of no surprise since the PDRC page is administered by the same team that also managed Suthep's page and comments tended to be in response to page posts. But the comments of both pages did not exactly align: the PDRC's comments were heavily slanted toward nationalism topics, with keywords such as "our land," "our nation," "country," "Thai nation," "Thailand," and "nation" being very prevalent.

The fact that the promilitary sentiment is only concentrated among the comments of the Army Supporter and Thailand Informed suggests that popular support for the military as an institution important to Thai politics is not widespread even among the supporters of the movement demanding a coup. Promilitary sentiment is instead highly prevalent only in Thailand Informed, which constitutes the smallest number of "likes" across all five groups. A manual verification of promilitary comments also reveals that the sentiment tends to be general toward the military institution and not necessarily directly related to its role in politics. Nonetheless, the key terms associated with support for the military were well aligned with how Thais were brought up to believe in the military institution: "army," "protect," "safeguard," "sacrifice," and "survival." The military has long been understood as the protector of the Thai nation and these very words captured well the justification given by the military leaders for the May 2014 coup.

Crowdsourcing Support for Dictatorship

Did the sentiment among PDRC key groups on Facebook change after the coup? Are they still supportive of the military government whose takeover of power they facilitated? I conducted a similar analysis of all the comments on the five Facebook pages discussed in the earlier section with the addition of V for Thailand as a sixth page for analysis. The time frame of this postcoup analysis ran from May 23, 2014 to May 23, 2017—constituting a period of three years since the military coup. Online content and text analysis are an excellent way to uncover popular sentiment in a dictatorship like Thailand because there is no other reliable alternative to measure the pulse of the populace on political issues. Moreover, because these groups,

TABLE 7.3. Top keywords per topic, topic probabilities, and sentiment (precoup)

Topics	Sampled Keywords	Highest Topic Probabilities	Sentiment
Anti–Red Shirts	cheating, government, red shirt, burn, buffalo, red, stupid, die, dog, no brain, evil, bad mouth, hell, ungrateful, get out, very bad (vulgar), feeling sorry (vulgar), thief	Suthep (60%)	negative
Leadership	kamnan's fan, Thai people, heart, good wish, fight, our children, citizens, well wishes, Suthep, democracy, winning, PDRC, drive away, Ratchadamnoen stage, thank you, family, success, sacrifice	Suthep (33%)	positive
Promilitary	Citizens, army, nation, well wishes, thank you, sacrifice, Thailand, safeguard, protect, good people, prime minister, survive soldiers, congratulations, compliment	Thailand Informed (46%)	positive
Royalism	Wishing you (royal), the best, good people, protect, safety, king, monarch, Thai people, the royal institution, healthy, always of assistance, dharma, appreciative, fatherland, bow down, heart	Army Supporter (19%)	positive
Nationalism	Nation, bureaucracy, country, good wishes (Buddhist), Thai, reform, well wishes, sacrifice, winning for sure, come out, tyrant, army, police, our land, Thai nation, Thailand	PDRC (52%)	positive

Source: Author's calculations.

TABLE 7.4. Top keywords per topic, topic probabilities, and sentiment (postcoup)

Topics	Keywords	Highest Topic Probabilities	Sentiment
Royalism	king, beloved, salute, barami, bow down, Thai people, happy, good wish, monarchy, long live, institution, father, Thai people	Army Supporter (41%)	Positive
Nationalism	for the nation, patriotic, Thai, Thailand, Thai people, land, sovereignty, good living, sacrifice, everyone, protect, citizens, very good	Thailand Informed (24%)	Positive
Promilitary	soldiers, supportive, thank you, citizens, Thai, beautiful, protect, good wish, safe, bravery, tranquility, society, very good, good people, persevere	Army Supporter (30%)	positive
Policy Issue	(**Rubber**) rubber, price, low, clarity, children, southerners, bad, baht, money, rural people, help, die	PDRC (12%)	negative
	(**Constitution**) constitution, Thailand, disaster, Thai people, cheated, suffer, nation	Suthep (20%)	negative
	(**Sugar**) sugar, damage, Thailand, Malaysia, role, unsuccessful, government	PDRC (15%)	negative
	(**Corruption**) cheating, corrupt, sell, nation, bad deeds (karma), nation, power, rebels, too bad, very bad (vulgar)	PDRC (8%)	negative
Leadership	congratulations, Suthep, kamnan, Thai people, country, thank you, support, accolade, happiness, recover, goodness, protect	PDRC (25%)	positive
Anti–Red Shirts	stupid, buffalo, dog, no brain, intellect, red, Thailand, embarrassed, bad character, duped	V for Thailand (20%)	negative
Democracy	democracy, election, politics, vested interests, bad, politicians, citizens, clapping	Thailand Informed (4%)	negative
Buddhism	prayer, welcome (religious), good people, Buddhist monk, dharma, religion, protect, follow	Suthep (9%)	positive
Discontent	PDRC, power grab, lies, misbehave, politics, stupid, divisive, king, soldiers, disappointed	Suthep (25%)	negative

Source: Author's calculations.
Note: Excludes stop words.

in theory, are most likely to support the military government, there is less concern that the people would be too afraid to comment.

The results show a serious break from the precoup sentiment patterns across all five pages. There is no longer a unifying theme across the pages as both anti–Red Shirt and royalism sentiments were not prevalent in any of these pages. Indeed, anti–Red Shirt sentiment as a defining feature of pre-coup PDRC sentiment dropped off altogether for most pages, except for a small portion of the conversation on Suthep's page and a larger portion on V for Thailand's page. The disappearance of the anti–Red Shirt related conversations in most pages of the PDRC network suggests that Yingluck's removal from power eliminated the biggest threat to the nation—the Red Shirts—from the PDRC perspective. While the Red Shirt supporters were still around, the government in place would no longer be the de facto leader of the Red Shirt movement.

The findings from the topic modeling and manual comment analysis show a great variation across five pages in their emphasis on each topic discussion (figure 7.2). There were six salient topics overall: royalism, nationalism, promilitary, policy issues (rubber, sugar, constitution, and corruption), leadership, and anti–Red Shirts. Out of these six, no single topic had a high enough probability of saliency and relevancy for all pages. Royalism and promilitary sentiment seemed to be shared across four pages. The saliency of these two topics also varied widely across the five pages, with royalism being highly salient for Army Supporter but far less so for V for Thailand. Some topics, such as policy issues, were relevant to some pages but not to others.

The seemingly united PDRC-led opposition movement that successfully called for a military intervention to end democracy back in 2014 has shown considerable cracks since the coup. This chapter provides methodologically innovative empirical evidence for such cracks by mapping the motivations, sentiments, and networks of the most popular procoup groups in the first three years following military rule. The online population is targeted in this study not only because the online networks of supporters on Facebook were instrumental to the PDRC opposition movement prior to the coup but also because the offline environment made it hostile for the public display of dissent. While the online environment is not friendly for most antijunta or antimonarchy remarks, this study specifically examines groups that are most likely to be junta-friendly, monarchy-loving, and supportive of the military-backed authoritarian government. Thus, the key questions this chapter is concerned with are those regarding the motivations, sentiments, and networks of the procoup networks after the coup and whether or not there has

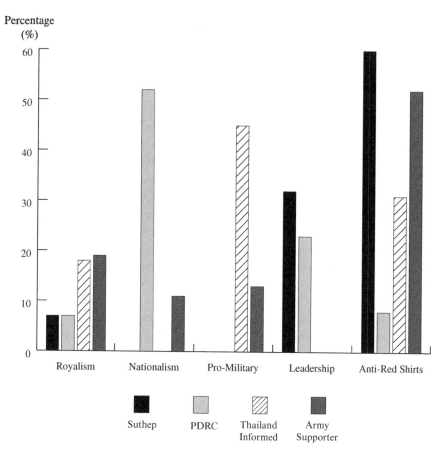

Figure 7.2. Results of topic probabilities by page during the Prayuth Chan O-cha government (May 23, 2014 to May 23, 2017)

been much variation across groups. The fragmentation of sentiment within the PDRC networks also indicates the diversity of the PDRC movement. Without the ultimate unifying theme of being anti–Red Shirt, as that which predominated in much of the PDRC conversations before the coup, the PDRC movement diverged in both the content of its conversations and in sentiment toward the PDRC movement itself.

The final analysis performed with the Facebook data is social network analysis. This approach allows us to better understand the qualities of the procoup networks over the course of the three years following the 2014 coup. Given what we know about the nature of the opposition forces prior to the coup, we would expect the procoup networks to be moderately united with some degree of community overlap. The generation of networks from the Facebook data resulted in five networks, variously colored, corresponding to the number of pages. I then created the one-mode "user co-comment" networks as previous analyses over the same three-year period. These networks depict users (nodes) and comment activity (edges), whereby an edge between two users means that they both commented at least once on any post within a given network over the three-year period. The clustering of nodes can suggest that there is a lot of within-page commenting by the same users. The overlapping of nodes can however suggest a high occurrence of co-commenting across pages. These one-mode projections of the networks provide a different picture of the procoup movement on Facebook, because the focus is on users and their comment activity rather than "likes." As discussed previously, commenting requires more effort and is more involved than simply "liking" a post. Comments also contribute differently to the spread of dictatorship support discourse in the postcoup environment, given that users can read each other's comments, interpret and learn from them, and engage in discourse by adding their own comments. Therefore, these networks provide specifically interesting perspectives on user (co)participation and discourse dynamics within each page and across the entire movement-level network (Smith and Graham 2017).

The social network analysis of the co-commenting across five pages shows the greatest overlap between the pages of Suthep and the PDRC (figure 7.3). This is hardly surprising given that Suthep is the leader of the PDRC and there are several cross-postings between the two pages, with the sharing of page administrators. The clustering patterns of commenters on other pages, however, seem separate from one another, suggesting a low degree of cross-page commenting. V for Thailand, Thailand Informed, and Suthep commenters are well clustered together, which means a high occurrence of within-page commenting—an indicator of a close community. The clustering of commenters on the PDRC page was moderate, while for Army Supporter it was sparse. This indicates that the latter's network was far from being a close-knit community in comparison to other groups.

The findings of the text and social network analysis produces three key results. First, the discourse and sentiment of those supporting the procoup groups vary widely in the postcoup environment. Contrary to popular belief, there is no single unifying motivation that is shared equally across the procoup movement. Royalism was used as a convenient ideology to unite the fragmented networks of the opposition prior to the coup. This has created an illusion that opposition forces were largely motivated by loyalty to the monarchy. This study has shown that some groups, such as Army Supporter and Thailand Informed, were far more overt in their support of the monarchy than others. Data from Suthep's and the PDRC's pages, which cumulatively represent the bulk of the coup supporters online, were far less engaged in discussion of the monarchy. The topic of royalism did not even register as significant among the networks of Suthep—the leader of the procoup opposition. V for Thailand, one of the first opposition groups to publicly exhibit its discontent toward the Yingluck government, was barely motivated out of a concern for the monarchy. Such low levels of discussion about the monarchy for some of these groups were most surprising, especially because the much-revered and beloved King Bhumibol Adulyadej died in October 2016 and the entire nation was in mourning mode for the following twelve months. One would expect much of the discussion on any of the procoup groups, if they were indeed motivated by royalism, to be about their monarch. But the text analysis paints a different picture. Moreover, the discussion over their support of the military—and by extension their overall sentiment toward the then military government—also varies widely. The two groups that were most royalist were also the most promilitary, and by the same token groups that were least royalist were also the least promilitary. The same goes for nationalism among both Thailand Informed and Army Supporter, as the two groups mostly likely to express their national pride and be concerned about sovereignty.

The most surprising finding related to the emergence of policy issues as focal points of discussion for those in the Suthep and PDRC supporter groups. The fact that the text analysis brings to the fore the importance of public policy and constitutional issues involving rubber, sugar, combatting corruption, and the constitutional drafting process is a strong indicator that PDRC and Suthep supporters may have been largely motivated by specific sets of policies rather than more amorphous ideological stances like royalism or nationalism. In retrospect, however, looking at how the Democrats had helped mobilize grassroots support for the PDRC and for Suthep personally, it was clear that Democrat-voting southerners were massively mobilized, especially offline, to support the opposition movement prior to the coup. Particularistic policies on rubber and sugar disproportionately affect southern Thai economies more than elsewhere. Beyond the regional issue, the constitutional drafting comments were highly aligned with the discontent toward Suthep and the broader PDRC movement—suggesting that there was growing unhappiness with Suthep as the leader as well as the broader PDRC movement generally.

The postcoup social media analysis suggests that there are three broad

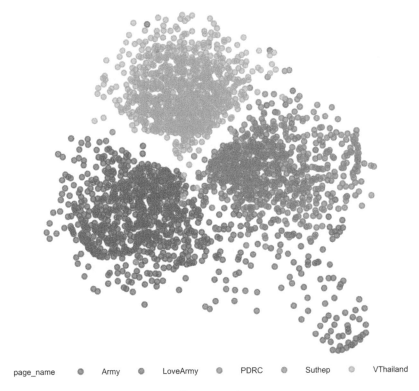

| page_name | ● | Army | ● | LoveArmy | ● | PDRC | ● | Suthep | ● | VThailand |

Figure 7.3. Co-commenting across five networks

categories of procoup supporters in postcoup Thailand: (1) royalists-nationalists; (2) identity-driven protagonists; and (3) policy-driven contingent supporters. The most conservative and ideologically driven groups are the royalists-nationalists, represented by the networks of Thailand Informed and Army Supporter. Supporters in this group are the most loyal to the military dictatorship—having justified the pivotal role of the military in safeguarding the monarchy and the nation. Their overwhelming gratitude toward the military—even three years on—is noted in their comments regarding the military being "brave," "selfless," "smart," and "good." Their communication patterns associate their promilitary sentiment strongly with their love of the monarchy and the nation. The second group, driven by identity politics, is represented by V for Thailand. Much of their comments on Facebook were about their identity being in opposition to the Red Shirts, the Thaksin regime, and majoritarian politics. Their sentiment toward "the other" was overwhelmingly elitist—labeling them as "stupid," "buffalo," "dog," and "easily duped." Electoral politics, to them, was merely a way for otherwise very corrupt politicians to lure support from uneducated country bumpkins (the Red Shirts) to sell their votes. V was not at all promilitary and its positive sentiment toward the institution held only insofar as the military was the only institution able to rid the country of its "evil doers" (the Shinawatras). They rarely discussed policy issues, which means that their support of the current military dictatorship was likely shaped by their overarching concern over the loss of political power and influence to the enfranchised and mobilized Red Shirts. The third group—the largest one of all—was largely policy-driven. Their support for the coup and subsequent military-installed government is contingent upon certain policies or agendas being activated in their favor. They are the least committed to the military and are not particularly royalist. Their discussion about their disappointment toward Suthep, their regret for supporting the PDRC, and their overall dissatisfaction with the 2017 Constitution indicates what may be a withdrawal of support for the causes of the coup and the military as a legitimate government on the whole.

The social network analysis demonstrates the fragmentation and the insularity of the procoup networks. Not only were the networks of these groups largely separate, cross-group communication was low. The one exception were the PDRC and Suthep networks, which were very similar. The insularity of their communication patterns meant that the benefit of communicating with other groups—even those likely to be similarly minded—was very limited. Users in these groups preferred to comment within their own pages and not on networks of similar groups. This potential echo-chamber effect across these Facebook pages of similar-minded groups means there was a lost opportunity to build a stronger and more frequent cross-group communication that might have helped to strengthen horizontal connections across networks.

PDRC Post-2014 Coup Politics

The precoup and postcoup sentiment comparative analysis reveals three key features about the PDRC online networks. First, royalism was not a prominent sentiment among PDRC online supporters—both before and after the coup. If at all, royalist sentiment is strongest among the royalist-nationalists, exemplified in the Thailand Informed and Army Supporter groups, which constituted a minority of the PDRC online support base.

This suggests that while leaders of both the PAD and the PDRC had long exploited the promonarchy agenda to gain popular support, royalism was not the main driving force for why people supported the PDRC online, bar for a minority few. But these staunch royalist groups were vocal and thus crucial to pushing the royalist agenda within the broader PAD and PDRC movements. Even after the passing of the much beloved and revered King Bhumibol, the constellation of conversation regarding the king on most PDRC pages was related only to his passing or his birthday and evoked little engagement with the PDRC movement beyond those explicit events.

Second, PDRC mass support for the military coup was largely concentrated around their anti–Red Shirt dissent; this masked other reasons for wanting to drive out Yingluck through whatever means necessary. The postcoup analysis demonstrated some aspects of what the PDRC wanted once the Red Shirts were no longer in charge, and these reflected different support bases within the PDRC. Groups that were royalist and nationalist were supporting the military government from an ideological perspective, while others continued to demand that measures be implemented so that once an election was called, a Red Shirt–aligned party could not return to dominate Thai politics. But most comments were policy-related and largely negative, indicating that support for the PDRC and the coup more generally was contingent upon the new government's performance in delivering public goods.

Third, the growing discontent within large sections of the PDRC Facebook conversation reflected the disappointment in both the PDRC as a movement and Suthep as its leader, on following through with reforms as per their campaign "reform before election." The conversation labeled under the "discontent" category, which occupied 25 percent of comments on Suthep's Facebook page, shows how unhappy the supporters were that Suthep had, in their view, turned out to be just like any other politician: lying, badly behaving, power grabbing, and disappointing. Such negative sentiment toward Suthep was again visible in policy-related conversations that demonstrated deep disappointment with the PDRC and Suthep as its leader. Further analysis would be required to investigate whether the growing discontent would be observable on Facebook conversations relating to Prime Minister Prayuth Chan o-cha. Promilitary sentiment, however, did not seem to waver, and in some cases grew, in the postcoup environment. The more conservative hardline groups, such as Army Supporter and Thailand Informed, had more positive conversations about the military after the coup, with keywords such as "bravery," "sacrifice," and "protect," than in the precoup period. This undercurrent of promilitary sentiment within the PDRC, even if among the less popular groups, still signified military support despite growing discontent with the military's policies and governance.

The divergent and contradictory identity of the PDRC in the postcoup period underscored how disunited and fragmented the PDRC support online was, even among those who seemed to be the "core" supporters of the PDRC. Before the coup, opposition to the Red Shirts served unify the movement. But once removed, it became clear how loosely organized the PDRC really was, with a negligible unifying theme and growing internal discontent and disunity. Unlike for the PAD, a new election was not held until five years after the 2014 coup; this left a vacuum for the PDRC in terms of having to establish a new direction for the movement after the coup. In the case of the PAD, after the 2006 coup, the 2007 election that followed immediately after ushered in another Thaksin-aligned party and give ammunition and cause for the PAD to regroup again. This was not the case for the PDRC as it had to scramble to find new meaning for the movement.

Suthep's Facebook page continued to act as the leading force of the PDRC postcoup, documenting his personal journey into monkhood and eventually as head of the PDRC and a nonprofit organization. The PDRC Foundation, established following the military takeover, operated largely out of Samui in Suthep's home province of Surat Thani. The foundation relied largely on key members of the former Democrat Party who became the engine of the PDRC protests prior to the coup, without reconnecting with leaders of other groups within the PDRC networks. In essence, the PDRC Foundation became a personal organization of Suthep's postcoup

TABLE 7.5. PAD/PDRC key figures across political parties in the 2019 election

Palang Pracharat	Ruam Palang Prachachat Thai (Action Coalition Party)	Prachathipat (Democrat Party)	Sangkom Prachatipatai Thai (Thai Social Democrat Party)
Nathapol Teepsuwan Puttipong Punnakanta	Suthep Tuagsuban Suriyasai Katasila Jatumongkol Honesakul Anek Laothamatas Katerat Laothamtas Petchompoo Kitburana	Chitpas Kridakorn Akanat Prompan Kalaya Sophonpanich Issara Somchai Sathit Wongnongteoy Choompol Julasai Thavorn Saenneam Witaya Kaewparadai	Somsak Kosaisuk Saneh Hongthong Chalee Loisoong

Note: This is not an exhaustive list, but includes only known politicians who were actively engaged with either the PAD or the PDRC.

that allowed him to maintain relevance while he contemplated his reentry into politics—notwithstanding his avowal to have permanently walked away from it.

While Suthep and the top echelons of the PDRC leadership that came from the Democrat Party vowed to not return to formal politics under the junta, other prominent members of the PDRC took positions inside various committees of the National Reform Council that was set up following the coup. Sombat Thamrongtanyawong became the head of the Political Reform Committee. PDRC supporters inside the constitutional drafting committee included Banjeod Singhanethi, Pakorn Preeyakorn, Preecha Watcharapai, Nareewan Jintanakanon, Jaras Suwannamala, Paiboon Nithitawan, Supatra Nacapew, Choochai Supawongsa, and Kamnoon Sithisaman, for example.[5] Some of these individuals were also active during the PAD rallies prior to the 2006 coup and had served in the subsequent military government. It is notable, however, that the PDRC did not become the watchdog of the junta government as the PAD did following the 2006 coup. The PDRC focused on carrying out civic work through its foundation; projects ranged from building a vocational college to organizing sufficient economy communities.[6] The PDRC Foundation ceased much of its activities by mid-2018 as it became clear that an election would soon be called.

The thin thread that held the PDRC and former PAD forces together broke apart and completely dispersed in the run-up to the March 2019 election. Key figures inside both the PAD and the PDRC could be found in at least four parties vying for positions scattered across Palang Pracharat, Ruam Palang Prachachat Thai (ACP), the Democrat Party, and the Thai Social Democrat Party. The faction of the PAD leadership that founded the New Politics Party continued on but under the revamped name of the Thai Social Democrat Party. Suthep Taugsuban founded a new party, the ACP, while allowing other former Democrat Party members who had left the party earlier to join the PDRC full-time to return. Palang Pracharat, the junta's new political party, took two of the most important and well-resourced PDRC leaders, Natthapol Teepsuwan and Puttipong Punnakanta. The splintering of the PAD/PDRC forces in this latest election vividly shows how little these yellow-shirted movement leaders had in common and that they were brought together only by an emergency crisis to resolve a political deadlock that had marred Thailand for a decade. The decline in support of the PDRC movement, evidenced by the social media data analysis of this chapter, presented a prelude to the electoral defeats of all successor parties to the PAD and the PDRC. The unofficial election results show that the Democrats came in fourth with 3,947,726 votes, Suthep's ACP came in eleventh with 416,324 votes, and the Thai Social Democrats came in fifty-seventh with 5,334 votes.[7] Palang Pracharat, while co-opting two top PDRC figures, could hardly be called a PDRC successor party given that it was a mix of key politicians from key political parties right across the Red–Yellow divide. But it was clear that Palang Pracharat had emerged as a winner in this election, not only because it exceeded most observers' expectations in garnering the largest number of popular votes, but also because of its clever tactic of co-optation.

Conclusion

While social media played a key role in uniting popular support for the PDRC's antidemocratic mobilization, it also helps make visible the cracks in popular support for the movement. Through a comparison of precoup and postcoup Facebook conversations of the PDRC's largest groups, the analysis shows a real divergence in the issues that mattered to different groups of supporters. While promilitary sentiment was driving the conversation of some PDRC groups, policy concerns were top priorities for others. The PDRC as a movement began to decline in popularity as discontent toward government policies and Suthep grew. Suthep's and PDRC's Facebook pages, totaling nearly three million "likes," constituted the largest majority support groups of the PDRC online. They ran on high popular support before the coup, with one-third of the conversations on those pages praising Suthep. After the coup, and noticeably after mid-2017, conversations on both pages turned drastically negative, with over half of the conversations expressing either discontent toward Suthep personally as the PDRC movement leader or toward the overall movement itself in venting that policy demands had gone unmet. The policy-driven discontent did not, however, correlate with precoup conversations about notable policy demands. Instead, in the precoup period PDRC conversations were overwhelmed with hatred toward their adversary—the Red Shirts—to the extent that their genuine reasons for supporting the PDRC were never actually articulated or made clear.

The return of all political parties and politicians associated with both the PAD and the PDRC to the electoral race in 2019 also shows that their support for the military coup was temporary and contingent upon their return to electoral politics. While demanding that the military "step in" and that elections cease, these yellow-shirted politicians never intended to permanently turn their back on democracy. The military coup was seen as a means to an end: they wanted the rules of the game to be rewritten to facilitate their electoral victories. Their gamble paid off in the short term: both the PAD and the PDRC helped to successfully engineer two annulled elections and the military coup d'états of 2006 and 2014. But the leaders of the PDRC were naïve if they thought they had brokered a win-win deal with the military. General Prayuth Chan o-cha decided to set up a party, Palang Pracharat, to run for election instead and, crucially, to use the same strategy that Thaksin had used to mobilize key political figures across multiple political parties, including two prominent PDRC leaders, into his orbit. Prayuth's political consolidation strategy worked: he was able to amass an influential team bent on continuing the work that was started by the junta following the 2014 coup. The Democrats, wanting to hedge against Prayuth, declared that they would not support Prayuth and the Palang Pracharat Party while Suthep was ready to support the junta, despite staying separate from him politically. The Democrats were the biggest losers in this election as the electoral base of the party had been frittered away by several parties that should have been their natural allies. What the social media data might also suggest is that the groups most promilitary during the dictatorship period likely became the electoral support base of Palang Pracharat, and not of any other PDRC-aligned parties.

EIGHT

Conclusion

After the 1991 coup d'état and the bloody popular uprising the following year, Thais were hopeful that would be the last: no more coups and no more military repression. The reformists worked hard to design a new constitution and pushed for a number of political and economic reforms to liberalize the political system, reduce the influence of the military in politics, and hamper the abuse of state power by politicians. A decade later many of the same reformists found themselves supporting and actively mobilizing antidemocratic movements to save democracy from itself. How did this happen?

In this book, I have advanced the argument that institutional blockage in Thai democracy drove the prodemocracy reformists into mobilizing against the democratic system. This antidemocratic mobilization, which drew largely on networks of civil society organizations and the urban middle class, was in response to what they perceived as an unacceptable "illiberalization" of a democratic regime. Ironically, the PAD and PDRC movements sought to reverse the tide of the growing "authoritarian democracy" by appealing for extraconstitutional interventions by nondemocratic institutions. The end results were military coups and repeated returns to the "real" authoritarian regime. Two democratic collapses in fifteen years in a moderately well-off middle-income country were not only catastrophic to the democratic development of Thailand but for other countries around the world.

Recently a growing number of Third Wave democracies have become more unstable and less free. Some of these democracies have reverted back to authoritarian rule, while others have remained in perpetual political instability. Scholars of comparative politics, particularly in the study of democratic consolidation, have provided a variety of explanations as to why young democracies face these challenges. This book presents a theoretical contribution to the understanding of how, why, and when democracies break down. I propose a novel approach to understanding democratic collapse through an examination of "antidemocratic mobilization." I fill a gap in the literature of democratization and regime study by bringing "ordinary people" back in to the debate when explaining the failure of a democratic regime.

My theory of institutional blockage offers a theoretical framework for understanding movement-induced democratic breakdowns in developing democracies. I argue that when a highly mobilized society perceives its access to channels of influence permanently blocked, we may see a rise of an antidemocratic movement. The role of popular mobilization takes center stage in my theoretical framework as a crucial factor in creating conditions for democratic collapse. I see institutional blockage as a process that is contingent on actors, institutions, and the interaction among them.

This book provides a typology of opposition movements: proreform, anti-incumbent, and antidemocratic. Popular movements in democracies often start out as being proreform or anti-incumbent (or both). They mobilize to voice their grievances and make their demands heard by the incumbent. Antidemocratic mobilization is only an available option in cases where there exist nondemocratic institutions. In my definition of antidemocratic movement, it must be able to appeal to nondemocratic bodies to extraconstitutionally intervene on its behalf. Ultimately, the actual collapse of democracy necessarily involves intervention from these nondemocratic bodies.

I provide an original contribution to the study of democracy and regime type by bringing "the people" back in to the debate. Political movements can bring a democratic regime down by creating conditions for extraconstitutional intervention by nondemocratic actors. Ordinary people in a democracy mobilize against the system because they feel "cornered" and "powerless" in a system that should, in theory, empower them. Their loss of access to power and the perception of permanent exclusion from power drive them to mobilize against the very system that is supposed to give them voice.

Media also play a central role in the rise of antidemocratic movements. In Thailand, both traditional and social media were crucial to the emergence of the PAD and the PDRC movements as they helped to unite opposition groups and advance an antidemocratic agenda. For both the PAD and the PDRC, leadership of the movement was decided based on which individual leader had the most access to the media. In the case of the PAD, Sonthi Limthongkul became the main leader of the movement because of his ownership of the Manager Media Group, which included print and online news, magazines, satellite TV, and radio. Sonthi was also the most antidemocratic PAD leader. His ownership of the media meant he had access to multiple platforms to push his antidemocratic agenda. Similarly, in the case of Suthep Taugsuban, leader of the PDRC, he won his leadership of the movement against other opposition leaders because of his access to a wide range of media platforms and his social media popularity.

My research on the People's Alliance for Democracy provides confirmation of the argument of institutional blockage as a central factor in antidemocratic mobilization in Thailand. It finds that the PAD initially emerged as a broad-based alliance of opposition against the government of Thaksin Shinawatra. Drawn largely from civil society organizations and the urban middle class, PAD supporters felt that channels for opposition voice in both formal and informal institutions were purposely closed off or rendered ineffective by the government. The growing authoritarian and illiberal rule of the Thaksin-led government appeared to threaten some of the basic democratic rights of the opposition. As such, the PAD began mobilizing and forming an opposition alliance to pressure for government change.

The emergence of the PAD had its seeds in the reformist politics following the Black May uprising. Reformers sought to make Thailand more democratic, open, and less dependent on the military. The political reforms in the postcoup period exemplify contestation over both the meaning of democracy and the way in which the current political system in Thailand ought to be changed. The compromise between the middle class, civil society, and elite conceptions of "democracy" resulted in the 1997 constitution (chapter 4). Reformists hailed the constitution as a major milestone in the country's political development for they believed it was the first time the constitution was written by the people and for the people. The 1997 constitution, however, provided grounds for both the rise of the Thai Rak Thai party and eventually the formation of the PAD.

The Thaksin government turned out to be the opposite of what the reformists had hoped. The 1997 constitution gave Thailand the first majority government, one that over time sought to consolidate its power through incorporating other parties. Newly created constitutional measures further strengthened the executive, while significantly weakening the opposition in formal democratic institutions. The growing power of Thaksin and his party alienated those who disagreed with them. Opposition forces began to emerge to protest against what they saw as the marginalization of opposition voices and encroachment on democratic rights. The biggest trigger to the opposition came when TRT won another landslide election in 2005. This brought with it the realization that the loss of power would become permanent. Facing a cohesive absolute majority in government, the opposition was losing both political space and access to power. To enhance bargaining leverage with the government, various opposition groups from both formal and informal realms banded together and formed the PAD movement.

The antidemocratization of the PAD occurred when the opposition perceived that their exclusion from power and marginalization likely would become permanent and that other strategies would not work. This perception was triggered by the fact that elections were no longer competitive and that there was "no way" electorally to get rid of the Thaksin government and his Thai Rak Thai party. As elections no longer seemed to be an option for punishing the incumbent, the PAD appealed to nondemocratic institutions—the military, the monarchy, and the courts. By appealing directly to these nondemocratic bodies and demanding extraconstitutional intervention, the movement effectively became antidemocratic.

In tracing the development of the PAD movement and its evolution into the PDRC, I also showed why the movement was *necessary* to the collapse of democracy in Thailand. While some sections of the political elites were not happy with the rule of the Thaksin government, there was no concerted effort to overthrow the regime until there was strong and clear signal from the PAD that any regime change would be legitimized and supported by "the people." Given the large support base of the PAD, measured in terms of both active (protesters) and passive (PAD media consumers) supporters, the opposition elites felt that any move against the Thaksin government would be successful. Extensive interviewing and discussion with key actors confirmed that the 2006 coup d'état was a response to the antidemocratic mobilization of the PAD.

The PDRC emerged as a successor movement to the PAD that was more firmly antidemocratic and wired online. Leveraging the affordances of social media in one of the world's most social media active countries, the online PDRC movement was vast, networked, and formidable. Social media have been shown to expand the reach of PDRC's antidemocratic voices and further deepen the Red–Yellow divide. It was also social media that helped forge the PDRC's agenda to oppose democracy not only by supporting military interventions in politics but also by changing the constitution to pave the way for more power for nondemocratic institutions.

Placing both the PAD and the PDRC movements in historical perspective, it is clear that Thailand possesses certain structural conditions that make a democratic collapse more likely (chapter 3). The country's political development was littered by long periods of authoritarian rule, frequent coups d'état, and a powerful military and monarchy. There was popular support for unelected leaders as well as for right-wing movements. While these factors matter to our overall understanding of the state of democracy in Thailand, they fail to account for why the PAD emerged when it did.

Given the conventional wisdom that democracy is the "best" political system that exists, why would ordinary people mobilize against democracy? A detailed analysis of the PAD's *and the PDRC's* discourse (chapters 4 and 7), coupled with participant-observation of the movement *and social media analysis*, reveals that different conceptions of "democracy" represent an underlying grievance of the movement supporters. In general, the movement was opposed to the idea of "majoritarianism" that was embedded in the democratic system. Civil society actors inside the PAD viewed democracy as an "inclusive," "participatory," and "consultative" political system where everyone's voice matters beyond election day. For many activists and NGOs, the true meaning of democracy is the power of the people and this can only occur in a grassroots democracy. As such, the current system of representative and electoral democracy is not the desired type of political system they see as empowering the people.

The middle class inside the yellow-shirted movements saw themselves as the enlightened group of citizens who believed democracy could only work if it were governed by the right people. They viewed moral authority, good governance, and traditional power holders (nondemocratic institutions) as being important to the political system. "Good" people, who are educated and righteous, should govern the uneducated masses until the latter becomes enlightened. The PAD's large support base in the middle class is both conservative and royalist in the sense that they believe that the monarchy should have veto power in the political system. The monarchical institution remains the pinnacle of the nation. Any attempt to undermine the power and authority of the monarchy (and to a lesser extent, the military) constitutes a threat to national sovereignty. Such a conception of "democracy" contradicts most basic definitions of democracy, as the former emphasizes strong roles played by nondemocratic institutions in the political arena.

The key point of this book, that mass political movements can play the central role in the collapse of democratic regimes, is underrepresented in both the popular and scholarly literature. Previous scholarship on anti-system/antidemocratic mobilization focuses largely on economic, elite-centric, and institutional explanations. Economic approaches typically argue that when new democracies face severe economic crisis, the public react negatively toward the regime by supporting antidemocratic/antisystem movements or political parties. I show in chapter 2 that such an economic explanation is unsuitable for the Thai case because the PAD movement emerged during a period of economic boom. While the growth was no match for the level experienced in the pre-1997 Asian Financial Crisis period, the economic conditions in which the PAD movement emerged were by most accounts good.

Some scholars believe the extent to which a democratic regime survives depends most critically on elite choices (Linz and Stepan 1978; O'Donnell, Schmitter, and Whitehead 1986; Ake 1991). It is the elites, not the people, who make or break regimes. Elites mobilize the masses to oppose democratic regimes for their own gains. This research does not disagree with the notion that elites matter in any regime change, but it challenges the centrality of elites in understanding antidemocratic mobilization and in democratic breakdown more generally. While elite action clearly matters in any regime change, this research suggests that social movements may have more agency than is typically assumed in such theories. Antidemocratic mobilization may rise not simply due to elite manipulation, but from mass movements that see no alternative to getting their voices heard.

To provide support for my argument, I ask whether the coup d'état in 2006 was contingent on the PAD movement. I show in chapter 6 that the coup would neither have been launched nor succeeded without mass support. Not only did the coup leaders admit that a popular opposition movement was crucial to their decision to overthrow an elected government, the PAD itself was calling for a military intervention. How do we know whether the opposition elites did not misconstrue or misinterpret public opposition toward the government as a signal for a military intervention? I provide public opinion support for antidemocratic mobilization through the use of both surveys and polling. Immediately following the 2006 coup d'état, two major pollsters reported more than 80 percent of the respondents nationwide agreed with the coup. Follow-up polls showed strong public support for the coup government in the rest of 2006. Moreover, the PAD was actively calling for extraconstitutional interventions, which garnered them much support from their members. It was not the case that the PAD was somehow "duped" into supporting nondemocratic elites.

The intraelite competition framework sees elite unity as crucial to regime stability. When elites are not unified, democratic breakdowns become more likely (Higley and Burton 1990; López-Pintor 1987). An antidemocratic movement is thus a reflection of the power struggle among rival elites. In the Thai case, scholars argue that the rise of the PAD movement and the eventual coup was a manifestation of the conflict between traditional elites—the military, the monarchy, and the bureaucracy—and new business elites led by Thaksin (McCargo 2008; Ockey 2008; Nelson 2007). The traditional power brokers were threatened by the new elites, most of whom were career politicians, over access to power and spoils. The traditional elites thus mobilized people to help them legitimize their seizure of power from a democratically elected government.

In chapters 4 and 5 I illustrate the importance of the masses in the PAD as driving the movement. The intraelite competition approach overlooks the very foundation of the PAD movement: its members. Indeed, the fact that so many PAD leaders took up political positions during the coup government signifies the importance the traditional elites placed on the PAD. This alliance was crucial to the coup being successful. Furthermore, elite-centric approaches fail to adequately capture how and why ordinary people joined the PAD in the first place. Clearly, they are not risking their lives to protect some self-interested, narrow-minded elites. Any elite-focused explanation for the PAD movement insufficiently captures the movement as a whole.

The class-conflict approach sees the conflict between the PAD and the incumbent government as a demonstration of deep-seated tension between the rural poor and the urban elites. Fearful of the rising political influence of the rural poor, the rich mobilize against them by seeking to subvert the democratic system that gives the former the power in the first place. The antidemocratic movement is thus an upper- and middle-class reaction to the threat imposed from below (Phongpaichit and Baker 2008; Pongsudhirak 2008; Funston 2009). An implicit assumption in this class-based framework is that economic positions shape groups in society along class lines and motivate their behavior. Yet I show that elites' preferences changed over the course of the PAD movement's development, which conflicts with key underlying assumptions of this revolutionary-threat hypothesis. If the PAD were to be made up of all the elites then they should always maintain their preferences and never leave the PAD.

This book fits most closely with the institutionalist approach, which sees institutions as critical to the success and failure of democracy. The weak political institutionalization argument (Huntington 1968; Berman

1997; Fiorina 1997; Armony 2004) sees democracies as most vulnerable when faced with a highly mobilized society and weak institutions. Poorly designed institutions are unable to cope with increasing societal demands, prompting society to mobilize against the democratic system as a whole (Berman 1997). While I agree with the focus on institutions, my approach addresses the flaws of the weak institutionalization framework in two key ways.

Antidemocratic mobilization emerges because institutional channels for the opposition are blocked, not because institutions are not sufficiently institutionalized to respond to the people. Indeed, the Thai case illustrates that the Thaksin government *was* responding to the people, largely through his propoor populist policies. His Thai Rak Thai party successfully enfranchised the majority of Thais, whose prior engagement in politics was limited to mere voting, by bringing them in to be an active part of the Thai political arena. But Thaksin was not responsive to the opposition. In fact, consistent with my argument, he was shutting the opposition out and taking their political space and access to power away, which resulted in them mobilizing to overthrow his administration. Furthermore, the weak political institution argument does not tell us what triggers democratic collapse. Under what conditions do states that are weakly institutionalized experience a breakdown? My institutional blockage theory addresses specifically the process, sequence, and conditions under which we can observe the emergence of an antidemocratic movement. The reemergence of antidemocratic forces, which culminated in the birth of the PDRC a couple of years after the PAD ended as a movement, reinforces the institutional blockage predicament. The PAD became less potent when democratic institutions were seen as more open to opposition grievances. Yet, as soon as there were signs the executive might be abusing his/her power again to the detriment of the opposition, antidemocratic mobilization restarted, even more determined to bring down a democratically elected government.

My research on antidemocratic movements contributes to the study of democratization and democratic consolidation in three major ways. First, by focusing on movements that oppose democratic regimes, I fill in the gap in the existing literature that focuses largely on prodemocratic movements. Understanding the process of antidemocratic mobilization is important to explaining the failures of democratization in developing democracies. Given that the majority of the countries in the world today has electoral democracy, it becomes especially important to understand the internal workings of democratic regimes that make them conducive to collapse. Political movements have been given little regard in contributing to democratic collapse in contrast to other factors, such as economic crisis, intraelite conflict, and class conflict. As such, my work in institutional blockage theory fills in the gap in our understanding of why democracies fall generally but also specifically how political mobilization plays a central role in regime breakdowns.

Second, this book illustrates how institutional engineering can have unintended consequences for a country's democratic development. Some of the scholarship on political institutions emphasizes the importance of crafting the "right" institutions in order to create a stronger and more institutionalized democracy. Yet the Thai case provides a warning to political reformers that perhaps devising new institutions to shape the behavior of political elites can have negative effects on democratic development as a whole. Perhaps it is not a question of crafting new institutions, but rather for whom these institutions are created. If political elites continue to find loopholes to get around the new institutions created to constrain them or, worse, create institutions to serve their vested interests, then institutional design alone simply cannot make democracy work better.

The PAD and PDRC movements also provide a valuable empirical contribution to the study of social movements by highlighting the importance of agency. Structural approaches dominate the existing literature on social movements due largely to the oft-cited political opportunity structure (McAdam, McCarthy, and Zald 1996; Tarrow 1994). Too much focus on structure, however, leads to theories that fail to explain the process and the timing of movement development. My theory on institutional blockage offers a more nuanced approach for understanding the dynamics of mobilization, by prioritizing the roles played by movement leaders and groups inside the movement. As such, my work helps to bridge the structure-agency divide that has characterized some works in the study of social movements.

Third, this book also contributes to the regime transition literature by providing a media-centric account of democratic breakdowns. Media is central to understanding not just how democracy collapses but also when. Instead of countering antidemocratic ideas, both the PAD and the PDRC leadership cleverly used a variety of media to galvanize support to overthrow democratically elected regimes. The irony of it all was that these opposition movements formed in retaliation against the incumbent's abuse of power and the marginalization of opposition media. By fighting what opposition supporters believed to be tyrannical governments, they in turn used the media to propagate their antidemocratic agenda. An opposition movement that has its own access to media outlets has in turn made military coups easier as they reduce the cost of elite-mass coordination and mobilization as well as establishing legitimacy for military interventions. Not only is media crucial to broadcasting antidemocratic ideas, its also provides new means to mobilize around them.

The focus on the use of social media in the case of the PDRC demonstrates the fundamental differences between social media and traditional media. Social media are the only media that truly give ordinary people the power to create content and mobilize around new ideas. Elites still matter a lot in the world of social media as tech-savvy elites can become influencers in the online world—amassing millions of followers and shaping behavior and discourse. But social media users also have the power to share and shape discourse online in their own right—even becoming influencers themselves without the networks and resources that elites normally possess. The content and social networking analysis of the PDRC networks both before and after the 2014 coup shows that the conversations among supporters did not always match what the leaders were propagating and that these conversations provide an important way to measure the pulse of the movement.

Future Research

Since 2000, more than half a dozen countries have witnessed a collapse of their democracy. Factors such as economic crisis, weak institutions, and social cleavages have been cited as explanations for these breakdowns, yet few have paid attention to the role of political movements and how they contribute to the fall of democratic governments. This book brings political movements back to the debate on the causes of democratic collapse. Specifically I focus on the phenomenon of antidemocratic mobilization. Democratic breakdowns have occurred in important countries like Egypt, Bangladesh, and Thailand in recent times. Why do people in democracies oppose their democratic regimes? How does antidemocratic mobilization contribute to our overall understanding of the state of democracy in the world today?

Institutional design is seen as a key factor in providing democratic stability in developing democracies. The main idea is that if institutions are properly crafted, democracies have a better chance of surviving (Power and Gasiorowski 1997; Robinson and White 1998; Lijphart 1999; Taagepera 2003). This conviction has spawned a vast research on electoral, party, and constitutional design that can contribute to the strengthening of democratic foundations. Efforts have been made to "engineer" democratic institutions in ways that would facilitate democratic success. The Thai elites have been obsessed with designing these institutions: from changing constitutions and electoral systems to creating new bodies to increase political participation. While there is no denying that efforts have been made to craft democratic institutions, the question remains: For whom? If institutions are designed to allow elites to ignore the voice of the people, why should we be surprised when people mobilize against democratic regimes?

The Thai case is one that has experienced both an antidemocratic movement *and* a collapse of democracy. The theory of institutional blockage should be able to "travel" and explain similar antidemocratic mobilizations in Egypt, Bangladesh, and Honduras, for instance. It should also shed light on cases of anti-incumbent mobilization that led to democratic collapse. In Venezuela, there was a civil society mobilization against the democratically elected Hugo Chávez, which created support for an eventual coup d'état in 2002. Encarnacion (2002) calls this a "civil society coup."

Table 8.1 provides recent examples of Third Wave countries that have faced either a democratic breakdown or a major mass political movement. A major extension of my future research should involve, first, the testing of my institutional blockage theory in countries that experienced both antidemocratic mobilization and democratic collapse, such as Egypt. Was the anti-Morsi movement in Egypt mobilized because of institutional blockage? If so, how?

Then I could test whether my theory would hold in cases where there is an antidemocratic movement but where democracy survives. The Philippines in 2001 witnessed a protest movement that called for extraconstitutional intervention, but its democracy ultimately survived. The anti-Estrada movement, or "EDSA 2," had some antidemocratic elements as the armed forces withdrew support from Estrada to join the movement, which was calling for a presidential impeachment. Yet their democratic sys-

TABLE 8.1. Classification of cases by regime and type of opposition movement

	Democratic Collapse	Democratic Survival
Antidemocratic Movement	Thailand (2006/2014) Egypt (2013) Mali (2012) Bangladesh (2007)	Philippines (2001) Thailand (2008)
Anti-Incumbent Movement	Venezuela* (2002) Honduras (2009)	Ecuador (2012) Turkey (2013)

* Venezuela notes a short-lived democratic collapse

tem survived a major political crisis as President Joseph Estrada eventually stepped down. Why?

Theoretically, the book is concerned with antidemocratic mobilization in developing democracies. Practically, this work is interested in the issue of democratic breakdown and survival in Third Wave democracies. What makes new democracies endure? Do measures aimed at strengthening young democracies have unintended consequences? If so, what? How do ordinary people play a role in the demise of the democratic system? To this end, I outline six key policy implications from my book.

First, the case of Thailand illustrates a sober reality: civil society is not always prodemocracy. Conventional wisdom seems to imply that civil society is a "good" thing and that the more of it, the better. What the PAD movement in Thailand has shown is the "dark side" of civil society. Civil society, under certain conditions, can be an illiberal force. As such we cannot assume that civil society is inherently democratic or liberal. Indeed, authoritarian rule is not antithetical to civil society; in some countries, authoritarian regimes support an expansion of civic life. Moreover, civil society is neither apolitical nor static. Just like interest groups, civil society organizations have their vested interests in maximizing their goals. For this reason, they can become political when their interests are threatened. Such interests can also change over time, making civil society organizations dynamic actors in the social *and* political arena. Given the key role played by civil society in recent cases of antidemocratic mobilization, policymakers of Western nations ought to be wary of blindly supporting "civil society development" in developing democracies as a matter of foreign policy. Civil society should not automatically be seen as "apolitical," "democratic," or "liberal." The key question foreign donors should address should no longer be about building civil society, but rather about building a "participatory" and "inclusive" civil society that will help a country's democratic development.

Second, a healthy democracy gives space for opposition voices. Democratic governments ought to ensure that regardless of the kind of government formation, there is space for the opposition both in the formal and informal spheres. Majoritarian governments are the most at risk of alienating opposition voices simply because their power is the most concentrated. Consequently, any attempt by a majority incumbent to further marginalize opposition voices can give rise to antidemocratic mobilization. To guard against this, opposition groups must be given appropriate space and channels to voice their concerns and grievances. There is merit to respecting opposition "rights" and giving them "voice" even if they are not able to affect any outcome. Respecting their space and the "right to oppose" and providing them with some form of power will result in a healthier and stronger democracy.

Third, the existence of *powerful* nondemocratic institutions makes democratic consolidation more difficult, but not impossible. These nondemocratic bodies are powerful because they provide alternatives to democratic institutions. In cases such as Thailand, where citizens accord more legitimacy to nondemocratic institutions as opposed to their democratic counterparts, consolidating democracy becomes especially hard. From a policy standpoint, one remedy to the problem of competing powerful institutions in a democratic polity is some form of power-sharing arrangement that sets out clear boundaries for each powerful entity in a democracy in the short term. Any attempt to undermine the power of one institution by the other will result in political conflict in the short term (as witnessed in the Thai case). In the long run, however, incremental steps can be taken to empower formal democratic institutions vis-à-vis nondemocratic ones, as has been the history in many "classic" cases of gradual democratization like the United Kingdom.

Fourth, building a strong party system weakens elite cohesion in the *short term* and can cause political conflict. While generally there is a consensus among scholars of party politics that a well-institutionalized party system strengthens democracy as a whole (Mainwaring and Scully 1995; Randall and Svasand 2002), the issue of short-term implications of party system institutionalization on the democratic polity has been largely neglected. What my book shows is that measures to better institutionalize the party system can have unintended negative consequences for the democratic regime. In cases where political elites are not fully committed to democratic ideas, party system institutionalization can weaken elite cohesion. A weakly institutionalized party system, in other words, produces elite cohesion. Political elites view the "democratic rules of the game" as a way to access power and rents. When the party system is weak (i.e., it has many patronage-based parties), there is no incentive for elites to subvert the system. However, strengthening party system institutionalization can prompt some elites to abandon the democratic system if they feel they will lose access to power and rents in the foreseeable future.

Fifth, the findings of my research suggest that the low quality of democracy can lead to a complete regime breakdown. In the democratization and democratic consolidation literature, there is an implicit assumption that there is a linear progression from a minimal/procedural level of democracy to a well-established democracy. Once elections are institutionalized then new democracies can work toward becoming more "mature" by developing democratic qualities such as responsiveness and accountability, so that eventually these countries will become "high quality" (Diamond and Morlino 2004). Yet, the Thai case shows that *institutionalized elections do not necessarily prevent regime breakdown*. Countries with routinized and institutionalized elections can still face democratic collapse if their quality of democracy is poor. Consequently, we need to break free from the order of "items" that democratizing states need to get right in order to become consolidated. O'Donnell (1996) is correct to point out the "illusion" about democratic consolidation as we prioritize formal rules of democracies before informal ones. Both ought to work hand in hand because a poor quality of democracy may be as much a threat to regime survival as not having routinized elections.

Finally, social media have shown to be a real bane to democracy. Instead of neutralizing radical voices online, they are forceful in emboldening them to the detriment of democracy itself. Once touted as a tool to democratize society, social media is also a potent platform for the anti-democrats to propagate, spread, and mobilize antidemocratic agenda. Yet to build a thriving democratic society, these radical voices online need to be accommodated and made public, not sidelined. Shutting down radical content would only drive it to encrypted platforms, such as LINE or WhatsApp, or worse to the dark net. By keeping these antidemocratic conversations alive on publicly accessible social media platforms like Facebook and Twitter, these radical thoughts can provide useful cues to understanding public opinion in general and identify organizations that nurture and promote them.

Notes

Chapter 1

1. Peter Meyer, "Honduran Political Crisis," Congressional Research Service, February 10, 2010. http://www.fas.org/sgp/crs/row/R41064.pdf

2. Meyer, "Honduran Political Crisis."

3. Asian Barometer, "Wave 4th Survey," 2016. http://www.asianbarometer.org/survey/wave-4th-survey

4. Freedom House, "Freedom in the World." 2019. http://freedomhouse.org/

5. Larry Diamond, *The Spirit of Democracy: The Struggle to Build Free Societies throughout the World* (New York: Macmillan, 2009).

6. Francis Fukuyama, "Preface," in *Political Order in Changing Societies*, ed. Samuel Huntington (New Haven: Yale University Press, 2006), xiv.

7. Monty Marshall, "Polity IV Project: Political Regime Characteristics and Transitions, 1800–2013." 2013. Accessed May 5, 2014. http://www.systemicpeace.org/polity/polity4.htm

8. Marshall, "Polity IV."

9. *New Zealand Herald*, "Clark: Bainimarama Attempting 'Thai-Style Coup,'" May 5, 2006. http://www.nzherald.co.nz/nz/news/article.cfm?c_id=1&objectid=10413816

Chapter 2

1. Freedom House, *Freedom in the World*. 2018. https://freedomhouse.org/report/freedom-world/freedom-world-2018

2. Diamond, *Spirit of Democracy*.

3. International Crisis Group, "Restoring Democracy in Bangladesh," *Asia Report* 151 (2008). http://www.crisisgroup.org/~/media/Files/asia/southasia/bangladesh/151_restoring_democracy_in_bangladesh.pdf

4. Baladas Ghoshal, "The Anatomy of Military Interventions in Asia: The Case of Bangladesh," *India Quarterly: A Journal of International Affairs* 65 (1) (2009): 67–82.

5. Michael Bernhard, "Civil Society and Democratic Transition in East Central Europe," *Political Science Quarterly* 108 (2) (1993): 307–26; Charles Kurzman, "Structural Opportunity and Perceived Opportunity in Social Movement Theory: The Iranian Revolution of 1979," *American Sociological Review* 61 (1) (1996): 153–70; Gary Rodan, *Political Opposition in Industrialising Asia* (New York: Routledge, 1996); Ronald Aminzade, *Silence and Voice in the Study of Contentious Politics* (Cambridge: University of Cambridge Press, 2001).

6. William Allen, *The Nazi Seizure of Power: The Experience of a Single German Town, 1930–1935* (New York: New Viewpoints, 1973), 276.

7. Adrian Lyttelton, *The Seizure of Power: Fascism in Italy 1919–1929* (Princeton: Princeton University Press, 1973), 41.

8. Stuart Woolf, ed., *Nationalism in Europe: From 1815 to the Present* (London: Routledge, 2002).

9. Juan Linz and Alfred Stepan, eds., *The Breakdown of Democratic Regimes, Latin America*, vol. 3 (Baltimore: Johns Hopkins University Press, 1978), 12.

10. Linz and Stepan, *Breakdown of Democratic Regimes*, 13.

11. Fukuyama, "Preface, in Huntington. *Political Order in Changing Societies*, xiv.

12. Pasuk Phongpaichit and Chris Baker, "Thailand in Trouble: Revolt of the Downtrodden or Conflict among Elites?," in *Bangkok May 2010: Perspectives on a Divided Thailand*, ed. Michael Montesano, Pavin Chacahvalpongpan, and Aekapol Chongvilaivan (Singapore: ISEAS Publishing, 2012), 214–29.

Chapter 3

1. Eva Bellin, "Contingent Democrats: Industrialists, Labor and Democratization in Late Developing Countries," *World Politics* 52 (2) (2000): 175–205.

2. Dan Slater, "Democratic Careening," *World Politics* 65 (4) (2013): 735.

3. David Morell and Chai-anan Samudavanija, *Political Conflict in Thailand: Reform, Reaction, Revolution* (Ithaca: Cornell University Press, 1981), 151.

4. Some scholars refer to this period as "semi-democracy." I believe such a term gives too much weight to democracy and prefer to use the more general term of political liberalization. See, for example, Likhit Dhiravegin, *Demi-Democracy: The Evolution of the Thai Political System* (New York: Times Academic Press, 1992); Clark Neher, "Thailand in 1987: Semi-Successful Semi-Democracy," *Asian Survey* 28 (2) (1981): 192–201.

5. Clark Neher, "Thailand in 1986: Prem, Parliament, and Political Pragmatism," *Asian Survey* 27 (2) (1986): 219–30.

6. Sathiern Chantimaporn, *Chatchai Choohavan: Thahan nak prachathippatai* [Chatchai Choonhavan: A democratic soldier] (Bangkok: Plan Publishing, 1989).

7. Sathiern Chantimaporn, *Chatchai Choonhavan*.

8. For a full official announcement of the NPKC for the takeover, see Meksophon, Rungmanee. *Bueang luek phruetsa pha 35 prachathippatai puean lueat muean ma klai tae pai mai thueng* [Behind the scenes and stories of May 35: Democracy

in blood, it seems we have come so far but we are never getting there]. (Bangkok: Tawan Ok Publishing, 2010).

9. Royal Thai Archive Online: www.geocities.com/thaifreeman/17may/may.html

10. Note that ironically but not coincidentally among the coalition partners is the party of Chatchai Choonhavan—Chart Thai—who was deposed in a coup.

11. *Matichon Weekly*, "Soldiers' Territory, No Trespassing! Chatichai Says 'I Never Interfere,'" February 24, 1991, 12.

12. Kobkua Suwannathat-Pian, *Kings, Country and Constitutions: Thailand's Political Development 1932–2000* (London: Routledge, 2003), 3.

13. For a detailed discussion of the concept of barami in Thai politics, see, for example, Peter Jackson, "Royal Spirits, Chinese Gods and the Magic Monks: Thailand's Boom-Time Religions of Prosperity," *South East Asia Research* 7 (3) (1999): 245–320; Patrick Jory, "The Vessantara Jataka, Barami and the Bodhisatta-Kings: The Origin and Spread of a Thai Concept of Power," *Crossroads: An Interdisciplinary Journal of Southeast Asian Studies* 16 (2) (2002): 36–78.

14. Suchit Bunbongkarn, "Thailand in 1991: Coping with Military Guardianship," *Asian Survey* 32 (2) (1992): 131.

15. Bangkok Post, *Catalyst for Change: Uprising in May* (Bangkok: Bangkok Post Publishing, 1992).

16. Charnvit Kasertsiri, ed., *Chak 14 Thueng 6 Tula* [From 6 to 14 October]. Bangkok: Thammasat University Press, 1998), 61–64.

17. Prajak Kongkirati, "Counter-Movements in Democratic Transition: Thai Right-Wing Movements after the 1973 Popular Uprising," *Asian Review* 19 (2006): 29.

18. "Contingent democrats" is a term coined by Eva Bellin in her article "Contingent Democrats."

19. Patrick McGowan, "African Military Coup d'États: 1956–2001," *Journal of Modern African Studies* 41 (3) (2003): 339–70. McGowan looks at all coups, failed and successful, and all coup plots in Africa between 1956 and 2001 (327 observations), and finds that a successful coup increases the chance of another coup, and that coups continue to be pervasive despite democratization (339).

20. "Popular support" is based in this instance on public opinion polls and the media interpretation of the coup.

21. Note that while the discourse and widespread media coverage of the Black May Incident point to the dominant role the middle class played during this uprising, several academics have challenged this view (Phongpaichit and Phiriyarangsan 1996; Ockey 2003)

22. Rodney Tasker, "Popular Putsch," *Far Eastern Economic Review* 151 (10) (March 7, 1991): 1.

23. *Economist*, "Seventeenth Time Unlucky," March 2, 1991.

24. Editorial Board, INN, *General Prem Tinasulanond: The Nation's Statesman*, 2nd ed. (Bangkok: T Film Publishing, 2009).

25. Su Anakhod, June 1, 1988, in Tamada (2009), 21.

26. Anand is married to M. R. Sodsri Jakrapan, a direct descendent of King Rama IV—King Bhumibol's great-grandfather.

27. PBS Interview, Tob Jode, June 20, 2011.

28. Interview with General Suchinda conducted by Rungmanee Meksophon in Meksophon, 2010, 165–71.

29. Manager newspapers, "From Tah Prachan to Sanam Luang," June 12, 1992, cited in BBC Black May, 371.

30. BBC Black May, 367–78.

31. "Friends of Anand: The Vaccine to Cure 'Good People' Is Losing Strength"— Special report, 10, March 26, 1993

32. "Friends of Anand," 10.

33. "Friends of Anand," 12.

34. Chaloemtiarana 2007; Chai-anan and Morell 1981.

35. Official website of the Thai government, produced by the Ministry of Foreign Affairs. They dedicate the entire section to the monarchy. http://www.thailandtoday.org/monarchy/thai-monarchy

36. 2007 Constitution, Section 2, "Regarding the Monarchy."

37. Official website of the Thai government, produced by the Ministry of Foreign Affairs. They dedicate the entire section to the monarchy. http://www.thailandtoday.org/monarchy/thai-monarchy

38. Pasuk and Baker, *History of Thailand* glossary, xi.

39. See "Tob Jode," PBS, January 4, 2013.

40. Sivaraksa was actually accused four times of lèse-majesté. See details in his biography on his website: http://www.sulak-sivaraksa.org

41. Gary Rodan and Caroline Hughes, *The Politics of Accountability in Southeast Asia: The Dominance of Moral Ideologies* (Oxford: Oxford University Press, 2014), 3.

42. Rodan and Hughes, *Politics of Accountability in Southeast Asia*, 13.

43. There were only seventy-six provinces at the time.

44. Dharma in Buddhism means the body of Buddha's teachings. It also refers to the moral transformation of human beings.

45. Prawes Wasi, "Happiness for All," 86–87.

46. KPI Congress IV, keynote speech by Professor Prawes Wasi.

47. Prasong Soonsiri, *Botrian khong phaendin* [Lessons of the land] (Bangkok: Naewna Press, 2000), 14.

48. Boonlert Kachayuthadej and P. Kongmeong, eds., *Ruam Sara Ratthathammanun Chabap Prachachon* [A Summary of the People's Constitution], 50–51 (Bangkok: Matichon Publishing, 1998).

49. Boonlert Kachayuthadej, *Ruam Sara Ratthathammanun*, 50.

50. *Naewna*, "Phong Thep Chin Thanachut 40 Phit Sa Ong Kon Itsara Ba Amnat" [Phonthep says 1997 Constitution creates power-hungry independent institutions], May 1, 2013. http://www.naewna.com/politic/43322

51. Saneh Jamrik, *Kanmueang Thai Kap Phatthana Kan Ratthathammanun* [Thai politics and constitutional development] (Bangkok: Thammasat University Press, 1997).

52. *Thairath*, "Panha Kanmueang Thai Kae Thi Khon Rue Ratthathammanun" [Problems with Thai politics: Is it because of people or the constitution?], February 9, 2009. http://www.thairath.co.th/content/pol/51952

53. King Prajadiphok Institute, *Five Years of Political Reforms under the New Constitution* (Bangkok: KPI Press, 2003), 453.

54. King Prajadiphok Institute, *Five Years of Political Reforms*, 454.

55. King Prajadiphok Institute, *Five Years of Political Reforms*, 436.

56. King Prajadiphok Institute, *Five Years of Political Reforms*, 437.

57. S. Lertpaitoon, *Ratthathammanun chabap mai tong di kwa doem* [The new constitution must be better than before] (Bangkok: Thammasat University Press, 2007).

58. Kachayuthadej and Kongmeong, *Ruam sara ratthathammanun chabap prachachon* [A summary of the people's constitution] 136.

59. Independent bodies include the (1) Election Commission of Thailand; (2) National Anti-Corruption Commission; (3) Office of the Ombudsman Thailand; (4) National Human Rights Commission; (5) Constitutional Court; (6) Central Administrative Court; and (7) Office of the Auditor General Thailand.

60. The actual wording of the constitution is that the prime minister advises the king to remove or appoint cabinet ministers.

61. See World Bank Education Statistics, "Country at a Glance: Thailand." Accessed July 7, 2020, https://datatopics.worldbank.org/education/country/thailand

62. An exception to this is for those who have been MPs before.

63. Somkid Lertpaitoon, *Ratthathammanun Chabap Mai Tong Di Kwa Doem* [The new constitution must be better than before] (Bangkok: Thammasat University Press, 2007), 8.

64. King Prajadiphok Institute, *Five Years of Political Reforms under the New Constitution* (Bangkok: KPI Press, 2003), 547.

65. *Thai Post*, "Kamnan Ma Ik 3 Muen—Si Khiao Chumnum Yai" [30,000 kamnans are coming—the Green protest], September 5, 1997. News Center Database.

66. *Khao Hun*, "Mop Fai Tan Yom Thoithap Thong Khiao Won Sanamluang" [Opposition groups willing to back down—their green flag all over Sanam Luang]. September 6, 1997. News Center Database.

67. *Thai Post*, "Kamnan."

68. *Khao Hun*, "Mop Fai Tan."

69. Rangsan Thanapornpan, *Kamnoet Ratthathammanun Thai 2540* [The birth of the 1997 constitution] (Bangkok: Thammasat University Press, 2002).

70. As Kasien Tejapira puts it, "As the crisis unfolded, nearly two-thirds of big Thai capitalists went bankrupt, thousands of companies folded, and two-thirds of the pre-crisis private commercial banks went under and changed hands. One million workers lost their jobs and three million more fell below the poverty line." "Thaksin Wat Fan Nang Kao-i "Nayokratthamontri" [Thaksin dreaming of a PM seat], *Thai Post*, July 4, 1998.

Chapter 4

1. *Isra News*, "Mia wara thep rattanakon ching on hun bo thua hai mae konsami nang ratthamontri" [Wife of Warathep Rattanakon rushed to transfer shares before husband becoming minister], January 1, 2013. Accessed February 9, 2013. http://www.isranews.org/investigative/investigate-asset/item/18533-วราเทพ-รัตนากร.html

2. *Thai Rath*, "Chi kanlaya khao khai on hun hai luk chaeng banchi pen thet" [Point: Kunying Kalaya transferred shares to son; financial fraud], March 10, 2010. Accessed February 9, 2012. http://www.thairath.co.th/content/pol/68014

3. Previously the Kijsangkhom party was formed by leading businessmen at the time but their wealth was dwarfed in comparison to those founding Thai Rak Thai.

4. J. Pinthong, ed., *Roo tan Thaksin* [We know what Thaksin's thinking] (Bangkok: Koh Kid Duay Khon, 2004), 94.

5. Data collected by author based on records from the National Statistics Office (Thailand).

6. C. Baker, "Thailand's Assembly of the Poor: Background, Drama, Reaction," *South East Asia Research* 8 (1) (2000): 1.

7. Siamrath, "Michai lopbi wutthi paiyannoi khia powo 281 khu chumnum yai tan" [Michai lobbies Senate to dismiss Poh Woh 281; threats of major protests], November 14, 2008. Accessed March 1, 2012. News Center Database.

8. Given that the majority of the brains behind TRT were not familiar with rural needs, they reached out to a number of key NGOs and activists for their input on propoor schemes, such as Professor Prawes Wasi and Praphat Panyachatruk.

9. Prachachat Thurakij, "Parakij Ti Yang Mai Set Khon Somkid Jatusripitak" [The unfinished business of Somkid Jatusripitak]. June 6, 2010. News Center Database.

10. Most graduated from top American MBA schools and have extensive experience in business and banking.

11. Thaksin's and TRT's main motto was 'Decrease Expenses, Increase Income, and Enhance Opportunity' (ลดรายจ่าย เพิ่มรายได้ สร้างโอกาส).

12. He served as the deputy prime minister (2001–06), minister of finance (2001–03), minister of commerce (2005–06), and was widely believed to be the engine of the TRT's economic policies.

13. *Prachachat Thurakij*, "Parakij ti yang mai."

14. Pran Pisitsethakarn, *Thaksinomics II: Thaksin Kab Naypobai Sangkhom* [Thaksinomics II: Thaksin and social policies] (Bangkok: Matichon Publishing, 2004), 267–68.

15. Referring to Thaksin's policy that helps to crack down on the mafia within the taxi community.

16. Taxi driver, personal communication, July 9, 2011.

17. Thaksin gave a speech at Bi-Tech on "Corruption." Cited in P. Pisitsethakarn, *Thaksinomics II: Thaksin kab naypobai sangkhom* [Thaksinomics II: Thaksin and social policies] (Bangkok: Matichon Publishing, 2004), 268.

18. *Khao Hun*, "Chao isan ruam khrueng saen hae hai kamlangchai atsawin khwai dam" [Nearly 50,000 people from Isan gave support to the black knight], June 15, 2001. Accessed February 10, 2012. News Center Database.

19. It is interesting to note that General Prem and Professor Prawes Wasi publicly supported Thaksin during the early stage of his administration.

20. Kraisak Choonhawan, an opposition MP from the Democrat Party, and also the son of Chatchai Choonhavan, who was ousted by the 1991 coup for "corruption," explains the difference between his family's corruption and that of the Shinawatras: "My father was the first elected prime minister. The military thought he was very corrupt, so they took him out. 'Extreme corruption' has always occurred in Thai politics but this paled in comparison to Thaksin's. My family . . . since Phin Choonhavan [grandfather; 1947 coup plotter] . . . can't compare to Thaksin's family, which is money politics. Children and grandchildren of Thanom [coup leader

and PM, 1963–73] drive Japanese cars. Families of past leaders may have privilege during their time of rule but not reproduction of wealth like Thaksin." Personal interview. During Thaksin's first term, Kraisak was a senator and was among the most vocal opponent of Thaksin from the senator 40 group.

21. Ukrist Pathmanand, "Thurakit thorakhamanakhom lae suesanmuanchon: Chak rabop khanathippatai su rabop phukkhat betset" [Mass media and telecommunications business: From cartel to monopoly], *Matichon Weekly*, March 2001, 16.

22. Veerachai Veeramethikul, TRT party list MP, is part of the Chiaravanont family. Thanin himself is an advisor to the finance minister.

23. *Matichon*, "Nak wichakarn panu ngo tan prae sanya mue thue khorapchan rupbaep mai rat sun 400 roi lan" [Academic joined force with NGOs to oppose mobile phone concessions worth 400,000 million]. December 2001. News Center Database.

24. Thai Rak Thai aide, personal communication, July 2, 2010.

25. Thaksin was known to be giving out Hernando de Soto's book *The Mystery of Capital: Why Capitalism Triumphs in the West and Fails Elsewhere* to his cabinet.

26. He viewed Thailand as a company and himself as a chief executive officer, which seems natural given that he was a business tycoon and that the TRT team was staffed with American MBA graduates.

27. Thaksin consolidated his political dominance on two levels: across parties and within the Thai Rak Thai party itself. When Thai Rak Thai was voted into office in 2001, its winning margin of 248 out of 500 seats was not enough for Thaksin, despite the fact that no party in Thailand had ever won more than a third of the votes. TRT proceeded to merge with the Kwam Wang Mai party and Seritham to gain an additional twenty seats—making it Thailand's first ever absolute majority government. Ironically, a stable and strong government is exactly what was intended by the 1997 constitution.

28. And because both the Kwam Wang Mai and Seritham parties completely dissolved when they merged with TRT, there was no threat of "defection" inside the governing party: something of a constant threat for every single coalition government in the 1990s. Even if TRT's coalition partner, Chart Thai, had defected to join the opposition (which it did not), TRT still held a majority and no minister could be voted out of a job as long as TRT MPs toed the party line.

29. Withaya Kaewparadai, personal communication, July 12, 2011.

30. Meaning that no matter what the election results are, the DP will never join forces with TRT or any other Thaksin-aligned forces.

31. Various Democrat MPs, personal communication, July 11, 2011.

32. Thawil Paison, personal communication, July 12, 2011.

33. For example, the first elected Senate included the following who were families of politicians or themselves politicians: Chumpol Silpa-acha, Chodchoi Sophonpanich, Sukhumpon Ngonekham, Rabiebrat Pongpanich, Veera Anantakul, Butsarin Teyapairat, Visit Techatheerawat, Sawat Amornwiwat, Kraisak Choonhavan, Pichet Pathanachode, Chaweewan Kajornprasart, Udsanee Chidchob, Den Toh-meena, Karun Sai-ngam, Surachai Pithutecha, Thavit Klinprathum, Athit Kamlang-ek, Wichian Pao-in, and Nitinai Nakornthap.

34. Such as Kasem Rungthanakiat, who ran for a MP seat with TRT and won in 2001.

35. *Matichon*, "Khrai sue siang—sue tua sowo siang woiwai chak phusong kiat ratthaban yuet wuthisapha?" [Who buys votes? buying off senators; complaints from the honorable; parliament seized senate?]. August 2002, vol 1. News Center Database.

36. *Matichon*, "Khrai sue siang."

37. The Tak Bai Incident, in which scores of men from the troubled Deep South were stripped, handcuffed, and stuffed into police vans and a further eighty-five suffocated to death, outraged anti-Thaksin senators.

38. Some of the early supporters of PAD from the Senate included Senators Kraisak Choonhavan (Nakorn Ratchasima), Maleerat Kaewka (Bangkok), Jermsak Pinthong (Bangkok), Winyu Ularnkul (Sakol Nakorn), Karun Sai-ngam (Buriram), Nirand Pitakwatchara (Ubolratchathani), Somboon Thongburan (Yasothorn), and Wongpan Takua-toong (Pang-nga).

39. *Krungthep Thurakij*, "2 Sapha leng yuen sakfok 'tak bai thamin'" [Two assemblies aim to question Tak Bai incident]. October 28, 2004. News Center Database.

40. Krungthep Thurakij, "Sapha leng yuen sakfok."

41. Such as Pichet Pathanachode, Wanlop Tungkananurak, and Winyu Urankul.

42. Newspapers include *Matichon, Thai Rath, Daily News, Bangkok Post, ASTV, Manager Khao Sod, Thai Post, The Nation, Khom Chat Leuk, Krung Thep Thurakij, Naewna,* and *Post Today*.

43. Kom Chad Luek, "Phon chi maeo khanaenniyom hot nakwichakan tuean rat rawang wikrit kanmueang" [Poll reveals popularity shrinks; academics warn government of pending political crisis]. February 25, 2004. News Center Database.

44. *Thai Rath*, "Op-ed: Yub ongkorn isara di mai?" [Dissolving independent institutions?]. December 3, 2005. News Center Database.

45. *Thai Rath*, "Op-ed: Yub ongkorn isara."

46. See Fah Diaow Gun web board on http://samesky.net

47. From 2001 to 2004, Shin Corporation's net profit jumped 260 percent while AIS increased its profit by 85 percent for the same period.

48. *Manager Daily*, "Khai chin paiyannoi khaichat liang phasi—bonthamlai khwam mankhong" [Selling out the nation, evading taxes, destroying stability]. January 24, 2006. News Center Database.

49. Hewison and Kittirianglarp 2009, 461.

50. J. Ungpakorn, "Thammai ngo kao kang ammat" [Why did NGOs side with ammat?], *Red Socialist*, February 28, 2011. Accessed May 14, 2012. http://redthaisocialist.com/2011-01-20-12-39-38/112-2011-02-28-16-44-45.html

51. Ungpakorn, "Thammai ngo kao kang ammat."

52. Pipob Thongchai, "Pathiroop prathet thai nai tassana khong pipob thongchai" [Political reforms in the eyes of Pipob Thongchai]. On Open, April 11, 2010. http://www.onopen.com/open-special/10-04-11/5337

53. Pipob, "Pathiroop prathet thai nai tassana khong pipob Thongchai."

54. Thai NGO, "The People's Assembly," n.d. http://thaingo.org/story3/par01_160146.htm

55. Thai NGO, "The People's Assembly."

56. B. Kayotha, personal communication, January 9, 2013.

57. *Thai Rath*, "NGO pen nai na khai kwam jon" [NGOs are brokers of poverty]. July 17, 2003. News Center Database.

58. *Thai Rath*, "NGO pen nai na."

59. B. Kayotha, personal communication, December 27, 2012.

60. Thai NGO, "The People's Assembly."

61. Thai NGO, "The People's Assembly."

62. *Matichon*, "Patibatkan popongo truatsop sapsin sue" [Suspicion over Poh Poh Ngo; checking finances of media]. June 11, 2002. New Center Database.

63. *Thai Rath*, "Samakhom nakkhao paiyannoi chae rat khukkham sue" [Journalist association believes government threatens media freedom]. January 3, 2003. Accessed June 2, 2012. News Center Database.

64. An ABAC poll showed that one in three respondents in Bangkok followed this show. http://www.positioningmag.com/content/talk-show-กรณีศึกษา-เอแบค-โพลล์-สำรวจคนกรุงเทพฯ-คัดค้าน-ปลดรายการช่อง-9

65. T. Songthai, *Kah Kue Nakrob Prachachon* [I am the people's warrior]. (Bangkok: GPP Publication, 2008), 38.

66. One of the biggest rallies was on February 4, 2006.

67. This happened despite the fact that Sonthi was considered an "outsider" by other PAD leaders, who were all drawn from the civil society sector.

68. K. Sithisaman, *Prakotakarn sonthi chak suea si lueang thueng phaphankho si fa* [Sonthi's phenomenon: From yellow shirt to blue bandana] (Bangkok: Ban Pra Athit Press, 2011), 280.

69. S. Katasila, personal communication, December 22, 2012.

70. *Prachatai*, "Khrapo sanoe tang "kammakan itsara" pracha phichan panha mop khru" [CPD proposed an independent committee to investigate concerns of teachers]. November 15, 2005. Accessed June 2, 2012. http://www.prachatai.com/journal/2005/11/6388

71. *ASTV Online*, "Mop khru khan thai-on at 'netiborikon' mai khaochai panha—rapphit chairon krit ron" [Teacher's mob opposed the transfer; claimed attorneys don't understand the problem], November 11, 2005. Accessed June 2, 2012. http://www.manager.co.th/Politics/ViewNews.aspx?newsID=9480000156529

72. The majority of Buddhist monks in Thailand are not vegetarian.

73. Sam Din, personal communication, June 24, 2011.

74. Y. Damchua, personal communication, June 21, 2011.

75. *Matichon*, "Chu wit 2 ma laeo khwang raboet sanghan nakkanmueang pan hun" [Chuwit no. 2 is here; threw a bomb; told politicians to tamper with stocks]. August 282004, 16.

76. This is a narrow definition of royalists.

77. As opposed to "antigovernment." The movement framed its cause as opposing Thaksin.

78. *ASTV Online*, "Thap phanthamit ku chat yan khluean phon khao lan phrarup 14.00 no" [PAD forces to save the nation confirmed mobilization at 2 p.m.], February 11, 2006. Accessed June 2, 2012. http://www.manager.co.th/Home/ViewNews.aspx?NewsID=9490000019100

79. Interviews with various PAD leaders confirmed this statement.

80. C. Sinsuwong, personal communication, July 10, 2011.

81. PAD leader, personal communication, December 19, 2012. The interviewee wished to remain anonymous.

Chapter 5

1. *ASTV Online*, "Patinya finlaen yutthasat thaksin" [The Finland manifesto: Thaksin's strategy]. May 15, 2006. http://www.manager.co.th/Daily/ViewNews. aspx?NewsID=9490000063603

2. *Manager*, "Chat satsana phramahakasatri lae chut chut patinya finlaen" [Nation, religion, king, and the Finland manifesto]. May 8, 2006. News Center Database.

3. Matichon Online, "Thorotho khu fong 'sophon' put patinya mua" [TRT about to sue Sophon for allegation of manifesto]. May 22, 2006. News Center Database.

4. S. Limthongkul and S. Pornudomsak *Muang thai rai sabda san jon* [Thailand Weekly mobile] (Bangkok: Ban Pra Athit Press, 2006), 339–43.

5. PAD supporter, personal communication, June 14, 2012.

6. *Thai News*, "Luan pen phuyai hai tham phuea chat rop chut khan rap—phrom harue 3 fai 'sonthi' yam chutyuen 'maeo' tong ok" [Let's be adults and work to serve the country; Sonthi insisted Thaksin must leave]. March 16, 2006. News Center Database.

7. *Matichon Weekly* ran a full cover story on Prem calling him the "fifth factor"—someone with significant barami who is being called to "step in" to resolve a growing political crisis. *Matichon Weekly*, February 17–23, 2006.

8. Other top leaders insist that the PAD, collectively, never supported the coup but each PAD leader differs on this. Such a statement contradicts a number of speeches PAD leaders made over the years.

9. *Manager*, "Thahan achip: 'Rua khong chat—kham banlang nai luang!'" [Professional soldiers: national defense to uphold the king]. November 22, 2005. News Center Database.

10. *Daily News*, "Phanthamit khuenchip lai thaksin chamlong yu thahan run nong patiwat phuea prachachon" [PAD reunited to chase away Thaksin; Chamlong told fellow soldiers coup was for the people]. June 25, 2006. News Center Database.

11. *ASTV Online*, "Thaksin yub sapha kohkohtoh sanong tan kwan leuk tung mai song mesayon see kao" [Thaksin dissolved parliament to call for a new election May 2, 2006], February 24, 2006. https://mgronline.com/politics/detail/9490000025604

12. *Thai Rath*, "Thaksin poet sapha ruam pha thang tan lo pao hai thalom 10 wan [Thaksin suggested a joint parliamentary session to find a solution]." February 22, 2006. News Center Database.

13. *Manager*, "Maeo plop khoromo mai yup—la-ok sang ham topto" [Thaksin consoled cabinet no dissolution or resignation; don't respond]. November 22, 2005. News Center Database.

14. *Thai Post*, "'Thaksin' yup sapha plueai that thae—su kan phachoenna" [Thaksin dissolved parliament; revealed his true self; confrontation]. November 22, 2006. News Center Database.

15. *Tnews*, "Mati pochopo mai song long leuk tung teng tang gug nud tok pak rum fai kan 26 kopo" [The Democrats confirmed boycotting the election, Teng still needing to discuss with opposition parties]. February 26, 2006. http://tnews.teenee.com/politic/143.html

16. A number of TRT members had begun to desert the party starting in early

2006. They included Korn Tapparangsi, Prapat Panyachartrat, Saranyu Wongkra-jang, Panlert Baiyok, Suvit Kunkitti, Thanit Thientong, Premsak Piayura, Sunai Sertbunsang, Likhit Dheravekin, and Sakrit Santimetanidol. There were many rumors that key people close to Thaksin were contemplating defection. They included Somkid Jatusripitak, Thammarak Isarangkul na Ayudhaya, Pongsak Ruk-tapongpaisal, Surakiat Sathiernthai, Jaturon Chaisaeng, and Somsak Thepsutin and his Wang Namyom faction. They left the party immediately following the coup to form breakaway parties.

17. *Krungthep Thurakij*, "Khon krungthep paiyannoi 42% tangchai ngot oksi-ang" [Bangkokians united to not vote]. April 23, 2006. News Center Database.

18. *Siam Rath*, "Phon chi pochocho chuea lang lueaktang sathanakan runraeng ban plai" [Polls reveal after election the situation will get worse]. April 2, 2006. News Center Database.

19. Kate McGeown, "Thai Result Points to National Divide," *BBC News*, April 4, 2006. http://news.bbc.co.uk/2/hi/asia-pacific/4874960.stm

20. McGeown, "Thai Result."

21. *Naewna*, "Thoi phuea chat 'thaksin' ramhai wen wak kanmueang" [Backing down for his country: Thaksin cried; stepped down]. April 5, 2006. News Center Database.

22. King Bhumibhol. 2006. Speech to the courts. April 25, 2996. http://kan-chanapisek.or.th/speeches/2006/0425-01.th.html

23. *Kom Chad Luek*, "San-aya phiphaksa 3 kokoto chamkhuk 4 pi doi mai ro long-aya lae mai hai prakan tua" [The court jailed ECT officers for four years with-out parole or bail]. July 25, 2006. http://news.sanook.com/politic/politic_10841.php

24. *Manager*, "Maeo 'tha chon khon mi barami khaen tham' witsanu—bawon sak thing phai" [Thaksin dared persons with barami, prompting Wisanu and Boworn-sak to leave]. June 30, 2006. News Center Database.

25. Wassana Nanuam, *Lub luang prang: Pathiwat prasat sai* [Secrecy and decep-tion: The overthrow of the sand castle] (Bangkok: Matichon Publishing, 2010), 48.

26. *Prachatai*, "Yan tham rat prahan tam withi prachathippatai phro mi pra-chachon yu khiang khang" [Insist coup was democratic because it was backed by popular support]. June 15, 2011. Accessed June 2, 2012. http://prachatai.com/journal/2011/06/35429

27. Sorayuth Suthachinda. "Ruang lao chao ni [Today's morning news], *Channel* 3, June 16, 2011.

28. Nanuam, *Lub luang prang*.

29. *The Nation*. "Kingdom 'Would Not Have Survived without Coup.'" October 6, 2006. Accessed July 10, 2012. http://www.nationmultimedia.com/2006/10/26/politics/politics_30017169.php

30. Nanuam, *Lub luang prang*, 48.

31. *Matichon*, "Mai mind" [Don't mind]. N.d. Accessed July 10, 2012. http://seri-chon.org/board/index.php?topic=7675.0;wap2

32. Nanuam, *Lub luang prang*, 48.

33. General Prayuth Chan o-cha, speech on Channel 5, June 14, 2011.

34. Although the army didn't outright endorse the Democrat Party, the chief made it clear that the army was against the pro-Thaksin movement and the

Thaksin-aligned party, Peau Thai. *Krungthep Thurakij*, "Anuphong bok yak hai banmueang sa-ngop khuan lueak phak lae khon di chut" [General Anupong warns if we want peace, we must vote in good party and good people]. June 9, 2011. Accessed April 24, 2012. http://www.bangkokbiznews.com/home/detail/politics/policy/20110609/394804/อนุพงษ์บอกอยากให้บ้านเมืองสงบควรเลือกพรรคและคนดี.html

35. Duncan McCargo, "Network Monarchy and Legitimacy Crises in Thailand," *Pacific Review* 18 (4) (2005): 499–519.

36. There were groups that came out against the coup but they were very small compared to the public support the coup leaders received.

37. Pipob Thongchai, personal communication, January 4, 2013.

38. Suriyasai Katasila, personal communication, June 19, 2012.

39. Somsal Kosaisuk, personal communication, July 11, 2011.

40. A. Paireerak, *Lao lung mai lai lung maeow* [Behind the scene talks to chase away Thaksin] (Bangkok: Ban Cheon Publishing, 2006), 137.

41. S. Pornwilai, *Pak panthamit* [PAD Party]. Bangkok: Ban Pra Athit Press, 2010), 63.

42. Pornwilai, *Pak panthamit*, 68.

43. P. Payutto, *Thammathipathai mai ma* [There is no dharmic democracy] (Bangkok: Pim Suay Publishing, 2006), 72.

44. R. Thanapornpan, *Jak Thaksinomics su Thaksinathipathai pak 1–2* [From Thaksinomics to Thaksinocracy: Part 1–2] (Bangkok: Openbooks, 2005), 141–42.

45. ABAC poll, November 2007. http://www.abacpoll.au.edu/in_news/2550/naewna231050.pdf

46. W. Limthongkul and D. Wongchukrue, *Pa hua jai pai gu chat* [Bring your heart to save the nation] (Bangkok: Ban Pra Athit Press, 2008), 49–51.

47. B. Kayotha, personal communication, December 27, 2012, .

48. K. Sithisaman, Speech on no confidence motion, National Assembly, June 23, 2008.

49. K. Worakul, "ASTV and the People's Alliance for Democracy," MA thesis, Chulalongkorn University, 2012.

50. Pornwilai, *Pak panthamit* [PAD party], 135–36.

51. Pipob Thongchai, "Pathiroop prathet thai nai tassana khong pipob thongchai" [Political reforms in the eyes of Pipob Thongchai]. On Open, April 11, 2010. http://www.onopen.com/open-special/10-04-11/5337

Chapter 6

1. For example, Jermsak Pinthong, Jaras Suwannamala, Karun Saeng-ngam, Klanarong Janthik, and Somkid Lertpaitoon.

2. Key PAD leadership figures then were appointed in the 242-member National Legislative Assembly. Of note include PAD leaders such as Prapan Koonmee, Chamlong Srimuang, Samran Rodpetch, Kamnoon Sithisaman, and Prasong Soonsiri.

3. C. Chanreong, "Ya rang ratthathammanun phiang phuea ni khon khon diao doi achan chamnan chan rueang" [Don't draft a new constitution to get rid of one person]. February 18, 2007. Accessed September 8, 2012. http://www.pub-law.net/publaw/view.aspx?id=1055

4. *Krungthep Thurakij*, "Samak 'yomrap chomna khoromo' khire" [Samak admits cabinet is ugly], February 3, 2008. Accessed April 24, 2012. News Center Database.

5. *Krungthep Thurakij*, "Samak 'yomrap chomna khoromo' khire."

6. *Matichon*, "Phuean ne win len bot ma phayot kem sang khaen—torong amnat" [Newin's friends betrayed to negotiate power], September 17, 2008. Accessed September 8, 2012, News Center Database.

7. *Matichon*, "Somchai sang 1 romoto kum soso samak ting hono" [Somchai told minister to control 10 MPs; Samak left the leader], October 1, 2008. Accessed September 8, 2012, News Center Database.

8. *Matichon*, "Somchai pob pa cheon meon tok 3 praden" [Somchai met with Prem; happy; discussed 3 issues], October 2, 2008. Accessed September 8, 2012, News Center Database.

9. *Prachatai*, "Theerayuth boonmee peud aekasan tulakarn piwat 2" [Theerayuth Boonmee open files for the second judicial coup], August 2, 2006. Accessed June 2, 2012. http://prachatai.com/journal/2006/08/9206

10. *Matichon*, "Pak ruam tahan tun potomo krob pochopo" [Party, military, finance, PAD took over the Democrat Party], December 19, 2008. Accessed September 8, 2012, News Center Database.

11. P. Pongpuapan, personal communication, January 8, 2013.

12. Referring to Princess Sirindhorn's interview with a Connecticut newspaper. See http://prachatai.com/journal/2008/10/18540

13. Suriyasai Katasila, "The Big Demonstrations," PAD press conference, Bangkok. http://www.manager.co.th/Politics/ViewNews.aspx?NewsID=9510000059495

14. *Prachatai*, "Theerayuth boonmee peud aekasan tulakarn piwat 2" [Theerayuth Boonmee open files for the second judicial coup]. August 2, 2006. http://prachatai.com/journal/2006/08/9206

15. Somsak Kosaisuk, personal communication, July 11, 2011.

16. Notable groups to protest against the coup in the aftermath of Thaksin's overthrow were the 19 September Anti-Coup Network, Saturday People Say No to Tyranny, Red Sunday Group, White Pigeon Group, 24 June Group, and the Tehmujin Network (Chanapat Na Nakorn and various academics).

17. Sombat Boon Ngam-anong, personal communication, June 10, 2011.

18. Kamol, personal communication, July 9, 2011.

19. A Democrat incumbent from Bangkok revealed, "Before the coup I was attending PAD rallies every day because the majority of people in my constituency went. . . . I went to garner votes. . . . now the Vote No campaign really hurt the Democrat Party. . . . I was even kicked out from some houses" (personal communication, July 14, 2011).

20. Rungmanee Meksophon, *Amnat III: sum ai thoy* [Power 3: Not backing down]]. (Bangkok: Baan Pra Athit Press, 2014), 207.

21. Nithithorn Lamleoa, *Rongtao pah bai kub jai tueng tueng* [A pair of sneakers and a big heart] (Bangkok: Baan Pra Athit Press, 2014), 34–35.

22. Nithithorn Lamleoa, *Rongtao pah bai kub jai tueng tueng*, 34–35.

23. *Daily News*, "Koh poh toh gonghtubtham kruekai jedsipjed joh ok Thalang khao yok radab" [SNT, the Dharma Forces, the 77-Province Network, declared they would escalate their mobilization], November 9, 2013. https://www.dailynews.co.th/politics/193627

24. Suthep Taugsuban, *The Power of Change* (Bangkok: LIPS Publishing, 2014), 244–46.

25. Suthep Taugsuban, *Power of Change*, 243–44.

26. T. Wutt, "Sonthi keon wethi kohpohpohsor tu taharn pathiwat" [Sonthi on PDRC stage calling for military coup]. *M Thai News*, May 10, 2014. https://news.mthai.com/general-news/328165.html

27. Naowarat Suksamran, "Peud jai Suthep jak na 1 Bangkok Post" [Suthep opened up his heart on *Bangkok Post*'s front page], *Post Today*, June 23, 2014. https://www.posttoday.com/politic/report/302501

28. *Manager Online*, "Rathaprahan pa tang tun" [Coup can resolve deadlock]. May 22, 2013. https://mgronline.com/daily/detail/9570000057257

29. *Thai Rath*. 2013. "Yon roi jed sip ha wan koh poh poh soh gon shut down muang krung" [A look back at the 75 days before the PDRC's Bangkok Shutdown], January 12, 2013. https://www.thairath.co.th/content/395551

30. National Statistical Office of Thailand, "Samruat kan mi kan chai theknoloyi sarasonthet lae kan suesan nai khruaruean phoso 2558" [Household survey of the use and access to ICT 2015]. 2015. http://service.nso.go.th/nso/web/survey/surtec5-1-3.html

31. *Prachatai*, "9 soso pochopo nam doi 'su thep' yuen bai la-ok thi sapha kokoto phrom chat lueaktang som" [Nine MPs led by 'Suthep' handed in resignation notice at the parliament; the Election Commission gets ready for a by-election]. November 12, 2013. http://www.prachatai.com/journal/2013/11/49748

32. *Kamnan* is a governing official at the subdistrict level (*tambon*). Suthep rebranded himself from a politician (a national level official) to an uncle or *kamnan* (used as terms of endearment) to increase his proximity to the populace and demonstrate his willingness to form and lead a "grassroots movement."

33. Suthep's Facebook profile: https://www.facebook.com/suthep.fb. Note that he changed his profile information from "politician" to "public figure"; his affiliation changed from "Democrat Party" to "Muan maha prachachon ratchadamnoen " (the masses of Ratchadamneon); and his short description was changed to "working on the street of *Ratchadamnoen.*"

34. Thai name: *Khanakammakan prachachon phuea kan plianplaeng prathet thai hai pen prachathippatai.*

35. Yingluck's Facebook profile page: https://www.facebook.com/cheeryingluck

36. See Facebook's definition of engagement: https://www.facebook.com/business/help/735720159834389

37. Some notable opposition groups included the academics group led by Sombat Thamrontanyawong, Silom Chamber of Commerce, and the Business Network for Democracy.

38. Nithithorn Lamleo, *Rongtaopabai kabjai teong teong* [Sneakers and fighting hearts] (Bangkok: Baan Pra-athit Press, 2013), 41.

39. Rungmanee Meksophon, *Amnat III Suu Mai Thoy* [Power III: Not backing down] (Bangkok: Baan Pra-athit Press, 2014), 260.

40. Asia Foundation, "Profile of the Protestors: A Survey of Pro and Anti-Government Demonstrators in Bangkok on November 30, 2013." Asia Foundation, December 2013. https://asiafoundation.org/resources/pdfs/FinalSurveyReportDecember20.pdf

41. Asia Foundation, "Profile of the Protestors."

42. Original posts: https://www.facebook.com/Y.Shinawatra/photos/a.10687 7456023385.4057.105044319540032/689551647755960/?type=3 (Yingluck) and https://www.facebook.com/209372495741907/posts/725168874162264 (Suthep).

43. Kom Chad Luek, *Khom Chatluek: Banthuek muan maha prachachon* [Memo of the People's Democratic Reform Committee]. Bangkok: Khom Chatluek Media, 2014).

44. In his interview with *Post Today*, Suthep said that the PDRC protests cost 1.4 billion baht. Out of this amount, 1 billion came from donations by his supporters, mostly in small amounts. https://www.posttoday.com/politic/report/302501

Chapter 7

1. The Facebook pages are Suthep: https://www.facebook.com/suthep.fb; PDRC: https://www.facebook.com/PDRCFoundation/; V for Thailand: https://www.facebook.com/V-For-Thailand-676553439464153/ (started in August 2018; the group's old, now-defunct page was https://www.facebook.com/V.For.Thailand); Thailand Informed: https://www.facebook.com/ThailandInformed (the translation of the group in Thai is "We are confident that more than a million Thais thank the military"; "Thailand Informed" is the English name the group has assigned itself); Army Supporter: https://www.facebook.com/armysupporter/ (the translation of the group in Thai is "Thai people support the military in protecting nation, religion and king"; "Army Supporter" is the English version of the group's name that it has assigned itself).

2. Pablo Barbera, "Rfacebook Package," *GitHub*, n.d., https://github.com/pablobarbera/Rfacebook

3. David Blei, Andrew Y. Ng, and Michael I. Jordan, "Latent Dirichlet Allocation," *Journal of Machine Learning Research* 3 (January 2003): 993–1022.

4. Fabian Pedregosa, et al., "Scikit-learn: Machine Learning Python," *Journal of Machine Learning Research* 12 (October 2011): 2825–30.

5. *Prachatai*, "Krai pen Krai nai 'kammathikarn yok rang rohtohnoh pob la ikon naew ruam nok weed" [Who's who in the constitutional drafting committee: Many found to be from the PDRC]. November 4, 2014. https://prachatai.com/journal/2014/11/56344

6. Website of the PDRC: http://www.pdrcfoundation.org/index.php/project

7. See the most recent unofficial announcement of the 2019 election results from the Election Committee of Thailand: https://www.ect.go.th/ewt/ewt/ect_th/download/article/article_20190328165029.pdf

Bibliography

Acemoglu, Daron, and James A. Ronbinson. 2006. *Economic Origins of Dictatorship and Democracy*. Cambridge: Cambridge University Press.

Adamic, Lada A., and Natalie Glance. 2005. "The Political Blogosphere and the 2004 US Election: Divided They Blog." In *Proceedings of the 3rd International Workshop on Link Discovery*, 36–43. https://doi.org/10.1145/1134271.1134277

Aeosriwong, Nithi. 2010. *Reading Thai Politics 3: The Politics of the Red Shirts*. Bangkok: Openbooks.

Ake, Claude. 1991. "Rethinking African Democracy." *Journal of Democracy* 2 (1): 32–44.

Allen, William. 1973. *The Nazi Seizure of Power: The Experience of a Single German Town, 1930–1935*. New York: New Viewpoints.

Aminzade, Ronald, et al. 2001. *Silence and Voice in the Study of Contentious Politics*. Cambridge: University of Cambridge Press.

Arato, Andrew. 2000. *Civil Society, Constitution, Legitimacy*. New York: Rowman and Littlefield.

Armony, Ariel C. 2004. *The Dubious Link: Civic Engagement and Democratization*. Stanford: Stanford University Press.

Arugay, Aries. 2005. "The Accountability Deficit in the Philippines: Implications and Prospects for Democratic Consolidation." *Philippine Political Science Journal* 26 (49): 63–88.

Asia Development Bank. 2010. *Key Indicators for Asia and the Pacific 2010*. http://www.adb.org/publications/key-indicators-asia-and-pacific-2010

Asia Foundation. 2011. *The National 2010 Survey of the Thai Electorate: Exploring National Consensus and the Color Polarization*. http://www.asiafoundation.org

Asia Foundation. 2013. "Profile of the Protestors: A Survey of Pro- and Anti-Government Demonstrators in Bangkok on November 30, 2013." December. https://asiafoundation.org/resources/pdfs/FinalSurveyReportDecember20.pdf

Asian Barometer. 2016. "Wave 4th Survey." Asian Barometer. http://www.asianba-
rometer.org/survey/wave-4th-survey

ASTV. 2009. "Mati ekkachan! mahachon phanthamit paiyannoi nun tang phak"
[Consensus on setting up a political party]. May 29. http://www.manager.co.th/
Politics/ViewNews.aspx?newsID=9520000058601

ASTV Online. 2005. "Mop khru khan thai-on at 'netiborikon' mai khaochai
panha—rapphit chairon krit ron" [Teacher's mob opposed the transfer; claimed
attorneys don't understand the problem]. November 11. http://www.manager.
co.th/Politics/ViewNews.aspx?newsID=9480000156529

ASTV Online. 2006. "Thap phanthamit ku chat yan khluean phon khao lan
phrarup 14.00 no" [PAD forces to save the nation confirmed mobilization at 2 p.m.]. February 11. http://www.manager.co.th/Home/ViewNews.
aspx?NewsID=9490000019100

Baker, Chris. 2000. "Thailand's Assembly of the Poor: Background, Drama, Reaction." *South East Asia Research* 8 (1): 5–29.

Baldassari, Delia, and Andres Gelman. 2008. "Partisans Without Constraint: Political Polarization and Trends in American Public Opinion." *American Journal of
Sociology* 114 (2): 408–46.

Bamrungsuk, Surachart. 2001. "Thailand: Military Professionalism at the Crossroads." In *Military Professionalism in Asia: Conceptual and Empirical Perspectives*,
edited by Multiah Alagappa, 77–91. Honolulu: East-West Center.

Bangkok Post. 1992. *Catalyst for Change: Uprising in May.* Bangkok: Bangkok Post
Publishing.

Barbera, Pablo. N.d. "Rfacebook Package." *GitHub.* https://github.com/pablobar-
bera/Rfacebook

Bellin, Eva. 2000. "Contingent Democrats: Industrialists, Labour and Democratization in Late-Developing Countries." *World Politics* 52 (2): 175–205.

Bellin, Eva. 2012. "Reconsidering the Robustness of Authoritarianism in the Middle East: Lessons from the Arab Spring." *Comparative Politics* 44 (2): 127–49.

Benkler, Yochai. 2006. *The Wealth of Networks: How Social Production Transforms
Markets and Freedom.* New Haven: Yale University Press.

Bennett, W. Lance, and Alexandra Segerberg. 2012. "The Logic of Connective
Action: Digital Media and the Personalization of Contentious Politics." *Information, Communication & Society* 15 (5): 739–68.

Berg-Schlosser, Dirk. 1998. "Conditions of Authoritarianism, Fascism and Democracy in Inter-War Europe." *International Journal of Comparative Sociology* 39 (4):
335–77.

Berman, Sheri. 1997. "Civil Society and the Collapse of the Weimar Republic."
World Politics 49 (3): 401–29.

Bermeo, Nancy. 2003. *Ordinary People in Extraordinary Times: The Citizenry and the
Breakdown of Democracy.* Princeton: Princeton University Press.

Bernhard, Michael. 1993. "Civil Society and Democratic Transition in East Central
Europe." *Political Science Quarterly* 108 (2): 307–26.

Bertrand, Jacques. 1998. "Growth and Democracy in Southeast Asia." *Comparative Politics* 30 (3): 355–75.

Blei, David, Andrew Y. Ng, and Michael I. Jordan. 2003. "Latent Dirichlet Allocation." *Journal of Machine Learning Research* 3 (January): 993–1022.

Boonmee, Theerayuth. 2007. *Khwamkhit song thotsawat* [Thoughts on two centuries]. Bangkok: Matichon Publishing.

Boonsuwan, Kanin. 2004. "7 pi patirup kanmueang: nisuea pa chorakhe?" [Seven years of political reforms: Running away from tiger to meet crocodile?]. Bangkok: SE-ED Books.

Bowie, Katherine. 1997. *Rituals of National Loyalty: An Anthropology of the State and the Village Scout Movement in Thailand.* New York: Columbia University Press.

Bratton, Michael. 1998. "Second Elections in Africa." *Journal of Democracy* 9 (3): 51–66.

Brustein, W. 1991. "The 'Red Menace' and the Rise of Italian Fascism." *American Sociological Review* 56 (5): 652–64.

Buachum, Singthong. 2010. *Bloody Songkran: Key Battle and Expensive Lessons for the Red Shirts.* Bangkok: Thongkamol Publishing.

Bunbongkarn, Suchit. 1992. "Thailand in 1991: Coping with Military Guardianship." *Asian Survey* 32 (2): 131–39.

Bunbongkarn, Suchit. 1999. "Thailand's Successful Reforms." *Journal of Democracy* 10 (4): 54–68.

Bunce, Valerie. 2000. "Comparative Democratization: Big and Bounded Generalizations." *Comparative Political Studies* 33 (6–7): 703–34.

Castells, Manuel. 2011. *The Rise of the Network Society.* New Jersey: John Wiley and Sons.

Ceron, Andrea, Luigi Curini, Stefano M. Iacus, and Giuseppe Porro. 2014. "Every Tweet Counts? How Sentiment Analysis of Social Media Can Improve Our Knowledge of Citizens' Political Preferences with an Application to Italy and France." *New Media & Society* 16 (2): 340–58.

Chachavalpongpun, Pavin. 2011. "The Necessity of Enemies in Thailand's Troubled Politics." *Asian Survey* 51 (6): 1019–41.

Chadwick, Andrew. 2007. "Digital Network Repertoires and Organizational Hybridity." *Political Communication* 24 (3): 283–301.

Chairak, B. 2006. "Po Cho Cho tung ruam kabuan isan dug thaksin prakat ruam pathiroop muang thai" [People in Isan joined the movement to halt Thaksin, claiming political reform]. January 15. http://thaingo.org/story3/par01_160146.htm

Chaisaeng, Chaturon. 2009. *Thai Democracy in Crisis: 27 Truths.* Bangkok: Institute of Democratization Study.

Chaloemtiarana, Thak. 2007. *Thailand: The Politics of Despotic Paternalism.* Ithaca: Southeast Asia Program Publications, Cornell University Press.

Chambers, Paul and Napisa Waitoolkiat. 2016. "The Resilience of Monarchised Military in Thailand." *Journal of Contemporary Asia* 46 (3): 425–44.

Changkwanyeon, P. 1999. *Dharmic State, Dharmic King.* Bangkok: Thammasat University Press.

Chanreong, C. 2007. "Ya rang ratthathammanun phiang phuea ni khon khon diao doi achan chamnan chan rueang" [Don't draft a new constitution to get rid of one person]. February 18. http://www.pub-law.net/publaw/view.aspx?id=1055

Chantimaporn, Sathiern. 1989. *Chatchai Choohavan: Thahan nak prachathippatai* [Chatchai Choonhavan: A Democratic Soldier]. Bangkok: Plan Publishing.

Chareonsin-olarn, Chairat. 2008. *Aesthetics and People's Politics.* Bangkok: Thammasat University Press.

Charumilind, Chatutong, Raja Kali, and Yupana Wiwattanakantang. 2006. "Connected Lending: Thailand before the Financial Crisis." *Journal of Business* 79 (1): 181–218.

Chiangkul, Withayakorn. 2010. *Pathirup prathet thai 1: sethakij kab karnmeong* [Reforming Thailand 1: Economy and politics]. Bangkok: Ban Pra-athit Press.

Collier, Ruth Berins, and James Mahoney. 1997. "Adding Collective Actors to Collective Outcomes: Labor and Recent Democratization in South America and Southern Europe." *Comparative Politics* 29 (3): 285–303.

Connors, Michael, and Kevin Hewison. 2008. "Introduction: Thailand and the 'Good Coup.'" *Journal of Contemporary Asia* 38 (1): 1–10.

Corsetti, Giancarlo, Paolo Pesenti, and Nouriel Roubini. 1999. "What Caused the Asian Currency and Financial Crisis?" *Japan and the World Economy* 11 (3): 305–73.

Croissant, Aurel and Philip Vokel. 2010. "Party System Types and Party System Institutionalization: Comparing New Democracies in East and Southeast Asia." *Party Politics* 18 (2): 235–65.

Daalder, Hans. 1984. "In Search of the Center of European Party Systems." *American Political Science Review* 78 (1): 92–109.

Daily News. 2006. "Phanthamit khuenchip lai thaksin chamlong yu thahan run nong patiwat phuea prachachon" [PAD reunited to chase away Thaksin; Chamlong told fellow soldiers coup was for the people]. June 25. News Center Database.

Del Vicario, Michela, et al. 2016. "The Spreading of Misinformation Online." *Proceedings of the National Academy of Sciences* 113 (3): 554–59.

De Zuniga, Homero Gil, Nakwon Jung and Sebastian Valenzuela. 2012. "Social Capital, Civic Engagement and Political Participation." *Journal of Computer-Mediated Communication* 17 (3): 319–36.

Diamond, Larry. 1996. "Toward Democratic Consolidation." In *The Global Resurgence of Democracy*, edited by Larry Diamond and Marc Plattner, 227–40. Baltimore: John Hopkins University Press.

Diamond, Larry. 2003. "Can the Whole World Become Democratic? Democracy, Development, and International policies." Irvine: UC Irvine, Center for the Study of Democracy.

Diamond, Larry. 2009a. "Democratic Governance and the Performance of Democracy." *CDDRL Working Papers* 117 (November).

Diamond, Larry. 2009b. *The Spirit of Democracy: The Struggle to Build Free Societies throughout the World.* New York: Macmillan.

Diamond, Larry, and Leonardo Morlino. 2004. "An Overview." *Journal of Democracy* 15 (4): 20–31.

Dhiravegin, Likhit. 1992. *Demi Democracy: The Evolution of the Thai Political System.* New York: Times Academic Press.

Dressel, Bjorn. 2010. "Judicialization of Politics or Politicization of the Judiciary? Considerations from Recent Events in Thailand." *The Pacific Review* 23 (5): 671–691.

Economist. 2002. "In Thaksin's Pocket." January 31. http://www.economist.com/node/966064

Eltantawy, Nahed and Julie B. Wiest. 2011. "The Arab Spring Social Media in the Egyptian Revolution: Reconsidering Resource Mobilization Theory." *International Journal of Communication* 5: 1207–24.

Encarnacion, Omar. 2002. "Venezuela's 'Civil Society Coup.'" *World Policy Journal* (Summer): 38–48.

Ferrara, Emilio, et al. 2016. "The Rise of Social Bots." *Communications of the ACM* 59: 96–104.

Fiorina, Morris. 1997. "Professionalism, Realignment, and Representation." *American Political Science Review* 91 (1): 156–62.

Freedom House. 2012. "Freedom in the World." http://freedomhouse.org/report/freedom-world/freedom-world-2012

Freedom House. 2013. "Freedom in the World." Freedom House. http://www.freedomhouse.org/report/freedom-world/freedom-world-2013

Freedom House. 2019. "Freedom in the World." http://freedomhouse.org/

Fukuyama, Francis. 1992. *The End of History and the Last Man.* New York: Freedom Press.

Fukuyama, Francis. 2006. "Preface" In *Political Order in Changing Societies*, edited by Samuel Huntington. New Haven: Yale University Press.

Funston, John. 2009. *Divided over Thaksin: Thailand's Coup and Problematic Transition.* Singapore: Institute of Southeast Asian Studies.

Galante, Laura, and Shaun Ee. 2018. "Defining Russian Election Interference: An Analysis of Select 2014 to 2018 Cyber Enabled Incidents." *Atlantic Council.* https://www.atlanticcouncil.org/wp-content/uploads/2018/09/Defining_Russian_Election_Interference_web.pdf

Gallagher, Michael. 2012. *Election Indices.* http://www.tcd.ie/Political_Science/staff/michael_gallagher/ElSystems/index.php

Garten, Jeffrey. 1999. "Lessons for the Next Financial Crisis." *Foreign Affairs* 78: 76–92.

Ghoshal, Baladas. 2009. "The Anatomy of Military Interventions in Asia: The Case of Bangladesh." *India Quarterly: A Journal of International Affairs* 65 (1): 67–82.

Gil de Zúñiga, Homero, Nakwon Jung, and Sebastián Valenzuela. 2012. "Social Media Use for News and Individuals' Social Capital, Civic Engagement and Political Participation." *Journal of Computer-Mediated Communication* 17 (3): 319–36.

Gilley, Bruce. 2010. "Democratic Triumph, Scholarly Pessimism." *Journal of Democracy* 21 (1): 160–67.

Groemping, Max. 2014. "Echo Chambers: Partisan Facebook Groups during the 2014 Thai Election." *Asia Pacific Media Educator* 24 (1): 39–59.

Groemping, Max, and Aim Sinpeng. 2018. "The 'Crowd-Factor' in Connective Action: Comparing Protest Communication Styles of Thai Facebook Pages." *Journal of Information Technology & Politics* 15: 197–214.

Gunitsky, Seva. 2015. "Corrupting the Cyber-Commons: Social Media as a Tool of Autocratic Stability." *Perspectives on Politics* 13 (1): 42–54.

Haggard, Stephen. 2000. *The Political Economy of the Asian Financial Crisis.* New York: Peterson Institute.

Hainsworth, Paul. 1994. *The Extreme Right in Europe and the USA.* New York: Pinter Publishers.

Hare, Christopher, and Keith T. Poole. 2014. "The Polarization of Contemporary American Politics." *Polity* 46 (3): 411–29.

Hargittai, Esther, and Yuli P. Hsieh. 2013. "Digital Inequality." In *The Oxford Handbook of Internet Studies*, edited by William H. Dutton, 129–50. Oxford: Oxford University Press

Hewison, Kevin. 1997. *Political Change in Thailand: Democracy and Participation.* New York: Routledge.

Hewison, Kevin. 2004. "Crafting Thailand's New Social Contract." *Pacific Review* 17 (4): 503–22.

Hewison, Kevin. 2012. "Class, Inequality, and Politics." In *Bangkok May 2010: Perspectives on a Divided Thailand*, edited by Michael Montesano and Pavin Chachavalpongpun, 141–60. Singapore: ISEAS Publishing.

Hewison, Kevin, and Kengkij Kittirianglarp. 2009. "Social Movements and the Political Opposition in Contemporary Thailand." *Pacific Review* 22 (4): 451–77.

Hicken, Allen. 2006. "Party Fabrication: Constitutional Reform and the Rise of Thai Rak Thai." *Journal of East Asian Studies* 6 (3): 381–407.

Hicken, Allen, and Erik Kuhonta. 2014. *Political Parties and Party Systems in Asia.* Cambridge: Cambridge University Press.

Higley, John, and Michael Burton. 1989. "The Elite Variable in Democratic Transitions and Breakdowns." *American Sociological Review* 54 (1): 17–32.

Howard, Philip N., and Muzammil M. Hussain. 2011. "The Role of Digital Media." *Journal of Democracy* 22 (3): 35–48.

Howard, Philip N., and Muzammil M. Hussain. 2013. *Democracy's Fourth Wave? Digital Media and the Arab Spring.* Oxford: Oxford University Press.

Huntington, Samuel. 1968. *Political Order in Changing Societies.* New Haven: Yale University Press.

Huntington, Samuel. 1993. *The Third Wave: Democratization in the Late Twentieth Century.* Norman: University of Oklahoma Press.

Jarusombat, Sopharat, and Siriporn Watchawalku. 2003. "Botbat khong nak rat-thasat nai kan patirup kanmueang" [The role of political scientists in political reforms]. *Rathasarnsart* 24 (1): 58–116.

Jenkins, Henry. 2006. *Fans, Bloggers, and Gamers: Exploring Participatory Culture.* New York: NYU Press.

Imai, Masami. 2006. "Mixing Family Business with Politics in Thailand." *Asian Economic Journal* 20 (3): 241–56.

International Crisis Group. 2008. "Restoring Democracy in Bangladesh." *Asia Report* (151). http://www.crisisgroup.org/~/media/Files/asia/southasia/bangladesh/151_restoring_democracy_in_bangladesh.pdf

International Labour Organization (ILO). 2013. *Economic Class and Labour Market Inclusion: Poor and Middle Class Workers in Developing Asia and the Pacific.* http://www.ilo.org/asia/whatwedo/publications/WCMS_218752/lang--en/index.htm

Isra News. 2013. "'Mia' wara thep rattanakon ching on hun bo thua hai mae kon 'sami' nang ratthamontri" [Wife of Warathep Rattanakon rushed to transfer shares before husband became minister]. January 1. http://www.isranews.org/investigative/investigate-asset/item/18533-วราเทพ-รัตนากร.html

Iyengar, Shanto, and Kyu S. Hahn. 2009. "Red Media, Blue Media: Evidence of Ideological Selectivity in Media Use." *Journal of Communication* 59 (1): 19–39.

Iyengar, Shanto, Guarav Sood, and Yphtach Lelkes. 2012. "Affect, Not Ideology: A Social Identity Perspective on Polarization." *Public Opinion Quarterly* 76: 405–31.

Jackson, Peter. 1999. "Royal Spirits, Chinese Gods and the Magic Monks: Thailand's Boom-Time Religions of Prosperity." *South East Asia Research* 7 (3): 245–320.

Jamrik, Saneh. 1997. *Kanmueang thai kap phatthana kan ratthathammanun* [Thai politics and constitutional development]. Bangkok: Thammasat University Press.

Jamrik, Saneh. 1998. *Than khit su thanglueak mai khong sangkhom thai* [New thinking for Thai society]. Bangkok: Withithas.

Jones, David Martin. 1998. "Democratization, Civil Society, and Illiberal Middle Class Culture in Pacific Asia." *Comparative Politics* 30 (2): 147–69.

Jory, Patrick. 2002. "The Vessantara Jataka, Barami and the Bodhisatta-Kings: The Origin and Spread of a Thai Concept of Power." *Crossroads: An Interdisciplinary Journal of Southeast Asian Studies* 16 (2): 36–78.

Kachayuthadej, Boonlert, and P. Kongmeong, eds. 1998. *Ruam sara ratthathammanun chabap prachachon* [A summary of the people's constitution]. Bangkok: Matichon Publishing.

Kasertsiri, Charnvit, ed. 1998. *Chak 14 thueng 6 tula* [From 14–6 October]. Bangkok: Thammasat University Press.

Kasertsiri, Charnvit. 2009. *Old Ginger vs. Thaksinocracy.* http://www.openbase.in.th/files/ebook/textbookproject/tbpj212.pdf

Katasila, Suriyasai. 2007. *Panthamit prachachon prachathipathai* [Alliance, people and democracy]. Bangkok: Openbooks.

Katasila, Suriyasai. 2009. "The Evolution of People's Politics towards Participatory Democracy: A Case Study of the People's Alliance for Democracy." MA thesis, Faculty of Political Science, Rangsit University.

Kempt, Simon. 2018. "Digital in 2018: World's Internet Users Pass the 4 Billion Mark." *We Are Social*, January 30. https://wearesocial.com/blog/2018/01/global-digital-report-2018

Kennedy, Charles H., and David Louscher. 1991. "Civil-Military Interaction: Data in Search of a Theory." *Journal of Asian and African Studies* 26 (1–2): 1–2.

Khao Hun. 1997. "Mop fai tan yom thoithap thong khiao won sanamluang" [Opposition groups willing to back down—their green flag all over Sanam Luang]. September 6. News Center Database.

Khao Hun. 2001. "Chao isan ruam khrueng saen hae hai kamlangchai atsawin khwai dam" [Nearly 50,000 people from Isan gave support to the black knight]. June 15. News Center Database.

Kim, Samuel, ed. 2003. *Korea's Democratization*. Cambridge: Cambridge University Press.

King, Gary, Jennifer Pan, and Margaret E. Roberts. 2013. "How Censorship in China Allows Government Criticism but Silences Collective Expression." *American Political Science Review* 107 (2): 326–43.

King Prajadiphok Institute. 2001. "Round-table on the New Government and Social Problems." http://www.kpi.or.th

King Prajadiphok Institute. 2003. *Five Years of Political Reforms under the New Constitution*. Bangkok: KPI Press.

Kitschelt, Herbert, and Anthony McGann. 1997. *The Radical Right in Western Europe: A Comparative Analysis*. Ann Arbor: University of Michigan Press.

Klanarong, Supinya. 2007. *Pud kwang jing* [Telling the truth]. Bangkok: Openbooks.

Klein, James. R. 1998. "The Constitution of the Kingdom of Thailand, 1997: A Blueprint for Participatory Democracy." The Asia Foundation Working Paper Series #8. http://constitutionnet.org/sites/default/files/Paper_on_the_1997_constitution_2.pdf

Knobloch-Westerwick, Silvia, and Benjamin K. Johnson. 2014. "Selective Exposure for Better or Worse: Its Mediating Role for Online News' Impact on Political Participation." *Journal of Computer-Mediated Communication* 19 (2): 184–96.

Kom Chad Luek. 2004. "Phon chi maeo khanaenniyom hot nakwichakan tuean rat rawang wikrit kanmueang" [Poll reveals popularity shrinks; academics warn government of pending political crisis]. February 25. News Center Database.

Kom Chad Luek. 2006a. "San-aya phiphaksa 3 kokoto chamkhuk 4 pi doi mai ro long- aya lae mai hai prakan tua" [The court jailed ECT officers for four years without parole or bail]. July 25. http://news.sanook.com/politic/politic_10841.php

Kom Chad Luek. 2006b. "Bueang luek patiwat!!! 'thaksin' moen pai doi di" [Behind the scene of the coup! Thaksin doesn't care]. September 20. News Center Database.

Kom Chat Luek. 2014. *Khom Chatluek: Banthuek muan maha prachachon* [Memo of the People's Democratic Reform Committee]. Bangkok: Khom Chatluek Media.

Kongkirati, Prajak. 2006. "Counter-Movements in Democratic Transition: Thai Right-Wing Movements after the 1973 Popular Uprising." *Asian Review* 19: 1–34.

Kozloff, Nikolas. 2007. *Hugo Chávez: Oil, Politics and the Challenge to the United States.* New York: Palgrave Macmillan.

Kreo-ngam, Wisanu. 2011. *Lok ni khue lakhon* [This world is drama]. Bangkok: Matichon Publishing.

Krungthep Thurakij. 2004. "2 Sapha leng yuen sakfok 'tak bai thamin'" [Two assemblies aim to question Tak Bai Incident]. October 28. News Center Database.

Krungthep Thurakij. 2006. "Khon krungthep paiyannoi 42% tangchai ngot oksiang" [Bangkokians united to not vote]. April 23. News Center Database.

Krungthep Thurakij. 2008. "Samak 'Yomrap chomna khoromo' khire [Samak admits cabinet is ugly]. February 3. News Center Database.

Krungthep Thurakij. 2011. "Anuphong bok yak hai banmueang sa-ngop khuan lueak phak lae khon di chut" [General Anupong warns if we want peace, we must vote in good party and good people]. June 9. News Center Database.

Kunmee, Prapan. 2008. *Chiwit ni koh pen ka prabat tat prachachon* [This life I dedicate to the king and to the people]. Bangkok: Green Panyayan Press.

Kurzman, Charles. 1996. "Structural Opportunity and Perceived Opportunity in Social Movement Theory: The Iranian Revolution of 1979." *American Sociological Review* 61 (1): 153–70.

Lamleo, Nithithorn. 2013. *Rongtaopabai kabjai teong teong* [Sneakers and fighting hearts]. Bangkok: Baan Pra-athit Press.

Laothamatas, Anek. 1988. "Business and Politics in Thailand: New Patterns of Influence." *Asian Survey* 28 (4): 451–70.

Laothamatas, Anek. 1996. "A Tale of Two Democracies: Conflicting Perceptions of Elections and Democracy in Thailand." In *The Politics of Elections in Southeast Asia*, edited by R. H. Taylor, 201–33. Cambridge: Cambridge University Press.

Lertpaitoon, Somkid. 2007. *Ratthathammanun chabap mai tong di kwa doem* [The new constitution must be better than before]. Bangkok: Thammasat University Press.

Levitsky, Steven, and Maria Victoria Murillo. 2003. "Argentina Weathers the Storm." *Journal of Democracy* 14 (4): 152–66.

Lewis, Paul. 1997. "Theories of Democratization and Patterns of Regime Change." *Journal of Communist Studies and Transition Politics* 13 (1): 4–26.

Li, Richard, and William R. Thompson. 1975. "The 'Coup Contagion' Hypothesis." *Journal of Conflict Resolution* 19 (1): 63–84.

Lijphart, Arend. *Patterns of Democracy: Government Forms and Performance in Thirty-Six Countries.* New Haven: Yale University Press.

Lim, Merlyna. 2012. "Clicks, Cabs, and Coffee Houses: Social Media and Oppositional Movements in Egypt, 2004–2011." *Journal of Communication* 62 (2): 231–48.

Limongi, Neto, et al. 1996. "What Makes Democracies Endure?" *Journal of Democracy* 7 (1): 39–55.

Limthongkul, Sonthi, and Sarocha Pornudomsak. 2006. *Muang thai rai sabda san jon* [*Thailand Weekly* mobile]. Bangkok: Ban Pra-athit Press.

Limthongkul, Warit, and Duangporn Wongchukrue. 2008. *Pa hua jai pai gu chat* [Bring your heart to save the nation]. Bangkok: Ban Pra-athit Press.

Linz, Juan, and Alfred Stepan, eds. 1978. *The Breakdown of Democratic Regimes: Latin America*. Baltimore: Johns Hopkins University Press.

Loader, Brian D., Ariadne Vromen, and Michael A. Xenos. 2014. "The Networked Young Citizen: Social Media, Political Participation and Civic Engagement." *Information, Communication & Society* 17 (2): 143–50.

Londregan, John, and Keith Poole. 1990. "Poverty, the Coup Trap, and the Seizure of Executive Power." *World Politics* 42 (2): 151–83.

Loveman, Brian. 1994. "Protected Democracies and Military Guardianship: Political Transitions in Latin America, 1978–1993." *Journal of Interamerican Studies and World Affairs* 36 (2): 105–89.

López-Pintor, Rafael. 1987. "Mass and Elite Perspectives in the Process of Transition to Democracy." In *Comparing New Democracies: Transition and Consolidation in Mediterranean Europe and the Southern Cone*, edited by E. A. Baloyra. Boulder: Westview.

Lyttelton, Adrian. 1973. *The Seizure of Power: Fascism in Italy, 1919–1929*. Princeton: Princeton University Press.

MacIntyre, Andrew. 2001. "Institutions and Investors: The Politics of the Economic Crisis in Southeast Asia." *International Organization* 55 (1): 81–122.

Mainwaring, Scott, and Timothy Scully. 1995. *Building Democratic Institutions: Party Systems in Latin America*. Cambridge: Cambridge University Press.

Mainwaring, Scott. 1999. *Rethinking Party Systems in the Third Wave of Democratization: The Case of Brazil*. Stanford: Stanford University Press.

Mainwaring, Scott, and Mariano Torcal. 2006. "Party System Institutionalization and Party System Theory after the Third Wave Democratization." In *Handbook of Party Politics*, edited by Richard S. Katz, 204–27. London: Sage Publications.

Maisrikrod, Surin. 1992. *Thailand's Two General Elections in 1992: Democracy Sustained*. Singapore: Institute of Southeast Asian Studies.

Maisrikrod, Surin. 1993. "Thailand 1992: Repression and Return of Democracy." *Southeast Asian Affairs*: 327–49.

Maisrikrod, Surin. 2005. "Making Democracy: Leadership, Class, Gender, and Political Participation in Thailand." *Contemporary Southeast Asia: A Journal of International and Strategic Affairs* 27 (1): 149–51.

Manager. 2005a. "Thahan achip: 'rua khong chat—kham banlang nai luang!'" [Professional soldiers: national defense to uphold the king]. November 22. News Center Database.

Manager. 2005b. "Maeo plop khoromo mai yup—la-ok sang ham topto" [Thaksin consoled cabinet no dissolution or resignation; don't respond]. November 22. News Center Database.

Manager. 2006a. "Khai chin paiyannoi khaichat liang phasi—bonthamlai khwam mankhong" [Selling out the nation, evading taxes, destroying stability]. January 24. News Center Database.

Manager. 2006b. "'Mai tha chon khon mi barami khaen thamwitsanu—bawon sak thing phai" [Thaksin dared persons with barami, prompting Wisanu and Bowornsak to leave]. June 30. News Center Database.

Manager. 2006c. "Chat satsana phramahakasatri lae chut chut patinya finlaen" [Nation, religion, king and the Finland manifesto]. May 8. News Center Database.

Manager. 2009. "Rang ngan deun kabuan lom thaksin ko rang ngan kan tum 223 baht" [Labor rally surrounding Thaksin to demand minimum wage of 223 baht]. May 1. http://www.ftawatch.org/node/8981

Marshall, Monty. 2012a. "Polity IV Project: Political Regime Characteristics and Transitions, 1800–2012." http://www.systemicpeace.org/polity/polity4.htm

Marshall, Monty. 2012b. "Coup d'états, 1946–2012." *Integrated Network for Societal Conflict Research (INSCR).* http://www.systemicpeace.org/inscrdata.html

Matichon. 2001. "Nak wichakarn panu ngo tan prae sanya mue thue khorapchan rupbaep mai rat sun 400 roi lan" [Academic joined force with NGOs to oppose mobile phone concessions worth 400,000 million]. December. News Center Database.

Matichon. 2002. "Patibatkan popongo truatsop sapsin sue" [Suspicion over Poh Poh Ngo; checking finances of media]. June 11. News Center Database.

Matichon. 2004. "Chu wit 2 ma laeo khwang raboet sanghan nakkanmueang pan hun" [Chuwit no. 2 is here; threw a bomb; told politicians to tamper with stocks], August 28, 16.

Matichon. 2006a. *Pha sowo thi phueng rue phu phang prachathippatai* [Dissecting senators: Promoting or destroying democracy?]. Bangkok: Matichon Publishing.

Matichon. 2006b. "Thorotho khu fong 'sophon' put patinya mua" [TRT about to sue Sophon for allegation of manifesto]. May 22. News Center Database.

Matichon. 2008a. *Lub luang luek* [Deep secrets and deception]. Bangkok: Matichon Publishing.

Matichon. 2008b. *Cha chae chao 2* [Slashing, revealing and withering away]. Bangkok: Matichon Publishing.

Matichon. 2008c. "Samak "at sue yu hai taek pat thuk phak ruam bip khia: [Samak told press stop trying to break us up]. June 28. http://www.matichon.co.th/news_detail.php?newsid=2379

Matichon. 2008d. "Somchai sang 1 romoto kum soso samak ting hono" [Somchai told minister to control 10 MPs; Samak left the leader]. October 1. News Center Database.

Matichon. 2008e. "Somchai pob pa cheon meon tok 3 praden" [Somchai met with Prem; happy; discussed three issues]. October 12. News Center Database.

Matichon. 2008f. "Popocho dude laew 252 ching nayok 15 thoko" [Democrat Party bought 252 MPs to contest for a leadership]. December 12. News Center Database.

Matichon. 2008g. "Pak ruam tahan tun potomo krob pochopo" [Party, military, finance, PAD took over the Democrat Party]. December 19. News Center Database.

Matichon. 2009. "193 wan chaichana khong panthamit 'bantuek tula deod'" [193 days of PAD's victory: Remembering the Black October]. December 31. http://www.manager.co.th/Politics/ViewNews.aspx?NewsID=9510000153554

Matichon. N.d. *Mai mind* [Don't mind]. http://serichon.org/board/index.php?topic=7675.0;wap2

McAdam, Doug, John D. McCarthy, and Mayer N. Zald, eds. 1996. *Comparative Perspectives on Social Movements: Political Opportunities, Mobilizing Structures, and Cultural Framings*. Cambridge: Cambridge University Press.

McCargo, Duncan. 1997a. *Chamlong Srimuang and the New Thai Politics*. London: Hurst.

McCargo, Duncan. 1997b. "Thailand's Political Parties: Real, Authentic and Actual." In *Political Change in Thailand: Democracy and Participation*, edited by Kevin Hewison, 114–31. London: Routledge.

McCargo, Duncan. 2000. *Politics and the Press in Thailand: Media Machinations*. New York: Routledge.

McCargo, Duncan. 2005. "Network Monarchy and Legitimacy Crises in Thailand." *Pacific Review* 18 (4): 499–519.

McCargo, Duncan. 2008. "Thailand: State of Anxiety." *Southeast Asian Affairs*: 333–56.

McCargo, Duncan, and Ukrist Pathmanand, 2005. *The Thaksinization of Thailand*. Copenhagen: Nordic Institute of Asian Studies.

McGeown, Kate. 2006. "Thai Result Points to National Divide." *BBC News*, April 4. http://news.bbc.co.uk/2/hi/asia-pacific/4874960.stm

McGowan, Patrick J. 2003. "African Military Coups d'État, 1956–2001: Frequency, Trends and Distribution." *Journal of Modern African Studies* 41 (3): 339–70.

Meksophon, Rungmanee. 2010. *Bueang luek phruetsa pha 35 prachathippatai puean lueat muean ma klai tae pai mai thueng* [Behind the scenes and stories of May 35: Democracy in blood, it seems we have come so far but we are never getting there]. Bangkok: Tawan Ok Publishing.

Meksophon, Rungmanee. 2014. *Amnat III suu mai thoy* [Power III: Not backing down]. Bangkok: Baan Pra-athit Press.

Meyer, Peter. 2010. "Honduran Political Crisis." Congressional Research Service, February 10. http://www.fas.org/sgp/crs/row/R41064.pdf

Montesano, Michael, Pavin Chacahvalpongpan, and Aekapol Chongvilaivan, eds. 2012. *Bangkok May 2010: Perspectives on a Divided Thailand*, Singapore: ISEAS.

Morell, David, and Chai-anan Samudavanija. 1981. *Political Conflict in Thailand: Reform, Reaction, Revolution*. Ithaca: Cornell University Press.

Muller, Edward N., and Mitchell A. Seligson. 1994. 'Civic Culture and Democracy: The Question of Causal Relationships." *American Political Science Review* 88 (3): 635–52.

Murray, David. 1996. *Angels and Devils: Thai Politics from February 1991 to September 1992, a Struggle for Democracy?* Bangkok: White Orchid Press.

Musikawong, Sudarat. 2006. "Thai Democracy and the October (1973–1976) Events." *Inter-Asia Cultural Studies* 7 (4): 713–16.

Naewna. 2006. "Thoi phuea chat 'thaksin' ramhai wen wak kanmueang" [Backing down for his country: Thaksin cried; stepped down]. April 5. News Center Database.

Naewna. 2008. "Ratchanikun rabu sathaban yu nai chuang antarai mi khabuankan min paiyannoi chi 'thaksin' yu nai ko sang khwam taekyaek won prachachon pokpong sathaban" [Royalists point out monarchy is in danger; antimonarchy movement; Thaksin creates division; plea to citizens to protect the monarchy]. November 11. News Center Database.

Naewna. 2013. "Phong thep chin thanachut 40 phit sa ong kon itsara ba amnat" [Phonthep points out that 1997 Constitution creates power-hungry independent institutions]. March 1. http://www.naewna.com/politic/43322

Nakornthap, Pramod. 2011. *Keng majak nai mai ao kasat* [How dare you not want the monarchy]. Nonthaburi: Green Panyayan Press.

Nanuam, Wassana. 2010. *Lub luang prang: Pathiwat prasat sai* [Secrecy and deception: The overthrow of the sand castle]. Bangkok: Matichon Publishing.

Nation. 2006. "Kingdom 'Would Not Have Survived without Coup'." October 6. http://www.nationmultimedia.com/2006/10/26/politics/politics_30017169.php

National Statistical Office of Thailand. 2015. "Samruat kan mi kan chai theknoloyi sarasonthet lae kan suesan nai khruaruean phoso 2558" [Household survey of the use and access to ICT 2015]. http://service.nso.go.th/nso/web/survey/surtec5-1-3.html

Neher, Clark. 1988. "Thailand in 1987: Semi-Successful Semi-Democracy." *Asian Survey* 28 (2): 192–201.

Neher, Clark. 1995. "Democratization in Thailand." *Asian Affairs* 21 (4): 195–209.

Neher, Clark. 1996. "The Transition to Democracy in Thailand." *Asian Perspective* 20 (2): 301–21.

Nelson, Michael. 2007. "People's Sector Politics in Thailand: Problems of Democracy in Ousting Prime Minister Thaksin Shinawatra." *Working Paper Series No. 87.* Hong Kong: Southeast Asia Research Centre, City University of Hong Kong.

Nelson, Michael H. 2013. "The Democrat and Pheu Thai Parties in Thailand's 2011 Elections: Thaksin Shinawatra Returns to Power." *Working Papers Series, the Southeast Asia Research Centre of the City University of Hong Kong.* http://www.cityu.edu.hk/searc/Resources/Paper/139%20-%20WP%20-%20Dr%20Nelson%20Thailand%202011%20Election.pdf

New Zealand Herald. 2006. *Clark: Bainimarama Attempting 'Thai-Style Coup.'* Accessed May 5, 2011. http://www.nzherald.co.nz/nz/news/article.cfm?c_id=1&objectid=10413816

Nikolov, Dimitar, et al. 2015. "Measuring Online Social Bubbles." *PeerJ Computer Science* 1: e38, https://doi.org/10.7717/peerj-cs.38

Nikomborirak, Deunden, and Somkiat Tangkitvanich. 1999. "Corporate Governance and the Challenge Facing the Thai Economy." OECD. http://www.oecd.org/corporate/ca/corporategovernanceprinciples/1931476.pdf

Nord, Philip. 2000. "Introduction." In *Civil Society before Democracy: Lessons from Nineteenth-Century Europe*, edited by Nancy Bermeo and Philip Nord, xiii–2. Lanham, MD: Rowman and Littlefield.

Nordlinger, EA. 1976. *Soldiers in Politics: Military Coups and Governments*. Englewood Cliffs, NJ: Prentice-Hall.

Norris, Pippa. 2001. *Digital Divide: Civic Engagement, Information Poverty, and the Internet Worldwide*. Cambridge: Cambridge University Press.

Ockey, James. 2003. "Change and Continuity in the Thai Political Party System." *Asian Survey*, 43 (4): 663–80.

Ockey, James. 2008. "Thailand in 2007: The Struggle to Control Democracy." *Asian Survey* 48 (1): 20–28.

O'Donnell, Guillermo, Philippe Schmitter, and Laurence Whitehead. 1986. *Transitions from Authoritarian Rule: Tentative Conclusions about Uncertain Transitions*. Baltimore: John Hopkins University Press.

O'Donnell, Guillermo, Philippe Schmitter, and Laurence Whitehead. 1996. "Illusions about Consolidation." *Journal of Democracy* 7 (2): 34–51.

O'Donnell, Guillermo, Jorge Vargas Cullell, and Osvaldo Iazetta. 2004. *The Quality of Democracy: Theory and Applications*. Notre Dame: University of Notre Dame Press.

Oliveira, Daniel, José Silva, and Paulo Henrique de Souza Bermejo. 2017. "Social Media and Public Administration: Social Sentiment Analysis about the Performance of the Brazilian Federal Government." *Organizações & Sociedade* 24 (82): 491–508.

Olukoshi, Adebayo. 1998. *The Politics of Opposition in Contemporary Africa*. Cambridge: Cambridge University Press.

PAD. 2009. *PAD Saving the Motherland: Proof of Bravery, Sacrifice and Ahingsa*. Bangkok: Tawan Aok Publishing.

PAD. 2011. *33 Praden tham tob khao pra vihan* [Thirty-three Q&A about Khao Pra Viharn]. Bangkok: Ban Pra-Athit Press.

Paireerak, Anchalee. 2006. *Lao lung mai lai lung maeow* [Behind the scene talks to chase away Thaksin]. Bangkok: Ban Cheon Publishing.

Pathmanand, Ukrist. 2001a. "Globalization and Democratic Development in Thailand: The New Path of the Military, Private Sector, and Civil Society." *Contemporary Southeast Asia* 24–42.

Pathmanand, Ukrist. 2001b. "Thurakit thorakhamanakhom lae suesanmuanchon: chak rabop khanathippatai su rabop phukkhat betset" [Mass media and the telecommunications business: From cartel to monopoly], *Matichon Weekly* (December 2001), 16.

Pathmanand, Ukrist. 2008. "A Different Coup d'État?" *Journal of Contemporary Asia* 38 (1): 124–42.

Payutto, P. 2006. *Thammathipathai mai ma* [There is no dharmic democracy]. Bangkok: Pim Suay Publishing.

People's Alliance for Democracy (PAD). 2008. Official press release. January 26. http://www.manager.co.th/Politics/ViewNews.aspx?NewsID=9510000036181

Pearce, Katy E., and Sarah Kendzior. 2012. "Networked Authoritarianism and Social Media in Azerbaijan." *Journal of Communication* 62 (2): 283–98.

Pedregosa, Fabian, et al. 2011. "Scikit-Learn: Machine Learning Python." *Journal of Machine Learning Research* 12 (October): 2825–30.

Phongpaichit, Pasuk, and Sangsit Phiriyarangsan. 1996. *Corruption and Democracy in Thailand*. Bangkok: Silkworm Books.

Phongpaichit, Pasuk, and Chris Baker. 2004. *Thaksin: The Business of Politics in Thailand*. Copenhagen: NIAS Press.

Phongpaichit, Pasuk, and Chris Baker. 2008. "Thailand: Fighting over Democracy." *Economic and Political Weekly* 43 (50): 18–21.

Phongpaichit, Pasuk, and Chris Baker. 2010. "The Mask-Play Election: Generals, Politicians and Voters at Thailand's 2007 Poll." *Asia Research Institute Working Paper Series* 144: 1–34.

Phongpaichit, Pasuk, and Chris Baker. 2012. "Thailand in Trouble: Revolt of the Downtrodden or Conflict among Elites?" In *Bangkok May 2010: Perspectives on a Divided Thailand*, edited by Michael Montesano, M., Pavin Chacahvalpongpan, and A. Aekapol Chongvilaivan, 214–29. Singapore: ISEAS Publishing.

Pinthong, Jermsak. 2004. *Roo tan Thaksin* [We know what Thaksin's thinking]. Bangkok: Koh Kid Duay Khon.

Pintobtang, Prapas. 2007. "Thaksina Prachaniyom" [Thaksin's populism]. *Fah Diaow Gun* 5 (January–March): 144–55.

Pintobtang, Prapas. 2010. "The *Yodya* Fights Back: A Political Analysis." In *Red Why: Thai Society, Problems and the Emergence of the Red Shirts*, 36–55. Bangkok: Openbooks.

Pisitsethakarn, Pran. 2004. *Thaksinomics II: Thaksin kab naypobai sangkhom* [Thaksinomics II: Thaksin and social policies]. Bangkok: Matichon Publishing.

Polbutra, Alongkorn. 2007. *Samut pok dam: Menu corruption rabob Thaksin* [The black book: Menu corruption of Thaksin regime]. Bangkok: Thammarat Thai Publishing.

Pongpaibul, Naowarat. 2004. *Koh kui gan khun anand* [We'd like to talk to Anand]. Bangkok: Matichon Publishing.

Pongsawat, Pitch. 2011. *The Politics of Prai*. Bangkok: Openbooks.

Pongsudhirak, Thitinan. 2008. "Thailand since the Coup." *Journal of Democracy* 19 (4): 140–53.

Pornwilai, Suwinai. 2010. *Pak panthamit* [PAD party]. Bangkok: Ban Pra Athit Press.

Position Magazine 360. 2005. "Chapta 'pra chai' phai amnat rat 27 michutyo ni ? ai mong yuet thi phi ai ! My Boss want it . . . ! pritsana chak ratthamontri"

[Watch Prachai lose power June 27; Men in black seized TPI; My boss want it! Mystery from minister]. June 24. http://www.positioningmag.com/magazine/details.aspx?id=73485

Power, Timothy, and Mark Gasiorowski. 1997. "Institutional Design and Democratic Consolidation in the Third World." *Comparative Political Studies* 30 (2): 123–55.

Prachachat Thurakij. 2010. "Parakij ti yang mai set khon Somki Jatusripitak" [The unfinished business of Somkid Jatusripitak]. June 6. News Center Database.

Prachatai. 2005. "Khrapo sanoe tang 'kammakan itsara' pracha phichan panha mop khru" [CPD proposed an independent committee to investigate concerns of teachers]. November 15. http://www.prachatai.com/journal/2005/11/6388

Prachatai. 2006. "Theerayuth boonmee peud aekasan tulakarn piwat 2" [Theerayuth Boonmee open files for the second judicial coup]. August 2. http://prachatai.com/journal/2006/08/9206

Prachatai. 2011. "Yan tham rat prahan tam withi prachathippatai phro mi prachachon yu khiang khang" [Insist coup was democratic because it was backed by popular support]. June 15. http://prachatai.com/journal/2011/06/35429

Prachatai. 2014. "Krai pen Krai nai 'kammathikarn yok rang rohtohnoh pob la ikon naew ruam nok weed" [Who's who in the constitutional drafting committee: Many found to be from the PDRC]. April 11, https://prachatai.com/journal/2014/11/56344

Prasertkul, Seksarn. 2005. *Karn meong phak prachachon nai rabob prachatipathai* [People's politics in democracy]. Bangkok: Wipasa Publishing.

Prasirtsuk, Kitti. 2009. "Thailand in 2008: Crises Continued." *Asian Survey* 49 (1): 174–84.

Pruksakasamesuk, Somyot. 2004. *Ka toh pluek Thaksinomics* [Crack Thaksinomics]. Bangkok: Puthuchon Publishing.

Przeworski, Adam, et al. 1996. "What Makes Democracy Endure?" *Journal of Democracy* 7 (1): 39–55.

Przeworski, Adam, et al. 2000. *Democracy and Development: Political Institutions and Well-Being in the World, 1950–1990*. New York: Cambridge University Press.

Putnam, Robert D. 1993. *Making Democracy Work: Civic Traditions in Modern Italy*. Princeton: Princeton University Press.

Putnam, Robert D. 2000. *Bowling Alone: The Collapse and Revival of American Community*. New York: Touchstone.

Qiang, Xiao. 2011. "The Battle for the Chinese Internet." *Journal of Democracy* 22 (2): 47–61.

Radelet, Steven, and Jeffrey Sachs. 2000. "The Onset of the East Asian Financial Crisis." In *Currency Crises*, edited by Paul Krugman, 105–62. Chicago: University of Chicago Press.

Randall, Vicky, and Lars Svåsand. 2002. "Party Institutionalization in New Democracies." *Party Politics* 8 (1): 5–29.

Reongwongwan, S. 1997. *Political History of Thailand since the Revolution of 1932 to the Present*. Bangkok: Ramkhamhaeng University Press.

Riggs, Fred. 1964. *Administration in Developing Countries: The Theory of Prismatic Society.* Boston: Houghton Mifflin.

Roberts, Kenneth, and Erik Wibbels. 1999. "Party Systems and Electoral Volatility in Latin America: A Test of Economic, Institutional, and Structural Explanations." *American Political Science Review* 93 (3): 575–90.

Robinson, Mark, and Gordon White. 1998. *The Democratic Developmental State: Political and Institutional Design.* Oxford: Oxford University Press.

Rodan, Gary, ed. 1996. *Political Opposition in Industrialising Asia.* New York: Routledge.

Rojanapruk, Pravit. 2008. "Wikrit kan muang lae akati noh soh poh thai korani prathep thob ruang panthamit" [Political crisis and criticisms towards Thai newspapers: the case of Prathep discussing the PAD]. *Prachatai,* https://prachatai.com/journal/2008/10/18540

Sachs, Jeffrey, Wing Thye Woo, and Klaus Schwab. 2000. "Understanding the Asian Financial Crisis." In *The Asian Financial Crisis: Lessons for a Resilient Asia,* edited by Jeffrey Sachs, Wing Thye Woo, and Klaus Schwab. Boston: MIT Press.

Saich, Tony. 1990. "The Rise and Fall of the Beijing People's Movement." *Australian Journal of Chinese Affairs* 24: 181–208.

Samudavanija, Chai-Anan. 1989. "Thailand: A Stable Semi-Democracy." *Democracy in Developing Countries* (3): 305–46.

Samudavanija, Chai-Anan. 1990. "Educating Thai Democracy." *Journal of Democracy* 1 (4): 104–15.Sanders, Thomas, and Howard Handelman, eds. 1981. *Military Government and the Movement toward Democracy in South America.* Bloomington: Indiana University Press.

Samudavanija, Chai-Anan. 1997. "Old Soldiers Never Die, They Are Just Bypassed: The Military, Bureaucracy and Globalization." In *Political Change in Thailand: Democracy and Participation,* edited by Kevin Hewison, 42–57. New York: Routledge.

Sartori, Giovanni. 1976. *Parties and Party Systems: A Framework for Analysis.* New York: Cambridge University Press.

Sathitniramai, Apichart. 2010. "Who Are the Red Shirts? Money-Hungry Mob, *Prai,* or the New Middle Class, Thailand at a Crossroad." In *Red Why: Thai Society, Problems and the Emergence of the Red Shirts,* 13–45. Bangkok: Openbooks.

Segerberg, Alexandra, and W. Lance Bennett. 2011. "Social Media and the Organization of Collective Action: Using Twitter to Explore the Ecologies of Two Climate Change Protests." *The Communication Review* 14 (3): 197–215.

Schedler, Andreas. 1996. "Anti-Political-Establishment Parties." *Party Politics* 2 (3): 291–312.

Schedler, Andreas, Larry Diamond, and Marc F. Plattner, eds. 1999. *The Self-Restraining State: Power and Accountability in New Democracies.* Boulder: Lynne Rienner.

Schlozman, Kay L., Sidney Verba, and Henry E. Brady. 2010. "Weapon of the Strong? Participatory Inequality and the Internet." *Perspectives on Politics* 8 (2): 487–509.

Schock, Kurt. 1999. "People Power and Political Opportunities: Social Movement Mobilization and Outcomes in the Philippines and Burma." *Social Problems* 46 (3): 355–75.

Senior Journalists. 1992. *Karn bariharn prong sai khong anand panyarachun* [Transparent leadership style of Anand Panyarachun]. Bangkok: Sarn Mualchon Press.

Shinawatra, Thaksin. 2003. "Speech at the Office of the National Economic and Social Development Board of Thailand." June 30. http://www.nesdb.go.th/portals/0/news/annual_meet/46/data11.pdf

Shirky, Clay. 2008. *Here Comes Everybody: The Power of Organizing without Organizations.* London: Penguin Books.

Siamrath. 2006. "Phon chi pochocho chuea lang lueaktang sathanakan runraeng ban plai" [Polls reveal that after the election the situation will get worse]. April 2, News Center Database.

Siamrath. 2008. "Michai lopbi wutthi paiyannoi khia powo 281 khu chumnum yai tan" [Michai lobbies Senate to dismiss Poh Woh 281; threats of major protests]. November 14. News Center Database.

Siamwalla, Ammar, and Somchai Jitsuchon. 2012. "The Socio-Economic Bases of the Red/Yellow Divide: A Statistical Analysis." In *Bangkok May 2010: Perspectives on a Divided Thailand*, edited by Michael Montesano, Pavin Chacahvalpongpan, and Aekapol Chongvilaivan, 64–71. Singapore: ISEAS Publishing.

Sinpeng, Aim, and Aries A. Arugay. 2015. "The Middle Class and Democracy in Southeast Asia." In *Routledge Handbook of Southeast Asian Democratization*, edited by William Case, 102-116. London: Routledge.

Sinpeng, Aim. 2017. "Participatory Inequality in Online and Offline Political Engagement in Thailand." *Pacific Affairs* 90 (2): 253–74.

Sinpeng, Aim, and Wimonsiri Hemtanon. 2018. "Change and Continuity in the Politics of the Media after the Coup." In *After the Coup: The National Council for Peace and Order Era and the Future of Thailand*, edited by Michael J. Montesano, Terence Chong, and Mark Heng Shu Xun. Singapore: ISEAS.

Sinpeng, Aim, and Erik Kuhonta. 2012. "From the Street to the Ballot Box: The July 2011 Elections and the Rise of Social Movements in Thailand." *Contemporary Southeast Asia* 34 (3): 389–415.

Sithisaman, Kamnoon. 2011. *Prakotakarn sonthi chak suea si lueang thueng phaphankho si fa* [Sonthi's phenomenon: From yellow shirt to blue bandana]. Bangkok: Ban Pra-athit Press.

Sivaraksa, Sulak. 2002. *Tuan krasae peu kwam swang tang sangkhom* [Alternatives for a better society]. Bangkok: Kled Thai Publishing.

Skoric, Marko, Jing Liu, and Kokil Jaidka. 2020. "Electoral and Public Opinion Forecasts with Social Media Data: A Meta-Analysis." *Information* 11 (4): 187, https:/doi.org/10.3390/info11040187

Slater, Dan. 2013. "Democratic Careening." *World Politics* 65 (4): 729–63.

Smith, Naomi, and Tim Graham. 2017. "Mapping the Anti-Vaccination Movement on Facebook." *Information, Communication & Society* (December): 1–18.

Songthai, Therdtham. 2008. *Kah kue nakrob prachachon* [I am the people's warrior]. Nonthaburi: Green Panyayan Press.

Soonsiri, Prasong. 2000. *Botrian khong phaendin* [Lessons of the land]. Bangkok: Naewna Press.

Stier, Sebastian, Arnim Bleier, Haiko Lietz, and Markus Strohmaier. 2018. "Election Campaigning on Social Media: Politicians, Audiences, and the Mediation of Political Communication on Facebook and Twitter." *Political Communication* 35 (1): 50–74.

Stiglitz, Joseph. 2000. "What I Learned at the World Economic Crisis." In *Globalization and the Poor: Exploitation or Equalizer?*, edited by William J. Driscoll and Julie Clark, 195–204. New York: International Debate Education Association

Suksamran, Naowarat. 2014. Peud jai Suthep jak na 1 *Bangkok Post* [Suthep opened up his heart on *Bangkok Post*'s front page]. *Post Today*, June 23. https://www.post today.com/politic/report/302501

Supkampang, P. 2010. *Sathaban tulakan thai khwam thathai nai kan sadaeng botbat amnat nathi nai yuk patirup kanmueang kap khwam chueaman khong sangkhom* [The judiciary: Challenges in the age of political reforms and public confidence]. Bangkok: King Prajadiphok Institute.

Suwannathat-Pian, Kobkua. 2003. *Kings, Country and Constitutions: Thailand's Political Development 1932–2000*. London: Routledge.

Svolik, Milan W. 2012. *The Politics of Authoritarian Rule*. Cambridge: Cambridge University Press.

Taagepera, Rein. 2003. "Arend Lijphart's Dimensions of Democracy: Logical Connections and Institutional Design." *Political Studies* 51 (1): 1–19.

Tamada, Yoshifumi. 1995. "Coups in Thailand, 1980–1991: Classmates, Internal Conflicts and Relations with the Government of the Military." *Southeast Asian Studies* 33 (3): 317–39.

Tamada, Yoshifumi. 2009. *Myths and Realities: The Democratization of Thai Politics*. Vol. 15. Tokyo: Trans Pacific Press.

Tarrow, Sidney. 1994. *Power in Movement: Social Movements, Collective Action and Politics*. Cambridge: Cambridge University Press.

Taugsuban, Suthep. 2014. *The Power of Change*. Bangkok: LIPS Publishing.

Taylor, James. 2011. "Larger Than life: Central World' and Its Demise and Rebirth—Red Shirts and the Creation of an Urban Cultural Myth in Thailand." *Asia Research Institute Working Paper* 150: 1–13.

Tejapira, Kasian. 2006. "Toppling Thaksin." *New Left Review* 39 (May–June). http://newleftreview.org/II/39/kasian-tejapira-toppling-thaksin#_edn21

Thabchumpol, Nareumol, and Duncan McCargo. 2011. "Urbanized Villagers in the 2010 Thai Red Shirt Protests." *Asian Survey* 51: 993–1018.

Thai News. 2006. "Luan pen phuyai hai tham phuea chat rop chut khan rap—phrom harue 3 fai 'sonthi' yam chutyuen 'maeo' tong ok" [Let's be adults and work to serve the country; Sonthi insisted Thaksin must leave]. March 16. News Center Database.

Thai NGO. 2003. "Sapa prachachon" [People's Assembly]. January 16. http://thaingo.org/story3/par01_160146.htm

Thai NGO. 2004. "Lod thaksin peum prachatipathai ruam kleonwai kan muang pak prachachon" [Reduce Thaksin, increase democracy, mobilize for the people's sector]. December 21. http://www.thaingo.org/HeadnewsKan/taksin211247.htm

Thai NGO. N.d. "The People's Assembly." http://thaingo.org/story3/par01_160146.htm

Thai Post. 1997a. "Kamnan ma ik 3 muen—si khiao chumnum yai" [30,000 kamnans are coming—the Green protest]. September 5. News Center Database.

Thai Post. 1997b. "Khowomo phueng amnat rat khwang rothono tuean ching yup sapha khon tem thanon" [Koh Woh Moh depends on state power to oppose constitution . . . warning if house dissolution then people out on the streets]. August 21. News Center Database.

Thai Post. 1999. "10 Ongkon pochoto thuang amnat khuen krathung ratthaban chatkan yup sapha" [10 organization Pochoto demand power back; pressured government to dissolve parliament]. January 11, 1999. News Center Database.

Thai Post. 2000. "Phon chi 'chuan' yup sapha prachachon rabu mai phochai thuk dan wang mai le 'chaturon' la-ok!" [Poll reveals house dissolution; people unhappy with government in every way; Wang Mai going down; Chaturon, quit!]. April 11. News Center Database.

Thai Post. 2006. "'Thaksin' yup sapha plueai that thae—su kan phachoenna" [Thaksin dissolved parliament; revealed his true self; confrontation]. February 26. News Center Database.

Thai Post. 2009. "Newin Chidchob: Anakhot nayok khon thi 28" [Newin Chidchop: Future PM number 28]. February 26. http://www.thaipost.net/news/160209/377

Thairath. 2003a. "Samakhom nakkhao paiyannoi chae rat khukkham sue" [Journalists association believes government threatens media freedom]. June 3 News Center Database.

Thairath. 2003b. "NGO pen nai na khai kwam jon" [NGOs are brokers of poverty]. July 17. News Center Database.

Thairath. 2005. "Op-ed: yub ongkorn isara di mai?" [Dissolving independent institutions?]. December 3. News Center Database.

Thairath. 2006. "Thaksin poet sapha ruam pha thang tan lo pao hai thalom 10 wan" [Thaksin suggested a joint parliamentary session to find a solution]. February 22. News Center Database.

Thairath. 2009. "Panha kanmueang thai kae thi khon rue ratthathammanun" [Problems with Thai politics: Is it because of people or the constitution?] http://www.thairath.co.th/content/pol/51952

Thairath. 2010. "Chi kanlaya khao khai on hun hai luk chaeng banchi pen thet" [Point: Kunying Kalaya transfered shares to son; financial fraud]. March 10. http://www.thairath.co.th/content/pol/68014

Thairath. 2013. "Yon roi jed sip ha wan koh poh poh soh gon shut down muang krung" [A look back at the 75 days before the PDRC's Bangkok Shutdown]. January 12. https://www.thairath.co.th/content/395551

Thanapornpan, Rangsan. 2002. *Kamnoet ratthathammanun thai 2540* [The birth of the 1997 constitution]. Bangkok: Thammasat University Press.

Thanapornpan, R. 2005. *Jak Thaksinomics su Thaksinathipathai pak 1–2* [From Thaksinomics to Thaksinocracy: Part 1–2]. Bangkok: Openbooks.

Thevarniramitkul, Parinya. 2006. "Tham yang rai prathet thai jung ja thung yuk lang Thaksin [How Thailand Could Transition to the Post-Thaksin Era]. *Prachatai*, July 23. https://prachatai.com/journal/2006/07/9080

Thongchai, Pipob. 2010. "Pathiroop prathet thai nai tassana khong pipob Thongchai" [Political reforms in the eyes of Pipob Thongchai]. *On Open*, April 11. http://www.onopen.com/open-special/10-04-11/5337

Traimas, Chaowana. 2007. *Koh mul peonthan 75 pi prachathipathai thai 2475–2550* [Basic data on 75 years of Thai democracy, 1932–2007]. Bangkok: Chulalongkorn University Press.

Tran, Mark. 2012. "UN Adopts "Momentous" Resolution on Universal Healthcare." *Guardian*, December 3. http://www.theguardian.com/global-development/2012/dec/13/un-momentous-resolution-universal-healthcare

Trippi, Joe. 2004. "The Revolution Will Not Be Televised." *Campaigns and Elections* 25 (8): 44–44.

Tufekci, Zeynep, and Christopher Wilson. 2012. "Social Media and the Decision to Participate in Political Protest: Observations from Tahrir Square." *Journal of Communication* 62 (2): 363–79.

Tungrapipakorn, Santi. 2010. *Tritsa di karn meong mai* [The theory of new politics]. Bangkok: Pim Dee Co.

Ungpakorn, Ji. 2010. *Thailand's Crisis and the Fight for Democracy*. London: WD Press.

Ungpakorn, Ji. 2011. "Thammai ngo kao kang ammat" [Why did NGOs side with ammat?] February 28. http://redthaisocialist.com/2011-01-20-12-39-38/112-2011-02-28-16-44-45.html

Uthakorn, Boonchana. 1993. *Kan patiwat khong khana rosocho 2534 kap prachathippatai* [The 1991 coup d'état of Roh Soh Choh and democracy]. Bangkok: Boonchana Uthakorn Foundation.

Voice TV. 2011. "Public Opinion on the Coup and Political Conflict." *ABAC POLL*, January 30, https://www.voicetv.co.th/read/3104

Vromen, Ariadne et al. 2016. "Everyday Making Through Facebook Engagement: Young Citizen's Political Interactions in Australia, the United Kingdom and the United States." Political Studies 64(3): 513–33.

Wasi, Prawes. 1990. *Thitthang anakhot thai phuea khwam suk thuan na* [The future direction of Thailand for the happiness for all]. Bangkok: Moh Chao Ban Publishing.

Whittington, Keith. 2001. "Revisiting Tocqueville's America: Society, Politics, and

Association in the Nineteenth Century." In *Beyond Tocqueville: Civil Society and the Social Capital Debate in Comparative Perspective*, edited by Michael W. Foley and Bob Edwards, 21–31. Hanover, NH: University Press of New England.

Wikileaks. 2006. "Ralph Boyce's Meeting with Sonthi Boonyarathklin." http://www.wikileaks.org/plusd/cables/06BANGKOK5811_a.html

Winichakul, Thongchai. 2008. "Toppling Democracy." *Journal of Contemporary Asia* 38 (1): 11–37.

Woolf, Stuart, ed. 2002. *Nationalism in Europe: From 1815 to the Present*. New London: Routledge.

Woolley, Samuel. 2016. "Automating Power: Social Bot Interference in Global Politics." *First Monday* 21. https://uncommonculture.org/ojs/index.php/fm/article/view/6161/5300

Woolley, Samuel, and Philip N. Howard. 2017. "Computational Propaganda Worldwide: Executive Summary." *Working Paper* 11. Oxford: Project on Computational Propaganda.

Worakul, Kamolporn. 2012. "ASTV and the People's Alliance for Democracy." MA thesis, Faculty of Economics, Chulalongkorn University.

Wutt T. 2014. "Sonthi keon wethi kohpohpohsor tu taharn pathiwat" [Sothi on PDRC stage, calling for military coup]." *M Thai News*, May 10. https://news.mthai.com/general-news/328165.html

Xenos, Michael, Ariadne Vromen, and Brian D. Loader. 2014. "The Great Equalizer? Patterns of Social Media Use and Youth Political Engagement in Three Advanced Democracies." *Information, Communication & Society* 17 (2): 151–67.

Yang, Guobin. 2009. *The Power of the Internet in China: Citizen Activism Online*. New York: Columbia University Press.

Yang, Guobin, 2014. "Political Contestation in Chinese Digital Spaces: Deepening the Critical Inquiry." *China Information* 28 (2): 135–44.

Index

Although family names are used in Thailand, Thais are normally known by their given names, which come first, as in English names. For this reasons people have been alphabetized under their first name.

Page references in italics are to figures and tables.

Red Shirts (United Front for Democracy against Dictatorship, UDD), 38, 47, 133; and 2014 coup, 176–78; composition of, 15, 154, 157; mobilization of, 149, 186; opposition to, 176–77, 181, 185, 188, 190; origins of, 13, 18, 149; and social media, 157, 160, 162, 176, 181
Red Sunday Group, 102, 219n16
religious networks, 8, 43, 107
rent-seeking, 82–85, 204. *See also* corruption
research methodology (of this book), 18–19, 157–59, 162–64, 170–76, 178–80, 182–83
royalist sentiment, 71, 76, 120, 131, 171, 181; in 2014 coup, 177–78, 181, 183–84; after 2014 coup, 185–87; in opposition to Thaksin, 108, 114; in PAD and PDRC, 37, 67, 108, 115, 131, 146–47, 177–78, 196
royal legitimization, 62
royalty. *See* monarchy (in Thailand)
Ruam Palang Prachachat Thai (Action Coalition Party or ACP), 189, 190
Russia, 141

Samakhi Tham Party (STP), 54
Samak Sundaravej (prime minister, 2008), 143–44, 146, 147
Sam Din, 106
Samran Rodpetch, 113, 218n2
Sangad Chaloryoo, 52
Sansit Chanpoon, 101
Santi Asoke, 106–7, 110, 150, 151
Saprang Kallayanamit, 127
Saranyoo Wongkrajang, 113
Sarit Thanarat, 64, 72
Sarocha Pornudomsak, 113
Sawat Amornwiwat, 213n33
Sawit Kaewwan, 113
Senate, 15, 16, 40, 45, 114, 139, 150, 214n38; popularly elected, 74, 95–96, 143, 145, 213n33
Seritham party, 213n27, 213n28
Shin Corporation, 12, 99, 100, 122, 214n47
Sinpeng, Aim: personal history, xi–xii

Sirichai Mai-ngam, 113
Sirindhorn (Princess), 147
Small-Scale Farmers' Assembly of Isan, 98, 102
socialism, 30
social media: and antidemocratic values, 167, 169; benefits of, 140; and class, 159; and democracy, 17, 140, 205; and electoral interference, 141; emergence of in Thailand, 19, 140; harm caused by, 141–42; and liberation, 16–17; and PAD, 140; partisanship of, 153, *158*; and PDRC, 140, 153–66; and polarization, 4, 17, 140, 164–68; and political engagement, 140–41, 159–60; reducing costs of coups, 4, 16, 140, 201; and regional divisions, 162, *163*, 166; significance of, 16–17; and socioeconomic profiles, 159–61, 166; and street protests, 160–62, 166, 168; use of by population, 6, 167
Sodsri Jakrapan, 209n26
Sombat Boon-Ngam Anong, 102
Sombat Thamrongtanyawong, 189, 220n37
Somboon Rahong, 63
Somboon Thongburan, 214n38
Somchai Wongsawat (prime minister, 2008), 144, 145, 148
Somkiat On-wimol, 96
Somkiat Pongpaibul, 73, 95, 109, 110–11, 151
Somkid Jatusripitak, 89, 212n12, 217n16, 218n1
Sompong Srakrawee, 96
Somsak Kosaisuk, 105, 109, 111, 112, 130
Somsak Thepsutin, 217n16
Sonthi Boonyaratklin, 126–27, 128, 129, 130, 194
Sonthi Limthongkul, 107, 118–21, 130, 150–53, 194, 215n67; and Manager Media Group, 104, 110, 134, 153, 194; opposition to Thaksin, 108, 109; popularity of, 104, 112; relationship with military, 127
Soonthorn Wilawan, 145
Sophonpanich family, 84, 213n33
Srivichai Warriors, 112

State Enterprises Workers' Relations
Confederation, 86, 105, 109, 111
state enterprise workers, 99, 105, 111
STP (Samakhi Tham Party), 54
STR (Student and People Network
Thailand Reform, Koh Poh Toh),
150–52, 156, 173
structural causes/explanations of anti-
democratic movements, 25, 30, 37
Student and People Network Thailand
Reform (Koh Poh Toh, STR or Uru-
pong protestors), 150–152, 156, 173
Student Federation of Thailand, 76, 108
student massacre (1976), 51, 52, 56
students, 86, 107–9, 146, 152; in 1973 upris-
ing, 51–52, 56, 61; in 2006 coup, 108
Suchinda Krapayoon (prime minister,
1992), 54–55, 56, 59, 60, 63–64, 67
Sukhumbhand Paribatra, 54
Sukhumpon Ngonekham, 213n33
Sulak Sivaraksa, 67, 101, 210n40
Sunthorn Kongsompong, 53, 54
Supatra Nacapew, 189
Supinya Klanarong, 100
Surachai Pithutecha, 213n33
Surayuth Chulanond (prime minister,
2006–08), 121, 128, 139, 142
Suriyasai Katasila, 104, 111, 112, 119,
121, 130, 134, 151, 156–57
Suthep Taugsuban, 150, 167, 189,
220n32, 221n44; antidemocratic prin-
ciples of, 168; loss of support for, 21,
187, 190; and media access, 194; and
the military, 152; and social media,
154, 156–58, *158*, 162–68, *163*, *164*,
173–78, 181–91, 194, 220n33; support
base of, 162, 168
Suwinai Pornwalai, 132

Tak Bai Incident (2004), 95, 96, 214n37
Tamarod, 5
Temasek Holdings, 12, 100
Thai Journalists' Association, 104
Thailand Informed, 173, 174, 176, 178,
183–87, 221n1
Thai Patriot Network, 149
Thai Rak Thai (TRT) party, 14, 36, 92,
123; corruption in, 96, 99; decline of,
123, 146, 149, 195; election in 2001,

213n27; election in 2005, 15, 16, 36,
45, 87, 135; election in 2006, 124–25,
133; membership of, 84, 87; philoso-
phy/policies of, 82, 88–89, 102, 146,
199; relationship with Red Shirts,
149; rise of, 81, 87, 194; successor of,
142. *See also* Palang Prachachon Party
(PPP)
Thai Social Democrat Party, 189–90
Thaksin Shinawatra (prime minister,
2001–06), xii, 32–34, 82, 87, 153; in
1997 financial crisis, 14; accountability
of, 131; coming to power of, 12–16,
42, 81, 212n19, 213n27; corruption
allegations against, 90–92, *91*, 99–100,
123, 132, 133, 146, 212n20; management style of, 92, 102, 132, 213n26;
opposition to, 91–106, 112, 146, 195;
overthrow of, 12–13, 62, 80, 87, 108–
10, 115–30, 139; policies of, 36, 80,
88, 88–89, 99, 199, 212n11, 212n17,
213n25; popularity and success of,
12–13, 36, 81, 87–90, 133; and Red
Shirts, 149; re-election in 2005, 42,
45, 135; and social media, 153. *See also*
Thai Rak Thai
Thammasat University, 108, 146; massacre at (1976), 52, 56, 61
Thanarat Samok-nae, 105
Thanin Chianravanont, 91
Thanin Kraivichian (prime minister,
1976–77), 52
Thanom Kittikajorn (prime minister,
1958, 1963–73), 51, 212n20
Thavit Klinprathum, 213n33
Third Wave democracies, 5, 8, 22, 31,
48, 192–93, 202–3
Tul Sithisomwongsa, 150
Turkey, 6
Twitter, 19, 140, 205

UDD (United Front for Democracy
against Dictatorship). *See* Red Shirts
Udsanee Chidchob, 213n33
unelected leaders, 6, 52, 53, 56, 60, 61–
64, 66, 196
unemployment, 29–30, 79, 81, 211n70
United Front for Democracy against
Dictatorship (UDD). *See* Red Shirts